Introduction
to
Fiscal Policy

SECOND EDITION

By

RICHARD W. LINDHOLM
Professor of Economics
Michigan State University

PITMAN PUBLISHING CORPORATION
New York • Toronto • London

Associated Companies
SIR ISAAC PITMAN & SONS, LTD.
London   Melbourne   Johannesburg
SIR ISAAC PITMAN & SONS (CANADA), LTD.
Toronto

PRINTED IN THE UNITED STATES OF AMERICA

DEDICATED TO THE

MEMORY OF MY MOTHER.

Preface

LIKE the first edition, this is a short and simple presentation of how the three government fiscal tools—taxing, spending, and debt management—affect prices, consumption (saving), employment, and income distribution. Desirable levels for these four economic relationships are established, and the analysis of the three fiscal tools relates the use of each in reaching the recommended level and retaining it.

This book is developed around four basic assumptions. The first is that fiscal policy is meaningless unless standards of achievement can be established which are superior to those set in the market place. The second is that understanding is improved if fiscal policies are not directly related to aggregate demand but instead are related to selected vital aspects of the economy which determine aggregate demand and which in turn are determined by aggregate demand. The third is that only a broad background in general public finance development is necessary, and detailed descriptive and analytical material may be limited to those aspects of taxation, expenditures, and debt management particularly related to the economic goals under consideration. And the fourth and last is that fiscal policy is such an actively current area that time should be available for discussing the developments reported in the daily newspaper.

The selection of the approach to fiscal policy and public finance presented here and the effectiveness with which it is developed are entirely my responsibility. However, I do wish to express thanks to my graduate professors, particularly to Alvin H. Hansen and C. E. Ayres, for the direction they gave to my economic training. I also wish to thank my colleagues, Professors Denzel C. Cline, Walter Adams, Lawrence S. Ritter, and Jacob Schmookler for their comments and assistance in developing and improving specialized sections in this book.

RICHARD W. LINDHOLM

Contents

vii

CONTENTS

Tables

Diagrams

CHAPTER 1

Fiscal Activities Surveyed

THIS is an explanation of the way in which the money-raising and spending activities of our governments in the United States affect the economy; of how our governments raise and spend their money; and of why governments raise and spend money as they do.

The money-raising and spending activities of any institution or individual are its fiscal activities. And the way in which the institution or individual carries out its fiscal activities is its fiscal policy. Hence, this book is a consideration of government fiscal policy.*

The importance of fiscal policy expands when the economic role of a government increases and contracts when the economic role of a government declines.

Government was very influential in establishing the tone of economic activities of the German states and free cities of the seventeenth and eighteenth centuries; therefore, fiscal policy was important to their economies. Government fiscal actions were carefully considered. As a result, a body of fiscal theory and fiscal administrative techniques was developed by the university professors who were the advisers of the German princes. Their writings are grouped under the name "cameralist school" of economic analysis.†

On the other hand, Adam Smith (1723-1790) of Scotland, the father of modern economics, and his followers assigned only a narrow field of activity to the public economy; that is, to fiscal policy. Under their influence, consideration of how the government could affect economic activity by the raising and spending

---

*Unless otherwise indicated, the term fiscal policy will be used to refer to government fiscal policy.

†From Latin *camera*, a room or chamber, the advisory conferences having ordinarily taken place in the princely chambers.

of money was neglected. It is sometimes said that the economists who followed the tradition of Adam Smith believed that the economic function of government should be limited to that of "a night watchman."

Gradually, as the modern economies of today have evolved, economists have become aware that the role of government must be considerably greater than that of "a night watchman" and that it is incorrect to assume that the best government is the cheapest government. This change of attitude has arisen from an abundance of experience which has shown that more government does not necessarily destroy the foundations on which a private capitalist economic system is built. Instead, experience has shown that more government can strengthen the foundations.

Comparing the Size of the Public and Private Economies

The economic role of government is not amenable to a single measurement.

One of a number of useful measures of the relative importance of the public and private economies of the United States is the number of individuals employed by each.

In 1939, the private economy employed 38 million individuals, and the public economy employed 4 million; thus, about 9.5 per cent of the full-time and part-time employees of the nation were employed by government. In 1944 (a war year), the private economy employed 47 million and the public economy 17 million, or about 26.6 per cent of the total. In 1954, the private economy employed 55 million and the public economy 10 million, or about 15.4 per cent.

The relative importance of the public economy as measured by the portion of total employment provided by government was 50 per cent greater in 1954 than in 1939. This comparison, which shows a considerable expansion in the portion of the labor force employed by government between 1939 and 1954, is not what it seems to be as there were about 9 million persons unemployed in 1939. If it is assumed that 4 million more of these unemployed were benefiting from government-provided assistance or work relief in 1939 than in 1954, the portion "employed" by government becomes 17.4 per cent for 1939 and therefore greater than in 1954.*

*The Economic Almanac, 1953-1954, (New York, Thomas Y. Crowell, 1953) and Survey of Current Business, July, 1954, p. S-10, 11.

Another measure of the relative importance of the public and private economies is the income originating in each. In 1939, the income originating in private business was $77,850 million and that in government $8,550 million or about 9.7 per cent of the combined income. In 1944, a war year, the income originating in private business was $144,907 million and that in government $34,366 million or 19.0 per cent of the total. In 1953, a postwar year, the income originating in private business was $261,000 million and that in government $34,000 million or 11.1 per cent. This measure of relative importance of the private and public economies indicates an increase in the relative importance of the postwar public economy of 1.4 percentage points, or 14 per cent.*

The validity of the second type of comparison—the national income ratio—is effected adversely by the fact that the amount of national income attributed to the public economy is greatly understated in the statistics because it does not include the contribution of government-owned capital and government-financed contracts. The amount of national income attributed to the public economy is not much more than the total of salaries and wages paid by the public economy, whereas in the case of the private economy the corresponding figure includes profits, interest, inventory adjustments, and the like, as well as salaries and wages arising from expenditures originating in both the public and private economy.

The first comparison—the portion of the total labor force employed by the public economy—is also inadequate as a ratio for appraising the private and public economies. The number of employees of the public and private economies would be comparable only if the government performed by forced account (employed directly the equipment and labor required rather than having the work performed by letting contracts to private firms) all activities that could be economically undertaken in this manner. Forced account type expenditure is relatively unimportant in the United States.

The relative importance of the public and private economies is shown best by the comparison of the total expenditure of the Federal and state and local governments with the gross national product or expenditure. This type of comparison is not perfect because it does not indicate the impact of government policy as shown in the type of securities issued to refund the debt, or of government economic policy indicated by other actions of the

*National Income Supplement to Survey of Current Business, July, 1954 (Washington, U.S. Government Printing Office, 1947), p. 5–10, 11.

Treasury or the Federal Reserve System or government lending agencies.

In 1939, the total expenditure of the private economy was $75,023 million and of the public economy $17,270 million. The expenditure arising from the public economy in 1939 was 19 per cent of the total expenditure made in the United States. In 1944, a war year, the total expenditure of the private economy was $107,435 million and of the public economy $103,116 million. The expenditure arising from the public economy in 1944 was about 49 per cent of the total expenditure made in the United States. In 1946, the first postwar year, the expenditure of the private economy totaled $153,379 million and the public economy $50,300 million or 24 per cent of the total. In 1953, the expenditure of the private economy totaled $279,622 million and of the public economy $85,235 million or 23.4 per cent, an increase of 4.4 percentage points or 23 per cent over the 1939 level.

It is only in the relative number employed that the public economy could be said to have contracted since 1939, and this statement would require the assumption that a large portion of reported unemployed were actually government employed.

Interrelationship between the Public and Private Economies

The public and private economies are intimately related and the activities of each vitally affect those of the other, even though they can be usefully distinguished for discussion purposes and even though tests of sound action that can be applied to either are not always applicable to the other. The services and functions performed by each economy are necessary for the efficient operation of the other. Their relative importance changes with time, but neither the public economy nor the private economy lives off the other.

From time to time, the initiative for most activity appears to be with one and then the other sector of the economy. During the period of the middle and late 1920's the initiative was with the private economy; during the middle 1930's the initiative was with the public economy; during the late 1930's and early 1940's the initiative was again with the private economy; during the middle 1940's the initiative returned to the public economy; and during the middle 1950's it went back again to the private economy.

Activity in the public economy is ordinarily prompted by stimuli different from those that affect the private economy. The demand that stimulates activity in the public economy may be labeled group demand and its analogy in the private economy may be labeled individual demand.*

For public group demand to become effective in stimulating a project or activity, the project must be politically acceptable—law, custom, public acquiescence, and the like are involved—and the necessary money must be in hand or obtainable. In a parallel situation in the private economy, political acceptability need not be considered; the desire, plus the purchasing power, is sufficient to make the demand effective. Consider the acquisition of a building by a municipal government and the acquisition of a building alongside it by a department store. Obviously, no sharp line separates the classes of activities. However, generally, it is group activities that are performed by the public economy. Certain activities—fighting wars, for example—are definitely a part of the public economy; but certain other group activities, such as the provision of opportunities for religious activities, are performed within either the public or the private economy.

Each of the two economies, in responding to the demands for the provision of goods and services, uses the other's facilities. Because the private economy in the United States provides the larger portion of goods and services, the public economy when it undertakes any important task must rely to a great extent on the private economy. Although the reciprocal dependence of the private economy upon the public economy is not so readily visible, it is nevertheless vital; for one thing, it would be quite impossible to produce any great quantity of goods and services without making use of the educated labor, the highways, and the police protection provided by the public economy.

When and how public funds are raised and spent affects the activities of the private economy. The services provided by the public economy are largely financed by the levy of taxes and the borrowing of funds from the private economy. Under modern conditions, the typical situation is that an expansion of one sector of the economy requires an expansion of the other.

An individual making an expenditure for an article at a commercial establishment considers as a fair exchange the transfer of a sum of money for a specifically desired good.

The goods made available through public channels are typically not enjoyed as the result of the individual's ability to

*Group demand as here used means demand for group use, and individual demand means demand for individual use. Consider the demand by a group of children or even a single child for public transportation to a public school as against the demand by thousands of children for bicycles to transport them on private affairs.

purchase them. Also, it is a frequent practice to charge through taxes high prices for the provision of goods and services from which the payer may receive no direct benefit. For example, the wealthy property owners of a city must make large contributions to cover the costs of public education, even though they send their own children to private schools. In the public economy the relationship between contributions, made by particular individuals or institutions, and the goods and services received need not bear close relationship.

When an individual makes a payment of taxes, the transaction is not usually an exchange of equals. The taxpayer typically does not receive direct or immediate benefit from the payment. Also, typically, the quantity of medium of exchange is not handed over to the government official because the taxpayer has decided that it is the best possible use he can make of his purchasing power, but rather it is paid into the government treasury because the law requires that it be done. A tax payment is a forced payment from which immediate direct benefits do not arise.

In private finance, the giving up of purchasing power to obtain a particular item of good is considered a voluntary action. The escape available is to keep the purchasing power and forgo the utilities which the good would furnish. But the purchaser does not always have a choice; if an individual refused to purchase all types of food because the prices were too high, he would soon be in the position of either giving up his purchasing power and living, or keeping it and dying. Modern governments in their collection of taxes never offer such harsh alternatives.

The individual consumer does not have a great deal of control over the prices charged for various goods and, after checking the possibilities of using substitutes, is forced to pay the sum demanded, if the particular need is going to be satisfied. (It should also be mentioned that for the vast majority of individuals these needs are usually necessities.)

Although neither the freedom of private economic operations nor the compulsion of public-finance fund raising are absolute, there is a considerable psychological difference between the payment of the typical tax and the completion of the typical commercial transaction.

FISCAL DEVELOPMENT,
WORLD WAR I TO WORLD WAR II

BETWEEN the two wars fiscal activity had two distinct phases, one lasting to 1930 and the other from 1930 to World War II.

Development in the 1920's

Professor Peck, writing in 1924, described the decline of Federal government revenues and expenditures and the expansion of state and local revenues and expenditures.* The decline in Federal expenditures and revenues arose from the cessation of hostilities, and the rise in state and local expenditures and revenues arose largely from the demand of the citizens for improved roads and schools. However, although this relationship between Federal and state and local fiscal activity existed, the Federal revenues and expenditures remained greatly above the pre-World War I level.

The interest payments alone on the Federal World War I debt were greater than the total Federal expenditures before the war.§ The expenditures of the Federal government during the 1920's were completely dominated by debt requirements.† The total budget of the Federal government averaged only $3,000 million, with interest payments making up a third of the total. In addition, revenues averaged almost $1,000 million above budgetary expenditures, so that the debt was reduced by nearly $8,000 million during the period. Therefore, the total receipts of the Federal government averaged about $4,000 million, interest expenditures about $1,000 million, and debt retirement the same amount. Thus, 50 per cent of the Federal government receipts were made available to Federal debt holders. In nearly all cases, these were persons in the upper income brackets.‡

The Federal tax system at the beginning of the 1920's provided for an excess-profits tax, a moderately progressive personal income tax, and many excise taxes. The first tax bill passed during this period provided for tax reductions, particularly of the excess-profits taxes and the high rates of the income tax.

The excess-profits tax has been used as a special war tax in the United States. The tax is assessed upon profits that are above those considered by the law to be normal. In the case of

*Harvey Whitefield Peck, *Taxation and Welfare* (New York, Macmillan, 1925), p. 3.

§Expenditures of the Federal government in 1916 were but $724 million, while interest payments on the Federal debt between 1923 and 1929 varied between $1,055 million and $680 million. William J. Schultz, *Financial Development of the United States* (New York, Prentice-Hall, 1937), pp. 524, 613, 615.

†When reference is made to government expenditures or revenues of a particular year, it is the fiscal year which is being referred to. The fiscal year 1949, for example, includes the last six months of 1948 and the first six months of 1949.

‡W. J. Schultz, *Financial Development of the United States*, pp. 613–615, 621.

the tax of the 1920's, it was levied upon corporation profits only and was based largely upon profits in excess of those made prior to World War I. A similar tax was levied during World War II and again during the Korean War.

The World War II excess-profits tax was removed on January 1, 1946 and the Korean War excess-profits tax was removed on January 1, 1954.

Prior to the passage of each of the tax bills adopted during the 1920's, the President and the Treasury recommended strongly that taxes bearing largely on small-income receivers should be retained and even expanded while the taxes bearing more heavily on the higher incomes should be reduced or remain unchanged. This advice had considerable influence on Congress.

The final burden of taxes is very difficult to determine, but certainly as a first approximation it can be stated that taxes on personal income, profits, and inheritances tend to remain upon the persons who make the payment. Also, as a first approximation, it can be stated that the burden of taxes upon goods and services rests upon the persons who purchase and consume the goods and services taxed. The term incidence is used to refer to this person upon whom the final direct burden of the tax rests.*

The Federal government during the 1920's obtained a large portion of its funds from the low-income recipients and made a large portion of its expenditures to high-income recipients. The fiscal activity of the Federal government during this period tended to take money away from persons of moderate means and make it available to the rich. Indirectly, this activity in turn made more funds available for speculation in the security market and contributed to the formation of the investment boom of 1928 and 1929.†

The changing of the portion of the total income of the nation received by different groups is called income redistribution. Income redistribution, when related to fiscal policy, usually refers to the reducing of the portion of total income received by the large-income receivers and the increasing of the portion received by the smaller-income receivers.

At the same time that Federal government fiscal activity was declining slightly, state and local activity was increasing. Also,

---

*See pp. 78–83 for further analysis of the burdens of different taxes.

†Also the sinking-fund scheme used brought about a greater reduction of debt during depression than prosperity. See Seymour E. Harris, *The National Debt and the New Economics* (New York, McGraw-Hill, 1947), p. 267.

rather than using revenues to pay off debt owned largely by the rich, the state and local governments were obtaining a large portion of their revenues by borrowing from the rich. These new borrowings by state and local governments were actually greater than the debt repaid by the Federal government. What the Federal government gave to the rich in debt repayment, the state and local governments took away in new borrowings. The net effect during the 1920's was that government debt activity was neutral. It failed to absorb any new savings, but it also failed to release funds that might have remained idle.

During the 1920's, the total annual expenditures of state and local government increased from about $5,500 millions to nearly $9,000 million. The total impact of state and local fiscal activities was, therefore, nearly twice as great as that of the Federal government. The funds for this great expansion in state and local expenditures were obtained from borrowing, as mentioned above, and from new tax levies.

The gasoline-tax and automobile-license levies developed during this period into important sources of state revenues. Between 1919 and 1929 all forty-eight states adopted a tax levied upon gasoline consumed in use of the highways. Also state inheritance and income taxes were adopted, or the rates were increased to obtain more revenues. However, the property tax remained the most important state and local tax, bringing in more revenues than all other sources combined.

The expanded expenditures of state and local governments were largely for welfare, school, and road purposes. These types of expenditure directly helped all classes but were certainly particularly beneficial to those in the lower income brackets. The tax revenues of state and local government took about an equal percentage of the income of the poor and the rich. The over-all tax burden could be called proportional. However, the expenditures certainly directly aided the middle and lower income brackets more than the upper. Thus, the over-all effect was, perhaps, slightly to increase the quantity of goods and services available to the lower-income receivers. In the 1920's, this was not true of Federal fiscal activity. A tax which takes a larger percentage of the income of the large-income receivers than of the small-income receivers is called progressive. An income tax such as the Federal income tax with steeply graduated rates is this type of a tax. A tax that takes a smaller percentage of the income of the large-income receivers than of the small is called regressive. A tax such as a poll tax, which is a certain number of dollars and paid by all persons, is a regressive tax. Also, a general sales tax levied as a uniform percentage of price is regressive because the lower-income receivers spend all of their income and therefore pay the tax on total income, while the high-income receivers save a portion of their income and avoid the tax on the portion saved. The total effects of fiscal action are considered regressive if, as a result of the action, the low incomes are decreased more or increased less than the higher incomes. The effects of fiscal action are considered progressive if the low incomes are decreased less or increased more than the higher incomes.

The Federal tax receipts during the 1920's were divided just about equally between excise-tax receipts and income-tax receipts; thus, the impact of the Federal tax system was not progressive as it is today but, perhaps, proportional. However, the expenditures of the Federal government, rather than being aimed at the poor as was the case with state and local expenditures, were received by the higher-income receivers—over 50 per cent of Federal expenditure was directly related to the debt. Therefore, fiscal activities of the Federal government during the 1920's tended to have a regressive effect; they increased the concentration of income in the upper brackets and intensified the problem of selling all goods produced. The state and local government fiscal activities absorbed savings and tended to equalize the distribution of goods and services. This is very nearly the reverse of relative effect of fiscal activities of the two levels of government during the 1930's.

Development in the 1930's

The period of the 1930's was the first time in the history of this nation that the governments of the United States, and especially the Federal government, entered into a program of spending and taxing aimed at eliminating an economic depression. The fiscal policy of the 1920's had been based on the idea that the nation's economy prospered best if the taxes levied upon profits were low and if every effort were constantly made to reduce government expenditure and the government debt. The last Federal revenue act passed prior to the great depression of the 1930's reduced the tax on corporate profits from 13½ to 12 per cent, and a temporary additional reduction of the taxes on profits was adopted by a joint resolution of Congress in December 1929—two months after the stock-market crash. However, prosperity did not return. Perhaps there was something wrong with the formula.

The expenditures of the Federal government and the state and local governments expanded slightly during the early 1930's, despite efforts to economize. At the same time, tax receipts began to fall off for all levels of governments. Federal receipts in 1933 were only slightly more than half as great as they had been in 1930, but expenditures had risen by a third. Desperate efforts were made by bewildered men to reduce Federal expenditures and increase Federal taxes. The administration continued to insist that the budget must be balanced, and most congressmen gave lip service to a balanced budget. But both the administration and Congress were unwilling to cut government expenditures; and Congress was unwilling to impose additional taxes upon individuals who were unemployed and upon business firms that were on the verge of bankruptcy. It was at this impasse between belief and reality that the concept of the cyclically balanced budget was born. (The expenditure of the government would equal the collection not within the fiscal year, but over a three to eleven year cycle.) The idea grew out of a need for a compromise between the balanced budget and the existing unbalanced budgets of the depression period. It was an attempt to rationalize the deficits of the period. Briefly, the idea was that budgets would be unbalanced during depressions and governments would expand their debt, but during prosperity there would be surplus of revenues and the debt would be retired. However, the presentation of the idea that debt increase might be good reduced the fear of government debt in the hearts of the people, and they became unwilling to pay taxes to reduce debt during prosperity. The Federal tax legislation of 1948 is an excellent demonstration of the weakness of the idea of a cyclically balanced budget. An idea born of desperate rationalization is seldom good, and the idea of a cyclically balanced budget may not be an exception.

The deficit of the Federal government grew as the 1930's advanced. The revenues of the Federal government were increased during the period to prevent the developing deficits, but the greater demands for expenditures more than absorbed these revenue increases. Federal fiscal activity began to approach World War I levels, and by 1939 Federal expenditures totaled $8,955 million, which was about equal to domestic expenditures in 1918. Federal revenues in 1929 totaled $3,833 million and by 1939 had grown to $6,742 million.* In 1929 over $1,000 million

*Data used in this analysis were taken from the *National Income Supplement* to *Survey of Current Business*, July, 1947, pp. 21–23.

had been available to apply on the Federal debt, while in 1939 the Federal government had a deficit of over $2,200 million. Federal expenditures for goods and services were about three times as great in 1939 as they had been in 1929.

State and local government expenditure also expanded during the 1930's, but this expansion was much less than the Federal expansion. Actually, most of the funds for expansion of state and local expenditure were provided by the Federal government. The use of Federal funds by state and local governments is as old as the nation, but the use of these grants, called grants-in-aid, expanded greatly during the 1930's. The average annual expenditures of state and local governments were $1,000 million greater in 1939 than in 1929, and their Federal grants-in-aid were up by about $850 million.

The social-security program, providing payments to the aged, the unemployed, and the handicapped, was established in the 1930's. By 1939 these new undertakings had expanded the expenditures of the Federal government by over $1,000 million and had expanded state expenditures by an even greater amount. A large portion of these expenditures was not actually made to individuals but was used to increase the totals of social-security funds and to increase the quantity of savings available for the purchase of Federal government debt. In addition, the Federal government expanded its expenditures on flood and erosion control. The Federal government also entered more actively into highway and public-building construction. The Federal expenditures to aid agriculture and housing also became much more important.

The types of expenditures expanded by the Federal government during the 1930's were aimed at increasing the scale of living of the people in the lower and middle income brackets. At the same time that expenditures of the Federal government became more closely related to the human welfare, the revenue system became more progressive. Thus, Federal fiscal activities began to increase the scale of living and decrease the savings of the citizens of the nation. In other words, the impact of Federal fiscal activities became progressive in its nature.

The large-scale use of borrowed funds made it possible for the Federal government substantially to increase real incomes of the lower income brackets without decreasing the real income of any individual. This relationship was possible because, as a result of government borrowing, large quantities of the factors of production that were unemployed became employed and produced goods.

The Federal tax revenues were expanded during the period by reintroducing and raising the rates of some of the excise taxes. The reintroduction of legal alcoholic beverages expanded the revenue of all levels of government. The Federal taxes on personal income and corporation profits were also increased. The general tax applicable to corporation profits was raised to 19 per cent in the Revenue Act of 1938. In 1936, the Federal government experimented with a tax on the undistributed profits of corporations, the purpose of which was to increase purchasing power through an expansion of corporate dividend payments.*

The state and local governments were greatly in need of additional revenues during the 1930's. The receipts from their established taxes had declined sharply. In order to get the money required for normal operation, many states introduced a general retail-sales tax. This tax has since developed into the most important source of state revenue. New taxes were not introduced by local governments; however, state aid to local government expanded, and in some states the property tax became exclusively a source for local revenue.

FISCAL DEVELOPMENT, WORLD WAR II AND AFTER

Government expenditures increased with the outbreak of World War II and continued at a high rate after the end of hostilities.

Size of War Fiscal Activity

The fiscal requirements of World War II necessitated a tremendous expansion of Federal revenues and expenditures. The attendant prosperity increased state and local revenues, but the rationing of raw materials and the shortage of labor reduced state and local expenditures. Although Federal tax revenues expanded greatly during the war and remained high in the postwar period, expenditures expanded much more rapidly and the gross Federal debt increased from $42,968 million in 1940 to $269,422 million in 1946 or $226,454 million.† At the time of

*In 1948, Great Britain utilized a tax on distributed corporate profits in order to decrease the quantity of purchasing power arising from corporate dividend payments.

†The gross per-capita debt increased from $325.62 in 1940 to $1,907.70 in 1946. *Annual Report of the Secretary of the Treasury for Fiscal Year ended June 30, 1947* (Washington, U.S. Government Printing Office, 1947), p. 356.

this unprecedented expansion of the Federal debt, the debt of state and local governments was being reduced. However, the total reduction of state and local debt was very small compared to the Federal expansion.*

In 1944, Federal expenditures alone were $95,559 million. This is greater than the gross national product of the entire nation for any year prior to 1941. During the years 1942 through 1945, Federal expenditures averaged nearly half the gross national product. The fiscal experience of World War II vividly shows that it is during these periods that the relative importance of the public economy, and particularly the Federal portion, expands. Also, the war experience of a gross national-product increase of over 100 per cent shows that government fiscal activity can increase tremendously the productivity of the economy. Government fiscal activity, which never quite succeeded in its efforts to utilize fully the productive resources of the nation in the 1930's, finally achieved its goal during World War II. But during the 1940's the pump was primed to overflowing and inflation resulted.

Government Revenue Sources During the War

The Federal government provided all of the funds for financing World War II and for the international postwar reconstruction. Table 1-1, given below, briefly summarizes Federal fiscal

TABLE 1–1. Federal expenditures, taxes, and deficits during World War II, 1941–1945 (in billions of dollars).

Year	1941	1942	1943	1944	1945	Total, five years
Federal expenditures........	14	34	80	95	100	323
Federal taxes...............	8	13	22	44	46	133
Federal deficit..............	6	21	57	51	54	190

Source: *Report of the Secretary of the Treasury for the Fiscal Year ending June 30, 1945*, p. 87.

activity during the five war years. The large portion of the financing done by expanding government debt was unfortunate. Certainly in 1943 more than slightly over one-fourth of Federal expenditures should have been obtained from taxes. During the entire five-year period, Federal borrowings were $57,000 million greater than tax receipts. About 60 per cent of the funds to

*State debt reduction from 1941 to 1946 amounted to $1,276 million or 35.1 per cent of the 1941 total. From the *Book of the States, 1948–49*, vol. 7 (Chicago, The Council of State Governments, 1948), p. 247.

finance World War II (1941-1945) were obtained by an expansion of the Federal debt. The great fiscal advantage of the Federal government over state and local governments in borrowing operations was demonstrated during World War II. Despite the fact that Federal debt was increasing at an unprecedented speed, the average rate of interest paid decreased. This ability of the Federal government always to obtain all the funds wanted is important in financing a war and is also very important in making Federal fiscal activity paramount during a depression.

War-finance policy has largely revolved around the determination of the correct portion of war expenditure that should be financed from tax levies and, on the other side of the same shield, the portion of total war revenues that should be obtained from loans. The more popular statement of the problem has been loans versus taxes; this, however, provides an incorrect emphasis. All major wars must be financed by the use of both loans and taxes, and the relevant discussion is related to the portion of each to be used.[*]

Merely because a war is financed partly by loans does not mean that the generation fighting the war is able to shift a portion of the economic cost to future generations. Most of the economic costs of war consist of the overtime put in by regular employees, the productive activity obtained from individuals temporarily drawn into the labor market, and the private consumption forgone. The hour of leisure lost or the steak that was not consumed will never be enjoyed. The scale of living of post-war generations will suffer particularly in those nations where destruction is severe or where a foreign debt has been accumulated.

The Federal government expanded its tax receipts largely by enacting a war excess-profits tax on corporate earnings and by increasing the rates of the individual and corporate income taxes. In addition, many new excise taxes were imposed and the rates of the old excise taxes were increased. Pressure to enact a Federal sales tax was resisted. These special rates and taxes, with the exception of the excess-profits tax, were largely continued until the spring of 1948. The excess-profits tax was repealed by Section 122 (a) of Revenue Act of 1945. The rates of the individual income tax were reduced and personal exemptions increased in the Revenue Act of 1948. The excise-tax rates in 1948 were still practically unchanged from their wartime levels.

[*]A. C. Pigou, *The Political Economy of War* (New York, Macmillan, 1941), pp. 72–86.

The expenditures of the state and local governments during World War II decreased by an average annual amount of $1,000 million. For this reason and because of the increased revenue receipts, a number of states reduced the rates of their income taxes. Also, the trend continued toward making a larger portion of the property tax available to local governments. Very few new state or local taxes were assessed. State and local governments during this period did not obtain net revenues from borrowing, instead state and local government debt was decreased.

Fiscal Trends Since World War II

It was hoped that Federal government defense and defense-related expenditures, and therefore Federal taxes, could be cut sharply as soon as the war between the United States and Germany-Japan ended. But this hope was not to be realized. First of all, large Federal government expenditures were required to assist in the restoration of the economies of our European allies. Second, despite the surrender of our enemies during World War II, international tensions have continued, requiring large government outlays. And, as a capstone to tax-cut hopes, on June 26, 1950, the United States as a member of the United Nations became the principal participant in the Korean War.

Table 1-2 shows the revenues of the Federal governments, state governments, and local governments for selected years since World War II.

Table 1-2. Federal, State, and Local Government General Revenue, 1946-1953 (in millions of dollars).

Year	Total Revenues Collected by All Levels of Government	Total Revenues of Federal Government	Total Revenues of State Governments	Total Revenues of Local Governments
1946	50,942	38,493	7,198	8,243
1948	57,224	40,890	10,025	11,036
1951	83,246	57,566	15,547	12,642*
1953	105,540	75,157	17,979	15,165*

Source: *Summary of Governmental Finances*, Bureau of the Census, Department of Commerce, Releases of October 20, 1954, November 2, 1953, and August, 1950. *Exclusive of grants-in-aid.

In 1946, the first year after World War II, revenues collected by the Federal government fell sharply; expenditures fell sharply

also but not rapidly enough to balance the Federal government's **budget.** It was not until 1948 that the Federal government collected more in revenues than it spent. For the next two years Federal revenues rose slightly, but expenditures increased slightly more, with the result that the Federal government's budget showed only a small deficit. The outbreak of the Korean War in the Summer of 1950 changed the situation, and both Federal revenues and Federal expenditures increased sharply. But again when expenditures reached their peak, revenues were inadequate; and the Federal deficit rose to $9,389 million in fiscal year 1953 (July 1, 1952-June 30, 1953).

While Federal expenditures did not fall as much as the Treasury had hoped that they would, they have not reached the $100,000 million level of the World War II period despite the rapid increase in prices. On the other hand, Federal revenues in 1953 reached an all-time high.

At the same time that Federal revenues were increasing, the state and local governments were also stepping up their tax collections and expenditures. The state and local governments had been forced to cut sharply their outlays during World War II, and as a result they had accumulated large numbers of projects which required immediate attention. To meet partially these demands, state and local governments doubled their revenues during the seven-year period between 1946 and 1953 (Table 1-2). This increase did little more than absorb the increase during the same period in the cost of goods and services which they purchased. Therefore, in order to catch up on postponed projects and to provide schools, highways, and other facilities for their expanding populations, state and local governments were forced not only to use the surpluses which they had accumulated during the World War II period but also to increase substantially their indebtedness. In 1953, for example, the combined debt of state and local governments increased by over $3,000 million. This was an 11 per cent increase in one year and brought the total debt outstanding of state governments to $7,824 million and of local governments to $25,735 million, for a combined total of $33,560 million.

Much of the expansion in revenues and expenditures of all levels of government since 1946 has been due to the inflation experienced not only in the United States but also to a greater or lesser degree in all countries of the world. Our Federal government cut taxes sharply in 1948, but in 1950 it found it necessary to increase the rates of the individual and corporate income taxes, to increase the number of excise taxes and their rates, and to restore the excess profits tax. State and local governments, too, increased some of their tax rates and in some cases introduced new taxes to enable them to collect the revenues required. However, the portion of total revenues arising from the principal sources of revenues has remained relatively constant.

The Federal government relies principally on the individual income tax for its revenue, with the corporation income tax a close second and during periods of war likely to be first. The state governments rely on the general sales tax and their special excise taxes, with the one on gasoline being by far the most important. Of course, many states collect individual and corporate income taxes, but they have never become a dominant source of revenues to states. The mainstay of local government revenues is the property tax which is collected as a per cent of the assessed valuation of property subject to the tax (Table 1-3). In practice the tax is collected largely from owners of real estate.

Table 1-3 shows the revenue sources, the uses of revenues, and the indebtedness of each level of government. The percentages given are for fiscal year 1953; however, these percentages remain relatively constant, and unless a great new fiscal development sweeps the country, they will be about as correct for 1963 as they were for 1953.

The expenditures of the Federal government continue to be dominated by national defense. These have been running in 1955 at the annual rate of over $40,000 million even though the United States is not involved in a shooting war. This amount is about a third more than the total expenditures of all state and local governments. In addition, the Federal government annually spends huge sums for purposes closely related to war. For example, the interest payments of the Federal government totaled nearly $7,000 million in fiscal year 1955, which is about as much as is spent on all public elementary and secondary education in the United States. (The colossal Federal debt of some $278,000 million arose largely from the costs of financing war—at least $200,000 million can be considered war debt.) Another Federal expenditure item closely related to war are the costs of services and benefits to veterans, over $4,000 million, or about the same as all expenditures on public highways.

The expenditures of state governments go largely for highways and education, which are of approximately equal importance when the budgets of all states are combined. In both

TABLE 1–3. Per Cent Distribution between Federal, State, and Local Government Revenue by Source, Expenditure by Purpose, and Debt, 1953.

Item	Federal Government	State Governments	Local Governments
General revenue, total—			
Net of intergovernmental	74.2	12.6	13.4
Taxes..................	75.1	12.6	12.2
Individual income.......	96.6	3.1	0.3
Corporation income.....	96.3	3.7	—
Sales, gross receipts, and customs..............	59.9	35.9	4.1
Property..............	—	3.9	96.1
Death and gift..:......	79.6	20.1	0.3
Licenses, permits, and other...............	17.0	66.1	16.9
Charges and miscellaneous	62.9	12.8	24.4
Direct general expenditures	72.4	9.2	18.4
National defense........	100.0	—	—
International assistance...	100.0	—	—
Education..............	7.2	16.2	76.7
Elementary and secondary schools....	0.6	1.9	97.5
All other..............	29.6	64.6	5.8
Highways.............	1.3	55.0	43.7
Public welfare...........	0.4	60.3	39.3
Total debt outstanding at end of fiscal year............	88.8	2.6	8.6

Source: *Summary of Governmental Finances in 1953*, Bureau of the Census, Department of Commerce, October 20, 1954.

these areas there is a recognized need for expansion, but expenditures have lagged behind what is generally considered a desirable level because of the problems of raising the money.

A third of all expenditures of local governments are made to finance education. The high birth rate since 1940 has caused such a shortage of classrooms and teachers that it can be safely forecast that education expenditures will increase in the future and with them the total expenditures of local governments.

CONCLUSION

THE public portion of the total economic activity of the United States is large and very important in establishing the level and direction of the whole economy. In view of the huge increase of the dollar amounts spent by all levels of government, the increase in the portion of total economic activity consisting of public expenditures has increased very little since the end of the 1930's. It appears that the mixture of public and private expenditures of about one dollar of public to three or four dollars of private suits the needs of the American economy, for it remains relatively stable. Either a severe depression or a war is necessary to disturb the one-to-three relationship and after the crisis has passed, there is a strong tendency to revert back to the former mixture.

The fiscal actions of the governments of the United States during the past thirty years show that taxes are pulled by two strong forces that are sometimes in conflict and also that expenditures are subject to two pressures that are very likely to conflict. On the one hand, there is the strong pressure to levy taxes in the old way and to avoid changing the rates, and especially to avoid raising the rates. This attitude has as its basic assumption the idea that taxes do not affect the level of economic activity. On the other hand, there is the pressure to change taxes and tax rates to encourage or contract the level of economic activity. The conflicting pressures on expenditures are, one, that certain things need doing and the government is the one to do them, and the other, that government expenditures are only partly related to the need for doing things. To this second group, government expenditures are a very important tool for maintaining the correct level of economic activity. The ups and downs of taxes and expenditures during the past thirty years are to a considerable extent an account of the way these diverse pressures—two for taxes and two for expenditures—have worked themselves out.

QUESTIONS AND PROBLEMS

1. Define fiscal policy; by the use of examples differentiate between fiscal policy and monetary policy. What are some of the difficulties related to separation of fiscal and monetary policy?

2. Compare the fiscal developments of the post-World War I period with those of the post-World War II period.

3. What is the relative size of the public economy? How has the growth of the public economy affected fiscal policy?

4. Why were the fiscal activities of the Federal government during the 1920's important in determining fiscal activities of the Federal government during the 1930's?

5. Give the principal causes of the growth of government expenditures during the post-World War II period. What do you think will be the trend of government expenditures during the next twenty years? What types of expenditures will show the greatest change? Why?

6. A decrease of government expenditure and a sales tax were advocated by the experts of the Treasury in January, 1933. Why, in your opinion?

CHAPTER 2

Terms and Concepts Used in Fiscal Policy Analysis

THE discussion of Chapter 1 summarized the fiscal history of the United States during the past thirty years. This chapter will define the economic concepts utilized in describing the level of economic activity and will briefly consider the determinants of the level of economic activity that are closely related to government fiscal decisions.

National Income

The term "national income" is used very frequently and has become the basis for the formulation of most economic plans. Although the term is now very common, its accurate measurement in the United States started in 1929 and the national income data of most nations are still not much more than informed guesses. In those countries where data for accurate measurement are available, disagreements still continue regarding the inclusion of particular items in the total—for example, the concept of national income used by the United States Department of Commerce has been recently revised upward by the inclusion of imputed rent of owner-occupied dwellings and corporate profits prior to payment of corporate-profit taxes.*

There are a number of terms which relate to the income of the nation. Briefly, the more common terms and their definitions are as follows:

National income is the aggregate earnings of labor and property that arise from the current production of goods and services by the nation's economy. Thus it measures the total

*See *Federal Reserve Bulletin*, Sept., 1947, vol. 33, no. 9, pp. 1105–1114, for excellent brief discussion of national income and product statistics.

factor costs of the goods and services produced by the economy. Earnings are recorded in the forms in which they accrue to residents of the nation, inclusive of taxes on those earnings. As such, they consist of the compensation of employees, the profits of corporate and unincorporated enterprises, net interest, and the rental income flowing to persons.

Gross national product or expenditure is the market value of the output of goods and services produced by the nation's economy, before deduction of depreciation charges and other allowances for business and institutional consumption of durable capital goods. The nation's economy in this context refers to the labor and property supplied by residents of the nation. Gross national product comprises the purchases of goods and services by consumers and government, gross private domestic investment, and net foreign investment.

Net national product or expenditure comprises the purchases of goods and services by consumers and government, net private domestic investments, and net foreign investment.

Personal income is measured as the sum of wage and salary receipts, other labor income, proprietors' and rental income, interest and dividends, and transfer payments.

Disposable income is the income remaining to persons after deductions of personal tax and other payments to general government.

The term national income in our discussions refers to the concept of gross national product (GNP) unless another concept is specifically named. If GNP is represented by Y, consumption purchases by C, gross private domestic investment plus net foreign balance by I, and government expenditures for goods and services by G, the concept can be expressed in the formula $Y = C + I + G$.

As will be pointed out, all government expenditures result in either consumption or investment just as do the expenditures of individuals and firms, but because government is frequently under special consideration, government expenditures are treated as of a different breed.

Also, all government expenditures are in a way group expenditures of the residents of the geographical area ruled by the government and therefore could be considered expenditures of the taxpayers. But again because of the desirability of frequently considering government separately, government expenditures are often assumed to be determined on quite a different basis from that of the expenditures of households and firms.

Investment

Investment activity is carried on by both the private and the public economy. Investment as a fiscal-policy concept is concerned largely with factors determining size of private investment and economic effects of public investment.

Investment, in the private economy, means the purchase of newly produced buildings, machines, inventories, residences, and the net foreign balance. These are capital goods which increase production or discharge utilities over a rather long period of time. The term "net foreign balance" refers to the amount that foreigners buy in this country over the amount that we buy in foreign countries. This latter type of investment was formerly made nearly entirely within the private economy, but since the middle of the 1940's it has been largely a public activity, and in addition in 1955 it meets few of the requirements of a investment—for example, the expenditures abroad of the Foreign Operations Administration. Also during World War II many additional factories and other productive facilities were financed by the public economy. The development of public-housing programs and government lending for residence construction is another example of the expansion of the public economy into areas of private investment.

Public investment, as shown above, can be and often is of the same type as private investment. In addition, public investment includes expenditures for highways, public buildings, dams, and the like, which are seldom purchased by members of the private economy. Sometimes other government expenditures —such as those for battleships, education, and health—are also considered investment expenditures. The justification for including a battleship is that it is certainly a good which will be used over a period of time. The justification for including education and health expenditures is that they certainly increase productivity over a period of time.

A private investment is made because of expected future returns over the cost of investment. Public investment is, or under ideal conditions would be, determined by the social values expected to arise from using funds in that particular way rather than in some other manner.

The term "investment" is not used here to refer to the purchase of securities or the purchase of homes or productive facilities which have already been produced. This type of investment is called financial investment; it does not lead to an increase of production but merely means that the bank account of one person has been increased and that of another reduced. Under certain circumstances—for example, if the security were owned by a commercial bank and the new owner were a private individual—the account of the purchaser is reduced but a compensating increase in the account of the seller does not take place.

Consumption

The meaning of the term "consumption" has been partly developed in our definition of investment. The purchases which are not investments are consumption expenditures. Consumption, defined in a positive fashion, is the use of economic resources by ultimate consumers.   The use of resources in consumption can take place in a number of ways. The resources can be utilized through the market as purchasable goods and services. The resources can be utilized in the home through self-production and consumption. Or consumption can arise through the medium of government provision of goods and services.

Consumption through the medium of government provision or public consumption varies from consumption through the market place or private consumption. The variation arises principally from the way that the quantity and the manner of resource use is determined. If consumption is determined by the market place, each consumer has as many votes as dollars (units of purchasing power) ; if determined through government action, each consumer has his own vote and as many votes as there are other individuals also desiring that type of consumption. Thus resource use in the private economy will be determined to a great extent by the *number of dollars* favouring a type of consumption, while government consumption will be determined by the number of *individuals* favouring a certain type of consumption.

Saving

Saving is one of the most difficult economic concepts to define, to calculate, and to apply correctly theoretically. It is also one of the most important concepts.

As calculated in our national income accounts, savings are made by all three sectors of the economy—government, corporate, and personal. Each of these three sectors is an important group of savers.

Table 2-1 shows for selected years the sources of gross savings. The largest item included in this concept of savings

during normal years is depreciation (the allowance permitted
by the Bureau of Internal Revenue in calculating taxable income
for the cost of machines and buildings used in production). De-

TABLE 2–1. Sources of gross savings, selected years, 1929–1953
(millions of dollars).

	1929	1944	1947	1950	1953
1. Personal saving...	4,168	36,928	4,043	12,104	20,019
2. Undistributed corporate profits.....	2,446	5,698	11,721	12,934	8,921
3. Corporate inventory reduction adjustment........	472	−287	−5,899	−4,864	−964
4. Business depreciation charges......	7,698	10,793	12,150	18,042	24,170
5. Capital outlays charged to current expense.........	506	854	1,401	1,858	2,248
6. Accidental damage to business capital	413	360	567	616	808
7. Excess of wage accruals over disbursements.......	0	−193	15	0	−76
8. Federal government surplus on income and product transaction.......	1,159	−54,577	12,222	9,229	−6,831
9. State and local government surplus on income and product transaction............	−128	2,689	1,044	−1,166	200

Source: *National Income, 1954, A Supplement to the Survey of Current
Business* (Washington, U.S. Government Printing Office, 1954), p. 164,
165.

preciation is not usually considered to be saving, but it is likely
to be the most important single source of funds for financing
investment-type expenditures. Also depreciation is a very important part of the concept of gross savings.*

In national income theory and in national income accounting,
investment-type expenditures can be made only with savings.
Also, all savings are used to make only investment-type expenditures. This equality of investment and saving in the national
income accounts is between gross savings and gross investment
and not personal saving and some other investment total.

*Depreciation allowances in tax returns are only indirectly related to the cost
of wear and tear of machines. See pp. 108–109 for a discussion of accelerated
depreciation (amortization).

Most theoretical analyses of savings are concerned almost exclusively with personal or household savings. In terms of national income accounting, the saving of households is the difference between disposable income and expenditures for consumption. Table 2-1 (line 1) shows that total personal saving was drastically decreased between 1944 and 1947. Actually, personal attitudes toward saving did not change nearly as much during this three-year period as the figures seem to indicate; the large reduction in the personal saving total for 1947 was due almost entirely to the way in which this figure is calculated.

Expenditures for durable goods such as automobiles and refrigerators are considered consumer expenditures in the year in which they are made. In 1944 consumers could not buy these goods. In 1947 they could buy them. Therefore, in 1947 consumers bought these goods with funds accumulated during previous years. The amount of these accumulations spent was deducted from current saving. However, in later years when accumulations were spent for housing, saving was not decreased, for this type of consumer expenditure is considered an investment.

There are many statistical and logical shortcomings hidden in the personal saving total; only two will be mentioned:

Payments made by householders to retire installment indebtedness, which has arisen largely from the purchase of durable consumer goods, are included in the personal saving total. This was the major cause of the rise of personal saving in 1953.

Inventory increases by all businesses not organized as corporations are included as personal savings. And it was the drop in the inventories of these businesses in 1947 that was another major cause of the low personal savings figure of that year. To provide a more meaningful designation of the difference between disposable income and consumer expenditures, one authority recommends the use of the term "private noncorporate saving" rather than "personal saving."*

Table 2-1 (line 2) shows that the portion of savings resulting from undistributed corporate profits has been very important since the World War II period and demonstrates every indication of remaining important. Undistributed corporate profits are savings which arise because corporate directors do not distribute

*George Garvy, Senior Economist, Federal Reserve Bank of New York.

corporate earnings as dividends. The attention that economists give this portion of savings, which in some years is as great and in some years is greater than personal saving, is very meager compared to the attention that they give personal saving.*

Information available on undistributed corporate profits permits little more than the conclusion that they are *not* determined by the same factors which determine personal or household saving. One very important determining influence on undistributed corporate profits, as we shall have an opportunity to see later, is the tax structure. In addition, undistributed corporate profits for a single year show a relationship to current earnings and to the level of dividends of the previous year.

Lines 8 and 9 of Table 2-1 show government—Federal, state, and local—savings data. These are another important component of gross savings.

Governments save when revenues are larger than expenditures. The major difference between the concept of saving as applied to governments and that applied to households and corporations is that governments save only when they have a budgetary surplus and dissave only when they have a budgetary deficit. A household saves when it does not spend all its income for consumption, and a corporation saves when it does not distribute all its profits as dividends and sets aside depreciation allowances The savings of a household or a corporation are not reduced when a household or a corporation uses its funds to finance the construction of a new building. However, the savings of a government are reduced when it uses its revenues to finance the construction of a new building.

Although by this point, "saving" seems to have so many meanings as to be almost meaningless, the discussion of "oversaving" in the following section will show how the concept, despite its shortcomings, is useful to economists in their efforts to understand how the economy functions.

Oversaving

The goals of fiscal policy are closely related to the economic concept of oversaving that has been developed since J. M. Keynes' *The General Theory of Employment, Interest, and Money.*

*See Sergei P. Dobrovolsky, *Corporate Income Retention, 1915–1943* (New York, National Bureau of Economic Research, 1951); and Franco Modigliani, "Fluctuations in the Savings-Income Ratio: A Problem in Economic Forecasting," *Part V, Vol. 11, in Studies in Income and Wealth* (New York, National Bureau of Economic Research, 1949).

Although the idea of oversaving—merely too much saving—is simple, the measurement of oversaving is so complicated that it requires more economic data than are available. The problem of determining the quantity of oversaving is closely related to the general problem of money flow.* Stated differently, oversaving exists when savings arising from a given level of income are greater than investment expenditure.

The problem of oversaving lies in the flow of money payments becoming inadequate to maintain an existing level of economic activity. At first glance, all saving may appear as money not spent for goods or services; however, on closer examination, it is seen that savings are often spent for goods and services used for production purposes rather than consumption. Oversaving arises when there is a greater quantity of money *not* spent on consumption goods than *is* spent on investment goods—that is, more is saved than is invested. This relationship brings about a reduction in the money flow and a consequent decrease in economic activity. However, whether money flows rapidly or slowly from groups to groups, the amount of money held at any one time is always equal to the total money of the society.

The requirement in a dynamic economy is not, however, just the maintenance of a particular size of income flow. The flow must be constantly expanding. This expansion of the size of the flow is necessary if the ever increasing quantity of goods and services is not to be sold at continually lower prices. A socialistic economy might be able to endure continually falling prices, but a capitalistic economy certainly cannot. The problem of a desirable quantity of saving is really nothing more than maintaining the proper-sized income stream and also providing for any desired expansion.

The quantity of the money flow is determined by the amount of money and its velocity. If there is no reason to expect an increase in speed of money flow, it is necessary to have an increase in the quantity of money.† In the past, the increase in money has taken place largely through investment that was in

---

*By money flow is meant "who has paid and who has received how much on account of various types of transactions or objects of payments." From "Tracing Money Flow through the United States Economy," by Morris A. Copeland, in the *American Economic Review*, vol. 36, no. 2, 1946, p. 31.

*An increase in the flow of a liquid can be accomplished by increasing the size of the pipe or increasing the pressure. Similarly, the quantity of money flow can be expanded by an increase in velocity of money turnover or amount of money.

excess of voluntary savings.* If savings available for investment are as great as the need for investment, this method of bringing about the expansion of money flow has been destroyed. Thus oversaving may in many instances be nothing more than the elimination of the shortage of voluntary saving which existed in the past. This shortage made necessary a desirable increase in the quantity of money through expansion of bank deposits. Oversaving, then, has become the term used to express an inadequate flow of money income, and the concept includes in addition an explanation of why this flow is inadequate. It is also quite possible that oversaving may arise from a decrease in speed of money flow as well as a decrease in the quantity of money; in fact, the former is the way in which it first appears.†

The acts of saving and investing usually take more time than the single act of spending for consumption. Even if every dollar saved is immediately set aside for the purchase of capital goods, the machinery of saving and spending is slower than that of merely spending. The same applies to taxes collected, unless expenditures are made in anticipation of tax receipts.

A result of a large quantity of voluntary saving is that investments can be made without any increase in the quantity of money, or with a smaller increase than would otherwise be necessary. For this reason, voluntary saving makes investment possible without the danger of inflation. Also, savings may produce conditions of deflation. The amount of savings is correct if the money flow with the existing quantity of saving is of the correct amount to maintain what is generally considered a desirable level of economic activity. If the savings are insufficient, inflationary tendencies will develop.

Logically, emphasis regarding the cause of insufficient money flow could be changed and placed upon consumption or upon the institutions having the power to increase the quantity of money. However, the emphasis has been placed upon savings and investment. This has been true because it has been the change in the relationship between these two economic phenomena that has created the new problems regarding the maintenance of an adequate flow of money. Another reason for

---

*Voluntary saving refers to income received but not spent for consumption. Forced saving is the bidding of factors away from consumption good production by increasing the quantity of money with a resulting inflatuation.

†Actually a common definition of saving is that it is that part of disposable income (earned yesterday but disposed of today) that is not spent on consumption.

this is that our economy is business directed. The decision to invest is determined by profit possibilities, and the persons who do the saving also do the investing and receive the profits.*

Deficit Finance

The term deficit finance is frequently used when referring to government fiscal activity related to the provision of a high level of national income. The term means that the government obtains an important portion of its budget by borrowing from individuals and commercial banks. When the government enters into borrowing activities, the budget is said to be unbalanced. What is meant is that the budget does not provide for tax receipts equal to expenditures. If the government obtains its revenues from borrowing, it is likely to bring about an increase in the effective demand for goods and services—that is, aggregate demand. This increase arises because the government has an additional quantity of money to spend but the quantity of money spent by individuals is not necessarily reduced. The borrowing of money from individuals often means that savings are used to purchase government debts. If the government had not borrowed, national income would have fallen. The refusal of the private economy to go into debt makes it necessary for the public economy to increase its debt—practice deficit finance—if deflation is to be prevented.

Deficit finance has been used by governments for many years in the financing of wars. However, it was considered an undesirable emergency measure that should not be resorted to unless the nation was in danger of being conquered by a foreign enemy. During the period of the 1930's, the obtaining of government revenues in this manner was seen to be a weapon that could be used to fight the internal enemy of depression and unemployment. It is in this second use that deficit financing is discussed in this section.

The Multiplier and Acceleration Effects and the Consumption Function

The multiplier, as used in fiscal policy analysis, relates to the increase in private consumption expenditures which arises from an increase in government expenditure. It is usually assumed that the government expenditure is made in the provision of

*Oversaving is related to investment opportunities. The reduction of investment opportunities is related to the concept of the mature economy. See George Terborgh, *The Bogey of Economic Maturity* (Chicago, Machinery and Allied Products Institute, 1945) and Alvin H. Hansen, *Full Recovery or Stagnation* (New York, Norton, 1938).

additional capital goods—for example, a public-works expenditure. The concept of the multiplier is only concerned with the increase in consumption expenditure that arises when the original government investment becomes income to individuals in the form of wages, profits, or interest. The portions of the original government expenditure which are drained off in savings and idle holdings of cash do not become a consumption expenditure and are called leakages.* The concept of the multiplier includes not only the original increase in private consumption expenditure that arises from the government investment but also the total increase in private consumption arising from the government investment. The additional leakages at each stage reduce the quantity of each successive private consumption-expenditure increase. The multiplier is said to be infinite if the leakages are zero, or if none of the income is saved, and one if 100 per cent of the government expenditure is saved. If the multiplier is assumed to be between two and three, the disposable income of individuals within a rather short period would increase by two or three times the government expenditure. This phenomenon is just as true of private investment activity as it is of government investment activity.

The accelerator principle is used in fiscal policy to describe the induced investment that arises from increased consumption expenditure. Thus the full effect of an additional government investment expenditure includes both the multiplier and accelerator effects.† The addition to national income that is provided by the accelerator leverage is determined by the relatively large expansion in investment that may arise from an expansion of consumption. This bunching of investment caused by the acceleration principle arises because a small expansion of consumption will bring about an immediate demand for a number of new machines. This will be the period of boom. However, if consumption does not continue to expand, the number of new machines demanded and produced will decline quickly. This will be the period of depression.

The accelerator will have an important effect if the industries producing consumer goods are operating at capacity when the

*For a good analysis and description of different kinds of leakages, see Henry Hilgard Villard's *Deficit Spending and the National Income* (New York, Farrar & Rinehart, 1941), pp. 238–257.

†Alvin H. Hansen, *Fiscal Policy and Business Cycles* (New York, Norton, 1941) and Gottfried Haberler, *Prosperity and Depression* (Geneva, League of Nations, 1940).

increase in demand arises.* Under these conditions, immediate orders for new machines must be placed to meet the demand. Also, the accelerator action will be more important if businessmen think the increase in demand for their goods will be maintained and may expand in the future.

The concept of propensity to consume, or the consumption function, refers to the portion of the income of an individual or an income group that is spent for consumption purposes. Keynes concluded that as the income of a community increased and decreased the amount of consumption also increased and decreased, but not as rapidly.† This relationship existed in the United States until the post-World War II period, when private savings decreased despite an expansion of income.‡ The propensity to consume is high if a large portion of income is spent on consumption and a small amount saved or invested. It is low if the reverse is the situation. The propensity to consume is high if the annual income of the individual or income group is low and low if the annual income is high. The portion of a particular level of income that will be consumed is considered to be constant.§ If the propensity to consume of the different income levels is constant, (1) it becomes possible to forecast the multiplier effect of particular expenditures, and (2) it becomes possible to estimate the quantity of savings that would arise from different levels of national income with a certain type of income distribution.‖ The general formula for calculating the multiplier from the marginal propensity to consume is:

$$\text{multiplier} = \frac{1}{1 - \text{marginal propensity to consume}}.$$

*The acceleration of investment in the United States arises when the Federal Reserve Board Index to production capacity approaches 0.85, disappears when it drops to 0.80.

†John Maynard Keynes, *The General Theory of Employment, Interest, and Money* (New York, Harcourt, Brace, 1936), p. 114.

‡In 1946, personal income was $177.2 billion and personal savings were $14.8 billion. In 1947, personal income increased to $196.8 billion but personal savings decreased to $10.9 billion.

§Keynes corrects for the secular drift and thereby provides a constant consumption function over time by stating his consumption function in terms of wage units. The use of wage units largely corrects for price and productivity changes.

‖The marginal propensity to consume determines the multiplier. "If the consumption psychology of the community is such that they will choose to consume, e.g., nine-tenths of an increment of income, then the multiplier is 10; and the total employment caused by (e.g.) increased public works will be ten times the primary employment provided by the public works themselves . . ." J. M. Keynes, *The General Theory of Employment, Interest, and Money*, pp. 116–117.

The multiplier is the reciprocal of the fraction that expresses the proportion of any given income increase that people save.

Efficient Resource Utilization

The efficient use of resources is their use in the fashion that will maximize the quantity of net utilities and also their use by the user offering the highest price. In economic theory, it has usually been assumed that the use of resources in the manner dictated by price relationships will also maximize the net utilities that could be obtained by the production of goods and services with the available resources. Public finance does not provide for the allocation of resources in any manner other than that dictated by the price relationships. Rather, the old price relationships are changed by changing the distribution of income through the collection of taxes and borrowing, by direct purchasing of goods and services by the government, and by affecting the quantity of monopoly in the private economy.

If the assumption is made that any distribution of income other than that determined in the traditional market place decreases the efficiency of resource allocation, then all activities of the public economy reduce the efficiency of resource allocation. However, in order to accept this assumption it is necessary to admit that the distribution of income indicated by Table 2-2 and 4-1 (p. 69) provides the consumption demand that would bring about the most efficient use of the nation's resources. This could be assumed only if it is believed that the additional desire to work arising from poverty combined with very high prizes for success increases productivity more than poverty and idleness of the rich reduces production efficiency. In addition, the increased utility obtained by making available additional units of goods and services to those in the lower income brackets must be assumed to be not much greater than the utility obtained by making available similar quantities of goods and services to high-income receivers. The writer does not believe these assumptions can be made.

The determination of the most efficient utilization of resources is necessarily a combination of uses in the manner that maximizes quantity of goods and services and net utilities. It is not possible to arrive at rather definite conclusions of the manner of resource use that will maximize the quantity of goods and services, but the determination of the quantities of particular goods and services that will maximize net utilities is quite another thing.

TABLE 2–2. Aggregate income and savings of United States consumers,* by 15 income levels, 1935–1936.

Income level	Number of families and single individuals	Aggregate income (mills.)	Savings		
			Amount (mills.)	Per cent of income	Per cent of net total savings
Under $500	6,710,911	$2,061	$ −800	−38.8	−13.4
$500–$750	5,771,960	3,615	−382	−10.5	−6.4
$750–$1,000	5,876,078	5,130	−254	−4.9	−4.3
$1,000–$1,250	4,990,995	5,589	−97	−1.7	−1.6
$1,250–$1,500	3,743,428	5,109	95	1.9	1.6
$1,500–$1,750	2,889,904	4,661	196	4.2	3.3
$1,750–$2,000	2,296,022	4,214	245	5.8	4.1
$2,000–$2,500	2,958,611	6,572	587	8.9	9.8
$2,500–$3,000	1,475,474	4,005	482	12.0	8.1
$3,000–$4,000	1,354,078	4,599	742	16.1	12.4
$4,000–$5,000	464,191	2,045	434	21.2	7.2
$5,000–$10,000	595,908	4,092	1,218	29.8	20.4
$10,000–$15,000	152,682	1,747	679	38.9	11.4
$15,000–$20,000	67,923	1,175	473	40.2	7.9
$20,000 and over	110,135	4,645	2,360	50.8	39.5
All levels	39,458,300	59,259	5,978	10.1	100.0

*Includes all families and single individuals but excludes residents in institutional groups.

Source: National Resources Committee, *Consumer Expenditures in the United States, 1935–36* (Washington, 1939), table 8, p. 48. Taken from Temporary National Economic Committee, Monograph No. 37, *Saving, Investment and National Income*, by Oscar L. Altman, p. 17.

The assumptions made when national income data are compared to determine utilization of resources from one period to another are that techniques have remained constant and that the relative prices placed upon different goods and services correctly determine value of the good or service to the nation. The value placed upon different goods and services is largely determined by income distribution; and, with the very unequal income distribution existing in the United States, it is very doubtful that relative prices correctly measure relative values.

Full Employment

Full employment is usually considered only in relation to the employment of labor, and it is assumed that when labor is fully employed other resources are also completely utilized.* It is

*Joan Robinson, *Essays in the Theory of Employment* (London, Macmillan, 1937), p. 15: "Conditions of full employment obtain when no one employer can increase his staff without reducing the staff of some other employer."

usually justifiable to make this assumption, for the available supply of labor is the basic determiner of the quantity of production. The experience gained during World War II has emphasized this fact. Of course, it is quite possible that other productive resources—through patent regulations, monopoly control, or inefficient management—are not being fully utilized even though labor is being completely utilized. Despite the importance of these factors in certain instances, it is reasonably accurate to consider full employment of labor and maximum productive effort as being identical.

The concept of full employment excludes the requirement that the full abilities of the working population must be used. Also, full employment does not require that every person be employed for the accepted normal number of hours per week. The conditions of full employment can be met even though a portion of the laborers able and willing to work at the prevailing wage scale and working conditions are temporarily unable to find employment. This latter type of underutilization of labor resources is frequently called frictional unemployment.

Frictional unemployment arises from labor turnover—that is, laborers temporarily out of employment while moving from one job to another. The term perhaps can be broadened sufficiently to include laborers being trained for a new type of job and those seasonally unemployed. Thus, in an economy as large as that of the United States, the conditions necessary to meet the requirements of full employment would exist with two to three million laborers temporarily unemployed.

The term "disguised unemployment" is used to refer to laborers that are employed but are engaged in activities that are generally recognized as being unproductive or are engaged in duties below their abilities.* The mass armies of Russia and China are excellent examples of disguised unemployment. Disguised unemployment frequently arises from the political necessity of providing work for all or at least for the vast majority of the able-bodied men and women of the nation. In the United States, there was a type of disguised unemployment in addition to reported statistical unemployment during the depression of the 1930's. This arose from the employment of highly trained men in positions far below those that they were capable of filling.†

*J. Robinson, *Essays in the Theory of Employment*, pp. 82–101.

†An excellent discussion of the nature of unemployment is in the *Monthly Labor Review*, vol. 64, no. 1, January, 1947, pp. 1–10.

The provision of full employment has become closely associated with a high standard of living. The attainment of full employment has been frequently advocated as the most important economic goal.

The analyses of the preceding paragraphs indicate the weakness of the term as an economic concept. The maintenance of full employment with a large amount of disguised unemployment does not mean that the quantity of enjoyable goods and services is maximized. Actually, the term "full employment" is much more meaningful as propaganda, than as an economic, goal. The shortcomings of the term were indicated during the Congressional hearings of 1946. The legislation finally passed provides the executive branch of the Federal government with sufficient economic information to enable it to pursue a policy aimed at full employment.

CONCLUSION

FISCAL policy utilizes terms and concepts that are in general use in the literature of economics. Because the desirability of utilizing the fiscal powers of the government to affect economic conditions developed during the severe depression of the 1930's and because this was also the period of considerable development in the study of economics under the leadership of J. M. Keynes, the concepts utilized in fiscal policy are closely associated with what has come to be known as Keynesian economics or "The New Economics." The result is that fiscal policy and its concepts are closely tied to depression destroying efforts of the government.

QUESTIONS AND PROBLEMS

1. What is Gross National Product? Why is it a better indication of the level of economic activity than disposable income? Discuss the correctness and incorrectness of including government as a separate aggregate of GNP.

2. Explain what you believe is meant by oversaving. Do you think it is a useful concept? Why? Are the two concepts related? How?

3. What does the term multiplier refer to? What is the relationship between the size of the multiplier and the propensity to consume?

4. Define investment. How is the accelerator effect related to the quantity of investment and fluctuations in investment?

5. What is disguised unemployment? Why do you think there is a tendency for it to be used by governments?

6. How would you define efficient use of resources? Can it be defined in a number of ways? Explain.

CHAPTER 3

Fiscal Tools

THE tools which the government uses to carry out its fiscal responsibilities can be grouped into three categories. These are revenues, expenditures, and debt management.

REVENUES

IN the first category of fiscal tools, revenues, taxation is by far the most important. In addition to taxes, the category includes grants and gifts, commercial revenues, and administrative revenues.

A workable definition of a tax is that it is a compulsory collection for a general purpose. Under this definition the payment for paving the road in front of your home, for example, is not a tax. It fits the definition to the extent of being a compulsory payment, but not to the extent that the money collected is spent for a general purpose; in this case the money collected is spent to benefit you directly as the owner of property fronting on the paved road. Neither is your payment for water provided by the city a tax because the payment is not compulsory since you can avoid it by not using water and because the payment is made for a personal purpose rather than for a general purpose.

Gifts and grants comprise the second type of revenue of governments. The meaning of gifts is obvious, and they are not important dollar-wise. Grants refer to grants-in-aid, and they are very important dollar-wise. Grants-in-aid are typically given by the higher level of government to the lower level. That is, grants are made by the Federal government to the state governments and by the state governments to the local governments. They are made largely to support social welfare programs, with education support granted by the states to the local governments being by far the most important. The avowed purpose in most cases is to equalize services offered in poorer areas with those available in the richer areas.

The term commercial revenues refers to government revenues that are earned in about the same way as revenues of business firms. That is, the government produces a service such as pure water, mail delivery, or passage through a canal and charges for the service much the same as would a private corporation. The justification for the the government furnishing services in this way in the United States is that private enterprise is unwilling to do it or that the government can do it better and more cheaply. The latter—that the government can provide a good or service better and more cheaply than private enterprise—is difficult to prove and is seldom used to justify government production and sale of goods and services. More often, goods and services produced and sold by the government include a subsidy because the government believes that the good or service provided is so beneficial to its citizenry that they should purchase more than they would if its price covered its full cost. In such a case, the price charged is not equal to all the costs that would have to be covered if the activity were carried on by private enterprise. The receipts from the sale of postal services partially exemplify this type of activity, but better examples are the tuition charged students at state institutions of higher education in the United States and the charges made for government-provided medical services in Great Britain.

Sometimes a government sells services at a price considerably greater than cost and uses the excess to cover the general costs of government. An example of this is at the municipal level where a city may use some of what it charges for municipally provided water or electricity as a tax.

A final type of commercial revenue of government arises from the sale of commodities previously purchased from private producers. Sometimes these revenues arise from the sale of products purchased to hold up prices or because the government had stockpiled to meet the possibility of a future shortage. At other times they arise from the disposal of facilities which the government no longer wishes to operate or goods which the government no longer finds useful.

The final general type of revenue is labeled administrative revenues. Many of these revenues come directly from medieval England where they were the principal sources of funds used to operate ordinary government functions after the breakup of the feudal system. Examples include a license to be married, a license to own a dog, and a permit to build a building (and a fine if the building is built without first obtaining a permit). The modern use of forfeitures of bond or bail posted are direct descendants of ransom payments of more romantic days. Also in this category are special assessments which would include the payment made to cover all or part of the cost of paving the road on which your property fronts. And a final and particularly interesting revenue are escheats which refer to the right of the government to the property of persons who die without legal heirs.

TAXES

THE different levels of government of the United States levy a variety of taxes. These taxes fall rather neatly into three major groups: income taxes, property taxes, and sales taxes.

Income Taxes

The income taxes produce the largest revenues. They are of two principal types: taxes levied on the income of individuals, and taxes levied on the income of corporations. Both types are used by the Federal government and by most of the states but are seldom used by the local levels of government. These taxes typically provide about four fifths of the revenues of the Federal government and about one sixth of the revenues of the state governments.

Although the individual income tax and the corporate income tax are separate taxes today, they grew up together and are still closely associated in the minds of many people. This close association partially accounts for the statement frequently heard that the taxation of the earnings of the corporation as income of the corporation and the taxation of the dividends paid by the corporation as income of the individual receiving the dividends is double taxation. To those who make the statement it is double taxation in the sense that the same income is taxed once as income of the corporation and again as income of the individual receiving the dividends. Other taxes are not considered double taxation of income; yet, of course, all taxes must be paid out of income and therefore one's income is taxed many times.

Development of Our Income Tax. Prior to the time of the Civil War, a number of state governments had experimented with the income tax, and some had used rates that were slightly graduated. But it was not until the Civil War that the Federal government made use of the tax. However, its adoption in 1861 was considered an emergency measure, which was judged by most writers of the period as the most unpopular tax introduced by the North. Whereas a number of taxes, such as those on tobacco and liquor, which were reintroduced during the Civil War, remained after the war and became permanent sources of Federal tax receipts, the income tax remained as a statute only until 1872.

From 1872 until 1894, the Federal government did not use an income tax. This was a period of generally falling prices and considerable economic hardship in the South and Midwest. The low incomes of farmers and laborers caused widespread opposition to the existing tax system. Taxes on goods sold and purchased were said to increase the cost of living of those already in the low income groups.

Finally, sufficient congressional support was found to attach an amendment to the Tariff Bill of 1894, providing for an income tax with a two per cent rate on the income of individuals and corporations, with individuals being allowed a personal exemption of $4,000. One year later, in 1895, the Supreme Court in the famous *Pollock v. Farmers' Loan and Trust Company* case declared the law unconstitutional.

Again the use of an income tax by the Federal government became a dead issue. This lasted until the Panic of 1907 when new agitation developed, and in 1909 the prospect of a Federal government deficit caused the enactment of a tax of one per cent on the net income of corporations in excess of $5,000. To make the tax constitutional, it was called a "special excise tax with respect to the carrying on . . . (of business as a corporation)." At the same time Congress provided for the submission of the Sixteenth Amendment to legalize the levy of a graduated income tax by the Federal government; and on February 25, 1913, the Amendment was adopted. The top rate of the first income tax enacted under the amended Constitution was 6 per cent. Today the top rate which applies to taxable income above $200,000 is over 80 per cent. The current tax rate on taxable income of medium- and large-sized corporations is over 50 per cent.

The high rates that those who opposed the income tax in the 1880's feared would destroy our free enterprise system are with us—but so is our free private enterprise system.

The Property Tax

Property taxes are the mainstay of local government revenues. The property tax alone provides more than 70 per cent of the locally collected revenues of local governments. Taxes labeled property taxes are paid by those owning real or personal property, and the amount of tax paid is determined by the valuation set on the property by the assessor to which is applied the tax rate. Included in "local governments" are cities, school districts, counties, townships, and special districts. The approximate portion of total collections used by each of these is given in Table 3-1. Forty years ago the property tax was also the principal source of revenues of state governments; today it accounts for only 4 per cent of state revenues.

TABLE 3-1. Distribution of property tax among the various types of local government.

	Percentage
Cities	38.0
School districts	32.5
Counties	21.4
Townships	6.0
Special districts	2.1

Source: *Summary of Government Finances in 1953*, Bureau of Census, Department of Commerce, October 20, 1954.

Development of the Property Tax. The property tax in the sense that it exists in the United States was not known in Europe and Asia in ancient times despite the fact that in those days nearly all wealth consisted of real property.

Similarly, when the United States was a young and struggling nation, most wealth consisted of the ownership of real property. However, the difference which caused the development of a different method of taxation in this country was that the early governments of the United States were much more democratic than the then contemporary governments of Europe. Therefore, the idea of exempting the property of the large landowners did not find government favor as it did in most other nations. Also, the United States was a new country with a rapidly expanding population and increasing real property valuations. Therefore property taxes did not cause property values to fall but merely somewhat slowed down their increase. That is, a tax which reduces the size of a capital gain is much more acceptable than one which causes a loss.

The property tax in the United States has always included livestock and buildings along with land. The early taxes upon property had provided that land of a certain type should bear a certain tax upon each acre. Also, they provided that each cow should be taxed so much, each barn so much, and the like. This method of taxing became very complicated as the types of property multiplied with the development of our economy. A movement for simplification of the early 19th century which recommended the collection of a general *ad valorem* property tax gained headway and was adopted by all the states. The simplification provided that the tax be levied as a certain percentage or millage of the assessed valuation of the different types of property. All property through assessment was reduced to a common denominator—its value in dollars. Upon this valuation was spread a uniform rate in the form of a certain portion or percentage of the determined valuation. However, the reformed property tax turned out to be neither uniform nor general despite the fact that the tax was levied on all property and was assessed at a uniform rate on the basis of determined value.

The assessor did not find the jewelry and the stocks and bonds owned by the rich, but it was easy for him to find and assess the simple house, the furniture, and the few cows owned by the poor. Moreover, the assessor did not know the value of the technical equipment used by large industries. The result was that the poor man paid a tax on all his property while the rich man and the large corporation paid a tax on only a portion of their property. Also to assure that assessors placed similar values on similar properties, boards of equalization to hear complaints and to make adjustments were established as early as 1820.

Because of these weaknesses and others, the general *ad valorem* property tax has been modified by all states. Some states have excluded personal property below a certain maximum value or personal property not used for productive purposes. Other states have assessed different types of property at different portions of the full and true value. Frequently different rates have been applied to different types of property. In some cases, public utility properties have been removed from the property tax rolls and have been subjected to special taxes. All these modifications have, of course, tended to make the property tax as complicated and varied as it was prior to the reform movement of the first third of the 19th century.

Sales Taxes

By far the most important revenue source of state governments are the general and selected sales taxes, sometimes called excise taxes. The general sales tax is collected by over thirty states and by many municipalities but not by the Federal government. And the selected sales taxes such as those on alcoholic beverages, cigarettes, and gasoline are collected by the Federal government as well as by the state governments and in a few isolated instances by local governments. The amount of these selected sales taxes collected by the Federal government is greater than that collected by the states, but because the total tax collections of the Federal government in a year of peace are over four times as great as the total tax collections of the state governments, these excise taxes are a much larger portion of state revenues. Excise taxes provide about 59 per cent of the total tax revenues of states.

Of the four principal excise taxes (general sales, tobacco products, alcoholic beverages, and motor fuels), the general sales tax is the newest in the United States. Elsewhere, however, the general sales tax has been used for a long time, and its analysis is entwined with the beginnings of the study of economics.

Historical documents show that the sales tax was a part of the tax system introduced by the rulers of ancient Rome to meet governmental expenses when the booty of war became insufficient. In medieval Europe, the sales tax was introduced when the development of commerce began. At that time it was considered a tax of the rich because it was the rich who were exempt from all other tax payments, and it was they who were the principal purchasers of goods in the market place.

During the 18th and 19th centuries, economists considered the general sales tax very undesirable on two principal bases: (1) the idea prevailed that the Spanish general sales tax (the Alcabala) had been largely responsible for the failure of the Spanish Empire to continue to prosper; and (2) the economic theory which was developed during the 18th century taught that taxes collected on items consumed by laborers (sales taxes) would result in higher wages and thus higher production costs and lower profits. And lower profits could not be tolerated, for it was believed necessary that large profits be made to increase the wealth of a nation.

The general sales tax was reintroduced in Western Europe at the end of World War I but did not become popular in the United States until the severe depression period of the 1930's.

Between 1933 and 1936, general sales taxes were imposed by 31 states. This great surge was stimulated by the demand for additional education expenditures plus the requirement that Federal funds for assistance to the aged, the blind, and dependent children be matched by the states. During World War II, a number of states abolished general sales taxes, but after the War they re-enacted them, not only to meet the needs of education again but also this time to meet the needs of veterans.

It is interesting to note that the enactment of state sales taxes in the 1930's was during a depression period with a prevailing buyers' market, whereas the new postwar spurt was during a boom period with a prevailing sellers' market. During the 1930's, sales taxes were justified on the basis that property tax delinquency was already high, and corporate profits and individuals' incomes were low. Sales taxes in the postwar period have been justified on the basis that a boom period exists and that sales taxes are deflationary; in addition, they bring in huge yields. It would seem that any economic climate is favorable for additional consumption taxes.

EXPENDITURES

GOVERNMENT expenditures in the economic literature of twenty-five years ago were almost always treated as being unproductive, and any increase in them was therefore to be abhorred. This attitude toward government expenditures had a long history leading directly back to the *Wealth of Nations* published in 1776 by Adam Smith, the father of modern economics. The concept is still frequently advanced by those who wish to pay lower taxes but at the same time continue to benefit from government expenditures.

The principal and the oldest form of government spending is for war, for preparation for war, and for rehabilitation and reconstruction after war. All direct war expenditures in the United States are made by the Federal government although state and local government expenditures are related to war through the effect which Federal government war expenditures have on prices and the availability of labor and materials needed by these governments to carry on the services which they are committed to perform. Even during periods of peace, such as the United States is experiencing as this is being written, expenditures for war account for over one half the total expenditures of all levels of government.

The basic underlying economic elements of war expenditure are (1) opportunity costs and (2) the impact on our fiscal system.

Opportunity costs, related to war expenditure, denote the uses to which the government could have allocated the funds which it spends on war. Fifty billion dollars could provide for much in the way of highways, schools, hospitals, old age assistance, and slum clearance. Whether or not the highways, schools, hospitals, old age assistance, and slum clearance would be provided if war expenditures were cut is not certain. A cut of war expenditures might only cause unemployment, or increase home construction and other personal expenditures, or increase the amount of leisure enjoyed by the average American.

The impact of war expenditure on our fiscal system is important because most of our taxes and the method of organizing and allocating responsibilities of different levels of government have resulted from the requirements of war finance. The income tax, the tobacco tax, the alcoholic beverage tax, and the excess profits taxes were first introduced during periods of war. During war the pressure to make those not fighting suffer along with the fighting man is very strong. The progressiveness of the Federal tax system and its emphasis on luxury spending has partially arisen from this austerity emphasis of war periods.

The procedures developed in administering the government debt are war babies, for war has been the period of debt expansion. Also, the growth of the dominance of the Federal government is traceable partially to war expenditures. While the war is in progress, the Federal government is easily able to introduce new taxes and to raise tax rates. When the war is over, even though the revenues which these taxes provide are no longer needed to meet the war expenditures, they are very convenient for use in financing peacetime projects. Elected representatives like to provide their constituents with the benefits they wish from government and to do this without increasing taxes. The continuation of war-introduced taxes and tax rates provide them with this possibility. The result is an increase in the portion of peacetime government activities carried on by the Federal government.

The second category of government expenditures are those made to carry on activities desired by the electorate, which they believe are best provided by government. Here we have the government paying for sewage disposal, streets, courts of law, and education. These services, and the many others provided by government, are as important as any provided in our economy and are therefore, of course, as productive. It is in the public economy's provision of streets, water, police protection, education of workers, unemployment compensation, old-age pensions, fire protection, sewage and sanitation facilities that the true meaning of "a mixed economy" (part private and part public) becomes apparent. These expenditures expand and contract as population shifts, technical developments, and production requirements are reflected in the voting of elected representatives.

The third category of public expenditures, those which are either increased or decreased to meet the requirements of economic stability, is very new and also very old. Historical references can be cited to show that ancient rulers constructed public works as a means of employing the labor supply; however, the development of public expenditures as a method of maintaining the "correct" level of economic activity arose largely during the deep depression of the 1930's. Basically the types of things that can be done with expenditures that can be used to provide the "correct" level of economic activity are those of categories one and two—war and socialized investment.

Responsible officials in the United States never publicly consider using war expenditures to achieve the "correct" level of economic activity. This is perhaps the true situation, for the level of war expenditures is caused by the actions of other nations which cannot be controlled by domestic officials. To the rather limited extent that normal expenditures of government can be increased and decreased, they are available to keep the level of economic activity "correct." Also during periods of extreme economic difficulties, extraordinary measures to increase or decrease government expenditures in particular areas may be taken. For example, under conditions of a severe inflation engendered by a large war, governments may cease all but the most necessary capital improvements while under conditions of a severe deflation, governments may spend for capital improvements that will not be immediately completely utilized. However, generally speaking, it is likely to be nearly as difficult to cause government expenditures as it is to cause the expenditures of individuals and businesses to change in such a way as to stabilize the level of economic activity.

DEBT

WHETHER a government increases or decreases its indebtedness depends on the size of revenue collections and expenditures. If revenues are larger than expenditures, the government will decrease its indebtedness; if they are smaller, it will increase its indebtedness. Therefore the size and trends of government indebtedness are directly determined by government revenue raising and expenditure actions. Indirectly, the size of the government debt is dependent on how the particular expenditure and revenue actions of government affect the level of economic activity. For example, if government expenditures were increased to develop a new source of power such as atomic energy and at the same time taxes were decreased, economic activity might be stimulated to the extent that tax receipts at the lower rate would be sufficient to cover the higher expenditures. This would be possible if government expenditure was very stimulating to the private economy.

In addition to its absolute size and its change of size, the debt of the government is important because its character and therefore its economic impact can be affected by decisions of government bodies. For example, if the Treasury and the Federal Reserve Board decide that an increase of indebtedness be offered to the public as short-term securities and if by monetary actions the commercial banks are encouraged to purchase these securities, then the increase of government debt will not absorb savings and is very likely to increase the supply of money of the country.* If on the other hand, long-term securities are issued instead, and if the interest rate is sufficiently high, the sale of these securities would absorb savings and increase interest rates but would not directly cause an increase of the money supply. Debt decisions of this type are included under the descriptive phrase "debt management."

Marketable Securities

The shortest-term security issued by the United States Treasury is the 91-day Treasury bill. On occasion this bill is issued for a longer period than 91 days—for example, the Tax Anticipation Bill (TAB's)—; however, the bill never runs for as long a time as one year. The bill is the only government security issued on a discount basis; that is, the return is the difference between the purchase price, which is lower than the par value,

*The way in which commercial banks expand the money supply when they extend loans or purchase securities is explained in *The Federal Reserve System, Purposes and Functions* (Washington, Board of Governors, 1954), pp. 14–30; *Money and Banking* by Raymond P. Kent (New York, Rinehart, 1951), pp. 238–247; and *Principles of Money and Banking* by Richard W. Lindholm, et al (New York, Norton, 1954), pp. 439–448.

and the par value which is received at maturity. The bill may be purchased by commercial banks in any quantity they wish, and it is a preferred security of commercial banks because of its short maturity period. In addition, the Federal Reserve permits commercial banks to convert bills into legal reserves with the minimum of inconvenience. If the administrators of the Federal debt wish the securities to be held with funds newly created by the banking system for that purpose rather than with savings, they issue bills; and the Federal Reserve stands ready to purchase them in case the commercial banks need additional reserves.

The next security in terms of length of time to maturity is the Treasury certificate. It matures in about a year and is also a favorite of commercial banks and may be bought in unlimited quantities by them. The government uses the Treasury certificate, too, when it does not wish to pay the interest required to attract savings or when it does not wish to have government debt held with savings. The holders of certificates receive the interest rate printed on its face. These securities were used extensively by the Federal government when its debt was expanding rapidly during the World War II and the Korean War periods.

The third security of the Federal government included in the short-term category, which commercial banks may also purchase in unlimited quantities, is the Treasury note which matures in not more than five years from its date of issue. Typically the interest the Treasury must pay per dollar of borrowed funds is higher, the longer the date to maturity of the issue used in the borrowing operation. Again extensive use was made of the note to borrow funds needed by the Treasury to meet the costs of World War II and also the Korean War.

The final category of marketable government securities are the bonds which are issued for a period longer than five years and on occasion for as long as forty years. The quantity of bonds which commercial banks may purchase prior to the time when the bonds become bank eligible is frequently limited. This limitation is imposed because the Treasury wishes to have these securities held with savings and not with money created by the commercial banking system. If the Treasury had wanted to have the securities held with funds created by the commercial banks, it could have saved itself interest costs by issuing bills, certificates, or notes. When bonds have only five years or so to run before they mature, they become bank eligible; and commercial banks may then purchase them in unlimited quantities. When long-term securities are near their date of maturity, they take on the characteristics of short-term securities except for one feature. Government bonds are issued with the condition that the Treasury has the privilege of calling them several years before the date of maturity, and holders of these securities do not know whether or not this right will be exercised until the first call date arrives. This feature makes a bond with four years to maturity more speculative than a note maturing in four years.

Non-marketable Securities

The cash value of marketable securities of the Treasury, like that of all marketable securities, rises and falls as the evaluations of buyers and sellers change. The cash value of non-marketable Federal government securities, on the other hand, is set by the Treasury. Thus, an owner of a non-marketable security can neither suffer a loss nor enjoy a gain. He can always receive a set number of dollars should he prefer cash to the security. However, he can turn the security into cash only by selling it to the United States Treasury or to an agent of the Treasury, which would more than likely be a commercial bank.

There are two large groups of non-marketable securities. The first group is the savings bond, of which the E-type savings bond is by far the most important. These securities of the Federal government are largely held by relatively small savers who want a relatively high interest rate and want to be certain that whenever they need the money they have saved they will be able to get it without suffering a dollar loss.

The second group of non-marketable securities is the special issues provided by the Treasury to the different Federal government agencies that invest a portion of their receipts. The most important of these agencies is the Federal Old-Age and Survivors Insurance Trust Fund. These trust funds will wish to turn their securities into cash when the benefits established under the law cost more than the payments received. Here again it is very important that it be possible to turn the securities into a definite number of dollars.

The purchase of government debt by the social security trust funds and other Federal government funds is the government purchasing its own debt. But the funds available to the government to purchase its own debt in this fashion are considered by the contributors to be a part of their savings and personal security program. Therefore it is correct to say that the special issue type of non-marketable securities is also held with savings. Also, because a person under social security cannot cash in his portion of the social security funds, it is possible to conclude that these securities are more securely held with savings than are any other type of government security.

PUBLIC FINANCE CONCEPTS

The Non-interventionist Attitude toward Public Finance

THOSE who believe in a minimum of government activity in the economy consider government fiscal activity as worsening economic conditions rather than bettering them. This attitude is based upon the idea that the removal of the basic causes of the difficulty is prevented by fiscal intervention of the government. For example, government coddling is considered to make the depression continue and become worse, because the economy is not permitted to arrive freely at an equilibrium from which sound recovery could start. The exception to the general opposition toward government fiscal activity of the *laissez-faire* economists is that the flexibility of economic life and freedom of movement of the factors of production should be encouraged.* This attitude toward government fiscal activity is completely out of touch with the realities of the world in which we live. Government expenditures and taxes aimed at breaking up the inflexibilities arising from modern technological methods would be a waste of government funds and, in addition, would destroy the efficiency of the private economy. The business of government in the foreseeable future will be to control and increase the efficiency of huge concentrations of capital and great labor organizations, and not to tear them into parts.

The Interventionist Attitude toward Public Finance

The interventionist believes that "the invisible hand" (the allocation of resources through prices determined in unregulated markets) of Adam Smith is inefficient and must be supplemented by government activity. The interventionist believes that sufficient economic data are now available and that the science of economics has developed to the point where it is possible actively to improve the economic conditions arising from the transactions

*The New Deal as a conscious and deliberate matter began in 1924 under the Coolidge administration. See "The Road Back to Full Employment," by Benjamin M. Anderson, in *Financing American Prosperity*, edited by Paul T. Homan and Fritz Machlup (New York, Twentieth Century Fund, 1945).

in the market place. An important portion of these positive actions is the revenue-raising and revenue-expenditure activities of government.

Also, the interventionist does not believe that an activity should be carried on by the private economy merely because such has been the case in the past or because the relative size of the private economy should not be decreased. Rather, the determination of whether a particular type of activity should be carried on in the private economy or in the public economy must be based upon the relative efficiencies of the two economies. This sort of attitude has determined that valley developments such as Tennessee Valley Authority be made with public expenditures and that the use of atomic energy in production should be carried on by the private economy. The traditional attitude that government should only perform the duties of a night watchman is completely abandoned.

Two Types of Government Fiscal Activity

All government fiscal activity affects the quantity of purchasing power available to the different portions of the private economy.* Also, all government fiscal activity affects the types of goods and services that will be consumed and produced. However, fiscal activity may be divided into two broad categories on the basis of the relative amount of voluntary fluctuation possible. The amount of voluntary fluctuation is important if government economic activity is expected to provide needed purchasing power when private economic activity begins to falter. Although the idea of public economic activity varying with fluctuations in the private economy possesses many undesirable features, it remains basic in the consideration of government fiscal action aimed at providing an efficient utilization of a nation's productive resources.

Expenditure for public works, farm relief, unemployment compensation, low-interest small security loans, and welfare are the principal types of government expenditures that can be rather readily varied depending on the amount of water the private economy is putting into the trough of total purchasing power. Government expenditure for courts, law enforcement, administration of legislation, interest on debt and war are examples of expenditures that cannot be readily varied. This

---

*Potential purchasing power consists of current income received plus assets possessed. The portion of income and assets actually used to purchase goods and services is the purchasing power.

type of division places international expenditure in a doubtful category. Experience in the middle 1950's seems to indicate that it is similar to war expenditure. International and war expenditures of the United States can be controlled only if we follow a conscious policy of aggression or if we refuse to be affected by developments in other nations. Neither of these possibilities appears probable.

Government revenues can also be separated on the basis of their variation between periods of prosperity and depression. In the case of revenues, the flexibility arises largely from the difference in the variation of the size of the base upon which the tax is levied during periods of high income receipts and low income receipts. Tax collections based on profits vary greatly in what is usually considered a desirable manner, while tax collections based on real estate change very little. Also, taxes levied upon luxury items vary greatly, while taxes levied on necessities such as cigarettes, gasoline, and food change much less. The taxes that bring in large quantities of revenue during prosperity and small quantities during depression are generally considered to be the more desirable because they help to keep the water trough of purchasing power full, when needed, and prevent it from overflowing, when that type of action is required.

The possibility of flexible government revenues is greatly affected by level of government. The Federal government can always borrow all the funds it requires. Therefore, it could greatly reduce its tax revenues without affecting expenditures. The state and local governments find it impossible to do this. As a result, the Federal government possesses much greater flexibility of revenue source. The state and local governments find it very difficult to borrow during the same period that members of the private economy find borrowing difficult. This is also the time when the water in the purchasing-power trough is getting low, but the state and local governments find it impossible to increase it by lowering their taxes and increasing their borrowings. However, this is exactly what the Federal government can do and did do during the 1930's.

CONCLUSION

THE three categories of fiscal tools are closely related; a decision to act in one way and to utilize one category directly in carrying out this decision will indirectly affect other categories. An increase of government expenditures is very likely to increase government revenues even though the taxes used and tax rates levied are not changed. It is not likely, however, to expand government revenues enough to avoid an increase of the government debt or a decrease of its surplus. The decision to increase expenditures is an independent decision which may or may not be dependent on revenue and debt considerations. This same high degree of independence exists in revenue and debt management decisions but there is also drifting in the background a degree of interdependence among the three categories of fiscal tools which when assumed away, as is done in the aggregate fiscal analyses of the last chapter, reduces the reality of the discussion.

The degree of usefulness of fiscal tools is largely dependent upon the control and flexibility which can be exercised in their use. If legislation closely restricts fiscal actions and if this legislation can only be changed with great difficulty, then the effectiveness of fiscal policy is greatly reduced. If the powers of a level of government, such as those of a municipality or of a state, are restricted, the fiscal policy possibilities of actions of that government are limited also.

QUESTIONS AND PROBLEMS

1. What are the three classes of fiscal tools?

2. Briefly outline the unique problems as you see them of each of the three groups of taxes.

3. Do you think it would be desirable to have only the Federal government collect income taxes, only the state governments collect sales taxes, and only the local governments collect property taxes? Give reasons for your answer.

4. Visit a local property tax assessor or collector of any tax and ask him to explain some of his everyday problems.

5. Explain the basic underlying economic elements of war expenditures.

6. On what basis would you consider government expenditures productive? On what basis would you consider them unproductive?

7. Do you think that it is correct to say that there is a special category of government expenditures for use in stabilizing the economy? Why or why not?

8. Use the concept of the multiplier to show how the government's budget might be balanced even though government expenditures are increased and tax rates are cut.

9. List the principal types of government securities. Get a recent copy of the *Treasury Bulletin* and (1) find out the quantity of each type of debt outstanding and (2) the average rate of interest for each type.

10. From the *Treasury* or the *Federal Reserve Bulletin* find out the distribution of the ownership of the different types of Federal government debt.

CHAPTER 4

Selected Goals of Fiscal Policy

CHAPTER 3 described the principal characteristics of the three kits of fiscal tools—revenues, expenditures, and debt. This chapter will describe the four economic facts or relationships selected for study and will point out briefly how they are affected by actions utilizing the three categories of fiscal tools. Also, it will point out how the attainment of the correct level for each of the four selected relationships becomes a goal of fiscal policy.

The goals established in this chapter for the selected relationships are other than those existing after the forces of the market place have worked themselves out. This must be the situation of any policy consideration other than that of *laissez faire*. The basic assumption is therefore necessarily that not all economic activity should be determined in the market place and that the decisions of the market place may be wrong and if wrong can be improved. However, improvement is only possible when there is a basis for judging what is good and what is bad, and part of the analyses of this chapter are aimed at establishing this basis in a general but, it is hoped, useful form.

All fiscal activity, and particularly fiscal activity which can be varied with the amount of private economic activity, is concerned with the determination of all fundamental economic relationships. The fundamental relationships of our economy can be stated in a number of ways, but the following four groups include most of the important economic relationships affecting efficiency of economic activity: (1) the values or prices of goods and services, (2) the portion of the income of the economy that is spent on consumption goods and services, (3) the degree of employment of labor, and (4) the manner in which the national income is distributed. The analysis of the effect of government revenues and expenditures upon these four relationships is the basis of the major portion of this book. They are discussed in relation to the effects upon them of (1) different methods of obtaining government revenue, (2) debt management possibilities, (3) various government expenditures, and (4) administration techniques.

Each of these goals is both an indicator and determiner of the general level of economic activity.

Stable or slightly rising prices indicate that the economy is functioning satisfactorily. Stable and rising prices also stimulate economic activity because they make it profitable to invest now rather than waiting and to buy the automobile now because the price will not be less next year and may be higher. The same is true of consumption. A high level of consumption expenditures is an indication of prosperity, and the fact that it is high helps to create and continue prosperous times. Employment levels possess the same two-fold character. Income distribution is less of an indicator of economic activity than the other three, but it also possesses this characteristic as well as that of being a determiner of the soundness of the economy. Therefore the effect of fiscal actions on prices, consumption, employment, and income distribution will show how fiscal policy can be used to preserve a healthy and highly productive economy.

PRICES

FISCAL activity can change the relationship between the quantity of purchasing power and the quantity of goods and can thus change the general level of prices. Fiscal activity can also change the relative prices of different goods and services and affect the quantity of particular goods and services produced and the manner of resource utilization.

General Price Level

The maintenance of a desirable general level of prices means, in a capitalistic system, that prices must not fall so much that debt burdens are greatly increased or inventories greatly decreased in value, and that prices must not rise so much that fixed incomes are greatly decreased in value or that a general hoarding of goods exists. The general level of prices is, of course, also greatly affected by monetary policy. However, it has usually been monetary activity dictated by fiscal requirements that has brought about a major change in the general price level.

A large portion of the economic difficulties of the 1930's arose from the severe fall in the general level of prices. The debt of agriculture became particularly burdensome as a result of sharp price declines. The sharp decline in inventory values that arose from the sharp fall of general prices also contributed to the intensification of the depression of the 1930's. The sharp rise of general prices during both world wars brought forth maladjustments in economic planning and income distribution and later caused serious economic problems.

The data of personal holdings of liquid savings of 1946 and 1954 which are given on page 72 and the data of Federal savings bonds in 1946 and 1954 given on page 204 show the effects of personal reserves of the very great increase in the general level of prices during the postwar periods. The decrease of these liquid reserves has reduced the ability of the people of the nation to purchase the goods and services produced at a most efficient level of production. The general level of prices best serves the needs of a capitalistic society if it is rising slowly; fiscal activities can and should be utilized to attain this ideal.

The stability of general prices is associated with economic stability. The most common test of the degree of economic stability is price movements. However, stable prices are largely the result of stable economic relationships and not the cause. Thus fiscal activities, to the extent that they maintain desirable economic conditions, have contributed to price stability. Also, fiscal activities can be used directly to affect certain crucial prices in a manner that will aid in preserving economic stability in a free enterprise society.

Either by a general rise (inflation) or by a general fall (deflation), prices can have a tremendous effect on the economy; that is, in addition to their function of allocating resources. The desirability of economic stability has always been recognized. However, the agreement has not been complete; there have been some that have considered violent price fluctuations desirable. This latter group believes that instability and insecurity provide a major portion of the basis for the progressive nature of our culture.

The theory of boom (inflation) and bust (deflation) determined government fiscal policy prior to the 1930's. It was assumed that the government could do little to prevent high prices and could do even less to prevent low prices. This meant that the government could do little to prevent the great economic wastes and maladjustments arising out of inflation and deflation.

In fact, the theory was that the inefficiencies arising from great price fluctuations were less than those to be expected if prices remained stable. The arguments (shake-out necessary to eliminate inefficient firms, high prices necessary to eliminate surplus of money, and so on) presented in 1946 and 1952 for the removal of price controls are evidences that the boom-and-bust theory is far from dead in the United States.

Particular Prices

The relative price obtained by an industry or a particular producer is affected by (1) the price that possible users of the product are able to obtain for the resources they possess, which is greatly affected by income distribution, and (2) the degree of bargaining advantage or monopoly possessed.

An increase in demand caused by change of income distribution would increase prices under either competitive or monopoly conditions. The increase in the demand for certain types of products and services caused by a change in income distribution brings about a transfer of resources through relative prices.

The manner of use of the resources of a capitalistic nation is determined largely by relative prices. If the price that can be obtained for the goods or services of a certain type of activity is high in relation to another type of activity, the first type of activity will be greatly encouraged and the resources of the nation will flow in that direction. For example, if the price that can be obtained for resort hotels in Florida is high and the price that can be obtained for worker's cottages is small, building materials will flow toward and be used in the construction of Florida hotels and not of worker's cottages. The use of resources in a capitalistic economy is determined to be most efficient if used in the manner dictated by relative prices. Although in many instances relative prices do not bring about the most efficient use of a resource, neither does the alternative of rationing and price controls, as an abundance of experience after World War II proved. In addition, rationing and price controls utilize a large quantity of resources in their administration. To the extent that fiscal activities can control prices so that prices do a better job of allocating resources, fiscal policy has eliminated a weakness of the price system and the apparently necessary inefficiencies of an administrated economy.

In a capitalistic economy, prices determine the relative portion of the national income received by the different factors of production. The price that a laborer obtains for his services determines his income and the portion of the national product that he can command. The same is true of the capitalist and the entrepreneur. By determining the portion of total income going to different groups, these same prices also largely determine the general types of goods that will be produced.

If the price obtained by labor is relatively high, the portion of productive facilities used to produce consumer goods will be increased. In the past, this relation has usually been characteristic of a depression period. If the return of the capitalist and entrepreneur is relatively great, the production of producer goods will expand. In the past, this has usually been a prosperity period. Desirable price relationships would exist if the prices obtained by the two groups were such as to provide a stable relative distribution of productive factors.

The prices paid for different products will also have a great effect on the manner in which natural resources—such as fertility and mineral deposits—are utilized. The determination of prices that will prevent the waste of natural resources would be another advance in the provisions of more goods and services.

Public finance activities can directly determine particular prices by relative tax burdens and the payment of subsidies. The levy of taxes can discourage the production of certain goods and, as a result, tend to influence the flow of resources toward the production of other goods bearing a lighter tax burden.

Relative prices of particular groups of goods determine the prosperity and efficiency of the different portions of the economy. Low prices for cotton, tobacco, and peanuts would prevent southern agricultural areas from obtaining the necessary fertilizer, machines, and labor required for efficient production. The relative price of a particular good or group of goods largely determines the quantity of resources that will be used in its production. Industries producing goods and services with high prices attract productive resources, and industries producing a product selling at low prices are forced to relinquish resources.

Effect of Monopoly

If a good is produced under monopoly conditions, the price will be higher and the quantity reduced. This reduction in the quantity of the good produced would mean that the factors used in its production would be decreased. Usually this results in a decline of the price of the factors and a subsequent increase of their flow into competitive areas where quantity restrictions do not exist. The flow of these raw materials away from the area that had become monopolized and toward the area still under competition would mean, under most circumstances, a reduced efficiency of resource use.

The effect of monopoly in the production of a good is to increase the price of the good produced and reduce the price of the raw materials required in its production. This effect tends to make the raw-material or resource owners combine to resist the pressure on their prices. A probable effect of this reaction would be reduced production throughout the economy and the great possibility of idle resources. High taxes on monopoly returns can reduce the bad effects of the distribution of income and inefficient allocation of resources arising from monopoly.

A monopolist producer uses a smaller quantity of raw materials and therefore produces a smaller quantity of goods, because his profits are maximized when prices are higher and quantity less, than is the case with a competitive producer. The monopolist could be induced to produce the same quantity of a good as a competitive producer if his profits would be maximized at this quantity of production. The government can induce a monopolist to expand production to this point through the payment of a subsidy per unit of output. The excess profits which the monopolist would receive as the result of this large subsidy could be mostly taxed away by the assessment of a lump-sum tax. The levy of the tax as a lump sum would not change the fact that maximum profits would be obtained when producing the same quantity of goods as a competitive producer.*

The monopolist can be induced to increase production by the payment of a subsidy, in the same way as he is induced to increase production when consumers become willing to buy a larger quantity of the products produced at a higher price. The change in the demand schedule changes the output and the price at which profits are maximized. A per-unit subsidy by the government has the same effect on production levels as an increase in demand. The difference in the effect, if the subsidy can be largely reclaimed by a lump-sum tax, is that a change in distribution of income is not necessary and the higher prices do not become a

*This relationship between a per-unit subsidy and taxation of profits has been mentioned by a number of economists. *Taxes Without Tears*, Donald Bailey Marsh (Lancaster, Penn., Jaques Cattell, 1945), discusses the idea very completely, pp. 99–151. "The criterion for a subsidy to induce the monopolist to expand to the optimum is that the subsidy per unit of output shall be equal to the difference between marginal costs and marginal receipts at the desired output (that is, the output where marginal costs equal price)"; p. 137.

part of the costs of some other producers. The object of the subsidy is to change the point where profits are maximized from low output to capacity output.

A monopolist could also be induced to produce up to the point where the additional cost per unit equaled selling price (point of optimum production) by merely reducing tax rates. The tax rates would induce this type of production if they were lowered as the output of the monopolist approached more closely the point of optimum production as determined by relative prices.

CONSUMPTION

The Quantity of Consumption

THE importance of the maintenance of the correct quantity of consumption in the preservation of the proper balance between savings and investment was pointed out in the definition of oversaving. If the portion of national income used to purchase consumption goods is too great, the quantity of saving and new investment will be insufficient to make use of the new technical developments and also replace worn-out capital goods. If the portion of national income intended for consumption is too little, intended saving becomes greater than intended investment, and as a result national income falls, bringing about a decrease of employment and inefficient utilization of resources. In addition, the quantity of consumption is related to the provision of the necessities required for an efficient labor force. The consumption level of food, shelter, clothes, medical care, and education of the humblest family must be adequate to maximize productive activity of its members. This correct level of consumption is vital to an efficient economy and is particularly vital to a capital-istic economy because of the relationship between quantity of savings and investment.

During the 1930's, consumption levels fell so low that all the goods and services consumed could be produced with over a fourth of the persons desiring work unemployed. However, this low level of employment was only in part directly caused by the decrease of consumption; it was to a great extent caused by the operation of the acceleration principle and the very nearly complete cessation of expenditure for investment. The consumption expenditures in 1929 totaled $78,761 million and private gross investment $15,824 million; in 1933, consumption equaled $46,346 million while investment was but $1,306 million. The dollar value of consumption decreased by 41 per cent, investment by 92 per cent.* The tremendous decrease in investment arose because, with consumption decreasing, the need for investment disappeared. The elimination of investment expenditure further decreased consumption through the reduction of consumer income.

The general low level of consumption of the 1930's reduced the quantity of goods and services obtained by many individuals to a point that was inadequate to provide even the basic necessities.† At the same time that this situation existed, persons were idle and natural resources that could have provided these necessities were wasted. The reduction of consumption of these low levels reduced the productivity of the people of the United States through inefficiency arising from malnutrition and inadequate housing, education, and medical attention. Also, productivity was reduced because the unemployed lost their skills through disuse and lost the incentive to improve their productivity and economic position because of the hopelessness of their economic position.

The portion of national income spent for consumption is likely to be too great during a period of war or of rapid preparation for increased future production. The consumption expenditure is usually not too great in the sense of providing more than an adequate scale of living; rather, the expenditure is too great to permit the use of the determined quantity of productive resources for war or investment. If the people believe it is for their best interests to allocate a very large portion of the nation's productive resources to war or to the expansion of the quantity of capital goods, then it is also to their best interests that provision be made for the reduction of consumption. The reduction of personal consumption will make possible large war expenditure or investment without a great general price rise. Some of the undesirable effects of a large general price rise were pointed out on pp. 55-56. The United States in 1955 is spending vast sums on armaments of all types, but the total is a sufficiently small portion of the national income (about 11 per cent) that it has not been necessary to reduce consumption.

*National Income Supplement to Survey of Current Business, July, 1947, p. 19.

†The analysis of income distribution on pp. 69–72 considers the problem of a subsistence level of consumption in greater detail.

The description of the goal of desirable prices included a brief statement of the ability of prices to determine the quantities of resources used and types of goods produced. It was pointed out that fiscal activities, through the levy of special taxes or special payments, could decrease or increase prices and thus affect resource use. These fiscal activities affect resource use largely because they decrease or increase the quantity of certain goods consumed. Fiscal activities can decrease or increase the quantities of particular goods consumed and in this way affect resource utilization. The levy by local governments of high property taxes upon houses decreases the quantity of shelter consumed. The Federal government provision of G.I. loans and payment of part of the costs in the provision of public housing increases the consumption of such resources as lumber and steel. They also determine the portion of the total quantity of these resources that will be used in the provision of shelter. Government action of this type can have a great effect on the way in which the consumer dollar is divided.

The achievement of a desirable level of consumption is an important part of the obligation of many sections of the business, political, social, and economic life of the nation. Government fiscal activities alone should not be assigned the duty of bringing about the best level of consumption. However, fiscal activities should and can have an important effect on the quantity of consumption.

Fiscal activity can increase consumption by providing for a reduction of the taxes levied upon persons within the lower income brackets—for example, by reducing general sales taxes and special excises upon necessities. Consumption can also be increased by obtaining a larger portion of government revenues from borrowing. Consumption of particular goods, especially luxuries, can be decreased by levying a special high tax upon them; and the general level of consumption can be decreased by increasing general sales taxes and excises levied upon necessities.

Government expenditures can affect consumption by subsidizing the production of certain goods—for example, during World War II the production of butter was maintained but the retail price was held down by the payment of a portion of the farmer's production costs by the Federal government. Government expenditures can also directly affect the general level of consumption by the payment of subsidies to low-income recipients.

The fiscal activities mentioned above and many others will always have an important effect upon the general level of consumption and the consumption of particular types of goods. Some of the possibilities are mentioned in this general description and analysis of the goal, but the full description of the manner in which fiscal activities have and can affect consumption is reserved for Chapters 5 and 7.

The proper general level of consumption and consumption of particular goods and services is to a great extent determined by income distribution. This relationship between the level of income and the portion of income consumed is shown in Tables 2-2 and 5-1 on pages 34 and 99. Therefore an important contribution to the solution of the continuing economic problem of the maintenance of the correct level of consumption is the manner in which the nation's income is divided. The goal of desirable income distribution is discussed on pages 68 through 76.

EMPLOYMENT

THE efficient employment of all productive persons is the most important single factor in the determination of the scale of living in a modern industrial nation.

Importance of Full Employment

"An hour of labour that is lost is lost forever." An hour of labor is the most perishable of all commodities and the most necessary element in production. Full utilization of labor is a *must* in the attainment of the maximum height of economic activity. It is also an important goal in the maintenance of political stability. Great emphasis has been placed upon the problem because of its importance and because of the apparent inability of modern industrial nations to provide for a desirable level of employment during periods of peace.

From the time of the American Revolution to World War I, while population, technology, and resources were expanding rapidly, full employment of labor and sufficient investment opportunities were not a problem. The mere recollection of conditions then existing is sufficient proof that this was an unusual period—for example, new areas were being explored and colonized and the industrial revolution was in progress. The opportunities offered for the use of savings assured that funds not spent for consumption would be quickly spent on investments. In fact, the demand for investment funds was so great that forced savings arising from expanded credit of commercial banks was likely. Because of this opportunity to use continually expanding quantities of savings, the private economy experienced no difficulty in maintaining aggregate demand—that is, the quantity of purchasing power arising from production was always available as effective demand.

The best-developed plans aimed at the provision of full employment* are the programs presented by Sir William H. Beveridge in *Full Employment in a Free Society* and Professor Alvin H. Hansen in *Economic Policy and Full Employment*.† Neither of the plans has been adopted by any nation of the world, but the fundamental principles, which are the same in both proposals, are very much a part of the economic thought in both England and the United States.

The plans proposed by both Hansen and Beveridge assign an important role to government revenue sources and government expenditure. The position of the government, however, is not all-inclusive as it is in Russia and the other control states. In Beveridge's opinion, the first and most important function of the public economy in providing full employment is the maintenance of expendable income at a size sufficient to purchase the goods and services provided by a fully employed working population. In Beveridge's words:

It must be a function of the state in the future to ensure adequate total outlay and by consequence to protect its citizens against mass unemployment, as definitely as it is now the function of the State to defend the citizens against attack from abroad and against robbery and violence at home. Acceptance of this new responsibility of the State, to be carried out by whatever Government may be in power, marks the line which we must cross, in order to pass from the old Britain of mass unemployment and fear to the new Britain of opportunity and service for all.‡

A desirable employment level has become synonymous with the popular term "full employment." Full employment is considered a necessity for political stability and maximization of production. More than any other goal, that of a desirable employment level is the aim of the entire economic and social system. The importance of full employment was expressed by Eric Johnston, former president of the United States Chamber of Commerce, in an even more forceful manner when he said:

*Full employment is defined on pp. 34–36
†William H. Beveridge, *Full Employment in a Free Society* (New York, Norton, 1945); and Alvin H. Hansen, *Economic Policy and Full Employment* (New York, McGraw-Hill, 1947).
‡*Full Employment in a Free Society*, p. 29.

Two powerful nations, Russia and the United States, will enter the postwar world representing opposite poles of economic and social thought. The Russian system will be propagandized. Ours will be, too— I hope, by example . . . . The test will be our ability to solve the problem of unemployment . . . I believe we can solve it on a democratic basis.*

The analyses of both Hansen and Beveridge largely assume that the expansion of purchasing power (aggregate demand) is the same as an expansion of employment.† Both Hansen and Beveridge are aware that the provision of full employment and a desirable level of economic activity is a very complicated business in a democracy. Hansen has pointed this out:

Thus in the "mixed economy" of modern political democracies, full employment must be achieved, not by the simple process of setting people directly to work, but by the far more complex process of ensuring an adequate volume of aggregate demand.

But even this is not the end of the problems facing a democratic capitalistic country attempting to provide full employment, for:

Though aggregate demand is adequate, a country may yet suffer from monopolistic restrictions, from strikes, from unbalanced wage-and-price structures, and from unemployment in stranded areas. All this is true, but it must nevertheless not be forgotten that aggregate effective demand is the *sine qua non* of full employment in a market economy.‡

The Direct and Indirect Methods of Obtaining Full Employment

Direct expansion of aggregate demand and employment arises when the government—through taxation, borrowing, sales, or expenditures—increases the quantity of funds used for the purchase of goods and services. This type of activity can be more effective in a largely socialized economy, where a large portion of the total economic activity is public. The increase in the portion of economic activity conducted by the governments of the United States has increased the possibilities of changing aggregate demand through direct action. In the United States, however, direct action upon aggregate demand cannot be expected to be as efficient as in a nation as largely socialized as Great

---

*Quoted by Randolph E. Paul in *Taxation for Prosperity* (Indianapolis, Bobbs Merrill, 1947), p. 235.

†"If we succeed in establishing an aggregate volume of output corresponding to full employment as nearly as is practicable, the classical theory comes into its own again from this point onward." Taken from "Keynes on Economic Policy" by Alvin H. Hansen, in *The New Economics*, edited by Seymour E. Harris (New York, Knopf, 1947), p. 203.

‡Alvin H. Hansen, *Economic Policy and Full Employment*, p. 42.

Britain. In any fiscal activity in a democratic capitalistic nation, not only the direct effects but also the indirect effects upon the private economy must be considered.

Aggregate demand and employment can be affected by indirect action largely through the stimulation or retardation of private investment. Investment is stimulated first of all by the maintenance of adequate aggregate demand. Private individuals certainly will not invest money to produce goods and services which cannot be sold. However, investment itself stimulates the sale of goods and services. To a great extent, therefore, aggregate demand is necessary for investment and investment is necessary for adequate aggregate demand. Investment is also stimulated by stable or rising prices, adequate net return on investment, cost reduction possibilities, and abundance of savings. The fiscal activity of the government can affect all of these factors necessary for large-scale private-investment activity.

The difficulties in the stimulation of private investment as a method of providing adequate employment lie in the disagreement over the manner in which stimulation of investment is to be provided rather than over its desirability (as has been true of direct activity). Much of this disagreement is because private investment will be affected by any action of government. Rapid technological progress and a mass consumer market are the best guarantees of a high level of investment. These favorable circumstances can be assisted somewhat by an income tax law that permits a rapid deduction of the cost of new investments from taxable income.

Fiscal policy can also indirectly influence employment by the assurances that it can provide for the typical worker and consumer; for example, by the provision of adequate social security and the elimination of violent economic fluctuations a decrease in the tendency to save might be effected with a resultant high level of consumption. This reduction of savings would aid in solving the problem of finding adequate investment opportunities for the savings arising at a particular level of national income.

Recent Employment Levels

Since World War II unemployment has risen high enough to be considered a problem in only two years; 1949 and 1953-54. However, unemployment was an important unsolved problem from 1931 to 1941. Throughout this entire period, over 20 per cent of the nonagricultural working population of the United

States was unemployed.* The importance of preventing unemployment is emphasized by the large portion of national income arising from employee compensation. In 1953, which was a year of very nearly continuous full employment, about 54 per cent of national income arose as employee compensation. A decrease in employment means a sharp drop in national income, which is indicative of decreased production. Unemployment is closely related to a reduced volume of consumption, the low morale of the workers, the breaking up of family units, the deterioration of trade skills, the loss of political democracy, and the breakdown of a free-enterprise economy. However, the mere provision of full employment, despite its close relationship to these problems, is not the long-searched-for panacea. This fact has been proved during the full employment existing since the end of World War II.

Full employment and inflation are very closely related. The possible evils of inflation must be risked in order to gain the great economic, social, and political benefits of full employment. Full employment is also closely related to reduced output per man-hour. Man-hour output in 1946 and 1947, periods of full employment, did not increase by as much as the prewar trend. Nevertheless, the total productivity of the economy was greatly above the prewar level.† The reduced man-hour output that arises during full employment does not indicate, as some have assumed, that the efficiency of the economy has been reduced. The reason for the apparent decrease is that the man-hour production of the man unemployed is not included in comparative man-hour production data. If the zero or nearly so man-hour production of the unemployed were included in the comparisons of man-hour production data of periods of full employment with periods of unemployment, the inefficiency of unemployment would be evident. In other words, man-hour production data only consider the efficiency of the employed and do not include the inefficiency that exists because of unemployment. Man-hour productivity measured in the traditional fashion increases during periods of full employment, maybe at an even more rapid rate than during periods of considerable unemployment, but the increase is from a lower base which exists because of the

*C. R. Daugherty, *Labor Problems in American Industry*, 5th ed., p. 65 (New York, Houghton Mifflin, 1941).

†The real income of workers in 1947 was substantially higher than in 1939; and, in addition, large quantities of goods were shipped abroad to rehabilitate Europe. *Survey of Current Business*, February, 1948, p. 25.

employment of the relatively inefficient. This relationship was shown in the 4-per-cent rise of man-hour productivity between the two full-employment years of 1946 and 1947.*

INCOME DISTRIBUTION

THE type of income distribution largely determines the type of economic activity and the amount of savings. These in turn are closely related to prices, consumption, and employment.

Importance of Income Distribution

Public finance can change income distribution by changing the portion of taxes collected and of expenditures made in the various income levels. The relative portion of income available to the low income brackets can be increased by decreasing their taxes and increasing expenditures that directly improve their income position. Also, the relative income of those in the high income brackets can be increased by decreasing their taxes and increasing the expenditures directly related to their income position. The many ways in which public finance activities can change income distribution are discussed in Chapters 6 and 8.

Fundamentally, income distribution is related closely to quantity of inherited wealth and equality in the provisions of income-making opportunities. Both of these can be affected by public-finance activity in a manner that will increase the equality of income distribution . A very unequal distribution of income, as will be shown, results in an inefficient use of the nation's resources, both human and natural. An unequal distribution of income results in a waste in some areas, while in others efficient productive activity is prevented because of shortages.

Unequal income distribution directly reduces productivity of human resources in two principal ways: (1) if persons capable of useful employment remain idle because they can enjoy all the material benefits of the society without working; and (2) if the goods and services that can be purchased with wages earned are fewer than those required to maintain good health and develop the productive abilities of the individual. Indirectly, unequal distribution of income could reduce productive activity through its tendency to increase the quantity of savings arising from a given-sized national income. The increase of savings

*The productivity in areas readily measureable increased by 4 to 5 per cent from 1946 to 1947; *Survey of Current Business*, February, 1948, p. 26.

reduces productivity of human resources when they rise to the point where they do not expand investment and cause the development of unemployment.

How Should Income Be Distributed?

Consumption Consideration. The idle rich, who are a product of unequal income distribution, are not undesirable because it is good in itself to work or because idle hands are likely to get into trouble. Idleness is undesirable because it reduces the quantity of goods and services which could have been made available for human enjoyment.

TABLE 4–1. Distribution of spending units and family units by size of income, 1953.

Annual money income before taxes	Per cent of spending units	Per cent of family units
Under $1,000	10	9
$1,000–$1,999	13	10
$2,000–$2,999	14	11
$3,000–$3,999	16	15
$4,000–$4,999	16	16
$5,000–$7,499	20	23
$7,500 and over	11	16

Source: *Federal Reserve Bulletin*, July, 1954, p. 701.

Much the more serious direct influence of unequal income distribution upon the productivity of human resources is the reduction of efficiency through inadequate income. Table 4-1 given above shows the distribution of income by spending unit and family unit in 1954. Table 4-2 (p. 70) gives the cost of a family budget, in a number of United States cities, that is sufficient to provide the goods and services required to maintain an adequate scale of living.*

The data presented in Tables 4-1 and 4-2 combine to show that a large portion of the families of the United States in 1953 received an income that was inadequate to maintain a budget that did not contain deficiencies in one or more aspects of family consumption.† In 1953 over 40 per cent of the families

---

*The Technical Advisory Committee of the Bureau of Labor Statistics defines a family budget as the list of goods and services required by an employed adult male, a housewife, and two children under 18 years of age.

†A spending unit is smaller than a family unit as used in the Federal Reserve study, there being 40.6 million families and single individuals and 46.3 million spending units. The spending-unit income is slightly less than that of the family and single individuals, but data for metropolitan areas for which budget data are available are given only in family units. The income of the family reported in the *Monthly Labor Review* is perhaps greater than that of the family unit reported in the *Federal Reserve Bulletin*. For this reason, of course, the data of the two tables are not completely comparable.

TABLE 4–2. Estimated cost in selected cities of a family budget, October, 1951.

City	Estimated total cost of budget
Washington, D. C.	$4,454
Seattle, Washington	4,280
New York, New York	4,083
Boston, Massachusetts	4,217
Detroit, Michigan	4,195
Pittsburgh, Pennsylvania	4,203
Chicago, Illinois	4,185
San Francisco, California	4,263
St. Louis, Missouri	4,112
Los Angeles, California	4,311
Cleveland, Ohio	4,103
Philadelphia, Pennsylvania	4,073
Cincinnati, Ohio	4,208
Houston, Texas	4,304
New Orleans, Louisiana	3,812

Source: *Monthly Labor Review*, May, 1952, p. 521.

The budget itself is a list of goods and services that, according to the prevailing standards of the community, are considered essential. The definition of the budget recognizes that in the actual experience of families there is a scale that ranks various consumption patterns in an ascending order from mere subsistence to plenitude in every respect. The budget level described here is at a point on this scale below which deficiencies exist in one or more aspects of family consumption.

Items that might not be considered necessary for production efficiency are considered necessities; for example, "Ice-cream cones and soft drinks have become essentials even for the poorest city family with children, who will sacrifice an otherwise adequate diet for a minimum of these items for their children." "The City Worker's Family Budget," Lester S. Kellogg and Dorothy S. Brady (*Monthly Labor Review*, February, 1948, vol. 66, no. 2), p. 142.

in the United States received an income that was insufficient to provide the standard American budget.* This is a very large percentage of the population of the United States. If it is assumed (and it is very difficult to assume otherwise) that productive efficiency of all persons with incomes below the standard budget has been reduced because of a shortage of purchasing power, the income distribution in the country, even in this favorable period, was far from the point that would maximize the utilization of human resources.* The consumer price index was three points lower in 1951 when the costs were established

*The Maintenance Budget for Families or Children developed "as a standard for good administration by relief agencies" by the Heller Committee for Research in Social Economics, University of California, required approximately a $2,000 annual income in 1946 for a family of four. The costs are for the city of San Francisco.

for a family budget than they were in 1953 the year for which family and spending unit income data are given. This compensates somewhat for the inclusion of families consisting of one person and rural families in the Federal Reserve Board data while the family budget data are designed to determine how much it costs a four-person urban family to purchase the goods and services it must have to finance a level of adequate living according to prewar standards existing in the large cities of the United States.

The situation during periods of depression and widespread unemployment are certainly much less conducive to a high utilazation of human resources than the situation that existed in 1951 or 1953.† The first fundamental basis for judging whether a particular income distribution is desirable is to determine whether it renders idle potentially productive individuals. The second fundamental basis of judgment is whether people in the lower income brackets have enough money to develop fully their productive potentialities. In the United States, the income distribution meets these tests better than in many countries, but great improvement is possible.

The manner in which income is distributed is also closely related to quantity of savings arising from a given national income. This relationship has been indicated by all income and savings studies that have been made in the United States. The most recent analysis of savings in relation to income was made by the Board of Governors of the Federal Reserve System.‡ Table 4-3, given below, shows the quantity of liquid savings held by members of different income brackets in 1945 and 1953. This table does not show all savings but refers only to liquid savings, which are usually considered the most important in analyzing the quantity of purchasing power that can be expected from disgorged savings. Therefore they are very important in forecasting the quantity of economic activity in the future.

The above analysis of the cost of a standard family budget in 1951 and of the distribution of the national income among the families of the United States shows that under the most favorable conditions the incomes of a large portion of the nation's producers are inadequate to maintain conditions correct for peak production.

†See Table 2–1 for income distribution during the middle 1930's. See *Quantity Budgets of Goods and Services Necessary for a Basic Maintenance Standard of Living and for Operation Under Emergency Conditions*, W.P.A. Division of Social Research, series 1, no. 21, 1936; *Intercity Differences in Costs of Living, March, 1935, 59 Cities*, W. P.A. Division of Social Research, Research Monograph 12 (Washington, U.S. Government Printing Office, 1937).

‡Quantity of savings arising from the different levels of income is also shown in Table 2–2 on p. 34 and Tables 5–1 on p. 99.

TABLE 4–3. Distribution of family units and liquid assets, by income groups, 1946 and 1954 (per cent).

Annual money income before taxes	1945	1946	1953	1954
	Spending units	Liquid assets held	Spending units	Liquid assets held
Under $1,000	20	7	10	4
$1,000–$1,999	27	14	13	6
$2,000–$2,999	23	17	14	7
$3,000–$3,999	15	16	16	10
$4,000–$4,999	7	10	16	11
$5,000–$7,499	5	13	20	22
$7,500 and over	3	23	11	40
All income groups	100	100	100	100

Source: *Federal Reserve Bulletin*, July, 1954, p. 701.

The data in Table 4-3 show that a small number of families in the highest income brackets possess most of the liquid savings. This corresponds with other earlier studies of the relationship between savings and size of income. The comparison between 1945 and 1953 indicates that liquid savings owned by the families in the upper income brackets increased between 1945 and 1953 but so did the number of families.

Saving Considerations. The importance of the relationship between savings and type of income distribution arises because it was believed during the 1930's that it was excess savings that largely caused idle men and idle machines. This is also very likely to be the cause of any depression of the future. It was not entirely the abundance of savings that caused the inadequacy of productive activity in the 1930's, but rather the quantity of savings combined with the investments that individuals and corporations planned to make. It was believed that the problem of idle men and idle machines could be removed by either decreasing the quantity of savings or increasing the amount of investment. Reducing the inequality of income distribution works at this problem from both ends. Savings are reduced because the portion of national income going to high-bracket income receivers is reduced. Investment is increased because demand for consumer goods and services is expanded through an increase of the portion of national income received by persons in the lower income brackets, where the propensity to consume is greater.*

The eighteenth- and nineteenth-century economists correctly urged that every effort should be made to expand savings. Shortage of savings was preventing the introduction of new machines and expansion into new geographical areas. Under these conditions, Benjamin Franklin's adage that "a penny saved is a penny earned" was excellent economic advice. Gradually during the twentieth century, production increased to the point where savings arising from the existing income distribution at full employment appeared to be in excess of desire for investment. The data presented at the Temporary National Economic Committee hearings showed that it was inability to use purchasing power accumulated as savings for investment that made men and machines idle.†

It has been as conclusively proved as any economic cause-and-effect relationship that excess of savings was responsible for the purchasing-power shortage that caused the decrease in productive efficiency evidenced by idle men and machines during the 1930's. The statistical proof was presented at the T.N.E.C. hearings, and the logical basis of the position is presented on pages 219 to 231 of this book.

The accumulation of savings during the eighteenth century can be compared to a man accumulating water in an area of seasonal rainfall and drought. The activity of building dams and cisterns and storing water in the reservoirs created is the most productive type of activity. This accumulation of water will help tremendously to expand the quantity of goods and services produced in the area. Accumulation of savings in the twentieth century can be compared to a person engaged in this type of activity in an area where the rainfall is always sufficient

*The point regarding the possibility of savings being very detrimental to efficient economic activity was very clearly brought out by Prof. Alvin Hansen during the Temporary National Economic Committee hearings in Congress. As an aside, it should be pointed out that the conclusion was supported by considerable statistical proof. ". . . . but it is extremely important to keep firmly in mind the fact that we cannot maintain full employment unless there is continuously going on a sufficient volume of plant and equipment expansion over and above replacement and renewals to absorb the full flow of savings. Savings do us good or harm according as they find or do not find investment outlets in productive expansion of plant and equipment and durable goods, including residential building and public works." *Hearings before the Temporary National Economic Committee, Congress of the United States*, Part 9, "Savings and Investment" (Washington, U. S. Government Printing Office, 1940), p. 3542.

†See the data given in Table 4–4 on page 74 regarding the relationship between national income, investment, and consumption during the late 1920's and the 1930's.

to meet the needs of productive activity. In this case the activity is a waste of resources; it decreases productive activity to the extent that the energies could be better spent in cultivating, fertilizing, and the like. Under the first set of circumstances the saver or dam builder was the most vital person in the community, while under the second set of circumstances he is a detriment.

TABLE 4–4. Net Capital formation and consumer's outlay, 1929–1937

(in millions of dollars)

Year	Net capital formation	Consumers' outlay
1929	10,082	73,342
1930	3,879	69,061
1931	− 278	56,288
1932	−4,427	44,055
1933	−2,987	42,270
1934	−1,533	49,704
1935	2,189	52,235
1936	6,301	58,906
1937	9,531	62,497

Source: *Hearings before the Temporary National Economic Committee, Congress of the United States*, Part 9, "Savings and Investment," pp. 4007–4008 (Washington, U.S. Government Printing Office, 1940).

Fiscal activity aimed at a more equal distribution of income reduces individual savings because persons in all income brackets typically cut down their quantity of savings before they reduce their scale of living. Statistics are not available to prove this relationship completely, and it is very doubtful if they could ever be gathered. The best data are perhaps those that show the fluctuations of consumption and saving. Table 4-4, given above, shows net capital formation (savings) and consumer outlay (consumption) for the years 1929 through 1937. The data cover two relatively prosperous periods, 1929-1930 and 1936-1937, and the serious depression period of 1931-1934. The data of this table leave no doubt that when income goes down, savings, as measured by net capital formation, are reduced before, and by much more, than consumption expenditures. This same relationship between savings and consumption is shown by the 1954 study of the Board of Governors of the Federal Reserve System (see Table 4-3). The study indicates that savings had begun to decrease in the lower income brackets and that amounts of disgorged savings had been used to meet general living expenses.

The quantity of savings arising in an economy producing a certain-sized income is certainly determined by a number of factors. The experience of the United States and other nations during World War II showed that price controls, rationing, and a strong propaganda program can greatly expand the quantity of savings. Also, certainly, political uncertainties, amount of savings already accumulated, and expectation of continued employment can have a great effect on the quantity of savings arising from a given-sized national income. Assuming all of these to be given, the quantity of savings is largely varied by changing the distribution of income.

Interrelationship between Fiscal Goals

The goals of desirable price, consumption, employment, and income-distribution levels are closely related to each other. It is very doubtful that any one of the goals can be reached and enjoyed without the other three also being largely achieved. However, the interdependence between the four goals varies. For example, it appears as though it would be possible to have a desirable level of prices without having full employment, or that full employment could exist with an undesirable price level, an undesirable level of consumption, and an undesirable income distribution. However, if these above conditions existed and a desirable level of employment were to be maintained by free private enterprise operating through the dictates of a market economy, the period of its continuance would be dependent upon large quantities of additional purchasing power being continually created. The latter method of maintenance would surely be brief and would end in the disorganization of inflation.

All four of the fiscal goals used here are related to the provision of a good allocation of resources. The worst allocation of the most important productive resource—labor—is idleness and the resulting poverty and loss of efficiency. However, the best allocation of labor in a market economy can be assured if consumption is maintained at a desirable high level and the distribution of income is good. For this in turn will result in price levels and relationships that allocate and utilize resources in a manner that will meet most standards of efficiency. (The adjective "good" is used here to refer to the conclusions of the analysis of consumption and income distribution that were presented earlier.) Therefore, a good allocation of resources would exist only if the the existing prices utilize resources in a manner that assures full employment, a desirable level of consumption, and an income distribution that is consistent with their maintenance.

CONCLUSION

THE data and the descriptive material of this chapter have indicated that each of the four relationships selected (prices, consumption, employment and income distribution) can be affected by fiscal actions. The basis for the selection of these four relationships has been presented, and in a general way the goal at which fiscal action is aimed in the case of each of the relationships has been established. When all four of the goals are reached, the result would be an economy operating at a high percentage of capacity all the time, and this benefit would be enjoyed with a minimum of government interference with the control and operation of the economy.

QUESTIONS AND PROBLEMS

1. Select a number of things that government can accomplish through raising and spending funds and relate their accomplishment to prices, consumption, employment, and income distribution.
2. Discuss the ways in which prices affect economic activity. How is relative price related to the problem of monopoly?
3. By the use of data mentioned in the chapter, or other reliable data, develop an income distribution that would provide the most efficient use of resources. Would this type of distribution provide for the most efficient use of resources under all conditions?
4. Do you think the interrelationships between the four goals of fiscal policy (prices, consumption, employment, and income distribution) are so close that they should be considered as one goal? Why?
5. Do you think it is just to take income earned by one individual and give it to another who has not earned it? Why? Do you think it is just to take wealth from one individual who has inherited it and give it to another? Why?
6. How is the problem of the mature economy linked with the concept of oversaving?
7. What is the concept of aggregate demand? How is it related to full employment? Compare the ways in which Sir William Beveridge and Professor Alvin Hansen would provide for an adequate aggregate demand.
8. It is sometimes said that the quantity of consumption is dependent upon investment; also, it is often pointed out that investment is dependent upon the prior amount of consumption. To what degree do you consider either of these concepts to be correct? Explain.

CHAPTER 5

Revenues in Relation to Price and Consumption Levels

CHAPTER 4 described what was concluded to be a "correct" level of each of the economic relationships: prices, consumption, employment, and income distribution. This chapter examines the possibilities existing in the first kit of tools—government revenues—to affect prices and consumption. Because taxes are by far the most important government revenue, our analysis is principally concerned with how prices and consumption are affected by them.

The effects of a particular tax are innumerable. This also is true of the other ways in which a government obtains its revenues. A listing of all possible effects will not be attempted at this time. The point that is being stressed here is that all revenue measures affect the type and quantity of economic activity. This is true whether the measure is undertaken to accomplish a particular fiscal goal, or whether it is used merely because it is the way revenues were obtained in the past, or whether it is just politically most acceptable. All revenue measure at the time of their adoption and during the period of their retention should be evaluated in regard to their possible impact upon the achievement of desirable fiscal goals.

Built-in Revenue Flexibility

The public-revenue system of the United States can aid in the achievement of the goals of fiscal policy without the initiating of new governmental action. The amounts of tax revenues obtained by the Federal and lower levels of government automatically (without a change in tax legislation) decline during periods of depression and increase during periods of prosperity. If the level of government expenditures remains constant during both prosperity and depression, the government must enter into deficit financing during a depression and accumulate a surplus or retire its outstanding debt during prosperity. Such an automatic corrective response of the revenue system is called built-in flexibility. However, built-in flexibility also exists in government expenditure.

Stable tax rates bring about variation in revenues, which aids in reaching fiscal-policy goals. Although this tendency has always existed, its impact has increased importance for the following general reasons:

1. Tax collections have become a larger portion of total economic activity.

2. The Federal tax system has become more progressive; therefore, receipts increase more rapidly with rising prosperity and decrease more quickly when depression sets in. An unemployed man will pay no income tax but will continue to pay excise and sales taxes on articles purchased.

3. The use of the withholding method of collecting the individual income tax and social security taxes, plus the payment of corporate income taxes within six months of the end of the tax liability period, and payment of estimated corporate tax liabilities during the last six months of the current tax year, have made tax receipts vary much more quickly as a result of a change in income than was previously the case.

If allowed to remain unchanged, during the different phases of the business cycle, the existing revenue system of the Federal government and, to a lesser extent, that of local governments can aid greatly in stabilizing prices, consumption, and employment, and in maintaining a desirable distribution of the national income.*

SHIFTING AND INCIDENCE OF TAXATION

THE incidence of a tax is briefly defined as the place where the burden of the tax finally comes to rest. The burden is taken from one person and placed upon another by the process called shifting. Shifting can take place only if an exchange transaction is involved. It is obvious that the location of the incidence and the manner of shifting are of vital importance in determining the effects of government revenues on the goals of fiscal policy. It is also true that it is very difficult to determine what the incidence of a particular tax is and the manner in which the tax will be shifted. A large portion of the difficulty arises from shortage of statistical

*Professor Arthur Smithies agreed with this evaluation when he wrote "Effective Demand and Employment" in The New Economics (New York, Knopf, 1948), edited by Seymour E. Harris, p. 566.

data, but an important additional factor is that the manner of shifting and the location of the incidence of a particular type of tax changes, depending upon the rate at which levied and the prevailing market and production conditions.*

A tax is said to be shifted *forward* if it is moved toward the consumer of the product or service taxed and *backward* if it is moved away. A very important factor in determining the direction of shifting is the price elasticity of demand. If the demand for the product is very inelastic—for example, the demand for salt or cigarettes—the full amount of the tax levied upon the product can be shifted forward without decreasing appreciably the quantity of the product sold. Under these conditions there is little doubt that the tax will be readily and quickly shifted forward. If the demand for a product is elastic, an increase in the price will decrease the quantity sold. An additional tax under these conditions is very likely to be either absorbed by the firm upon which it was orginally levied or shifted backward onto the firm's suppliers.

The elasticity of the demand for products or services produced and traded, upon which an additional tax burden has been placed, is determined by many factors. One important factor is the generality of the tax. If the tax covers a large geographical area and also includes all producers of substitutes as well as producers of a particular product, the demand for the taxed good and service will be inelastic. Also, if there is an abundance of purchasing power in relation to the quantity of goods, the demand will be inelastic; with either or both of these conditions prevailing, a tax increase will be rather readily shifted forward. If the reverse relationship exists between purchasing power and goods, the tax is likely to be absorbed by the firm upon which the tax is levied or shifted backward upon the resource providers. Therefore, the elasticity of demand is determined by the importance of the need filled by the good, cost in relation to the buyer's purchasing power, and the closeness of substitutes.

The degree of elasticity of supply is often more important in the shifting of taxes than elasticity of demand. A tax that is shifted in higher prices causes a reduction of consumption of the taxed product. This will decrease the price obtained by the producer, unless the supply is decreased. If the supply of a

*Otto von Mering, *Shifting and Incidence of Taxation* (Philadelphia, Blakiston, 1942); Marion Hamilton Gillim, *The Incidence of Excess Profits Taxation* (New York, Columbia University Press, 1945); Duncan Black, *The Incidence of Income Taxes* (London, Macmillan, 1939); John F. Due, *The Theory of Incidence and of Sales Taxation* (New York, Kings Crown Press, 1942).

product is inelastic, all taxes placed upon the product will tend to be shifted onto producers. Supply is apt to be inelastic if there are many producers (competition)—for example, agriculture—and elastic if there are only a few producers (oligopoly)— for example, manufacturers of farm machinery. Also, the supply of durable goods that can be used for a long period of time tends to be inelastic. In addition to current production, the supply of these latter goods includes many of the units produced during a number of years in the past—for example, homes and pianos.

Shifting of Income Taxes

The income tax of both the individual and corporate variety is called a direct tax. The term direct tax is used because it was believed they could not be shifted. This was largely true of these taxes when they were paid by only a small portion of income receivers and the rates were relatively low. Today the rates are high and most business and private income is subject to these taxes. The effect of this changed situation on the location of the incidence of these taxes is uncertain.

It was mentioned that the more general the tax, the greater the likelihood of shifting; but when the tax becomes so general that it includes all types of economic activities, shifting in the conventional manner is impossible. A worker cannot find employment in an industry where his income will not be taxed and it is difficult to engage in business without the income being taxed. Therefore these taxes have a relatively small effect on the types of products produced and types of economic activities engaged in.

It is sometimes said that the individual income tax can be shifted by deciding to work less because the purpose of work— income—is taxed whereas the purpose of not working—leisure —is not taxed. Studies attempting to find out if this logical possibility exists in the real world have concluded that it more than likely does not. A greater shifting likelihood has arisen from the growing consciousness of income earners that it is income after taxes that is important. On this basis the worker asks for higher wages because of an income tax increase.

If wages are increased to compensate for an individual income tax increase, resource owners (workers own their skills and strength) shift the tax to the consumers of the goods produced and to some extent to the other important group of resource owners, capitalists (owners of the machines and buildings). However, because the other resource owners would also be busy trying to shift their income taxes which would have also increased, the owners of labor and the owners of capital are very likely to get together and to shift their income tax increases in higher prices of goods and services. Here the owners of the resource labor (the workers) find themselves being the ones to whom the higher income tax is shifted because they are also the buyers of most of the goods and services. The owners of the resource capital are in a better strategic position to rid themselves of the burden of the income tax because their charges are a much smaller portion of the total cost of production and because the tax rate that they pay is higher than that of workers whereas the prices of the goods and services which they purchase would have gone up largely to compensate only for higher wages.

This advantageous income-tax-shifting position of capitalists, or of any relatively unimportant group with higher-than-average income tax rates, can be illustrated by a simple arithmetical example.

Let it be assumed that a product sold for $100 and that this $100 was distributed as follows:

$60—labor cost
10—capital cost (including normal profits)
20—all government costs
10—all other costs

$100

The income tax is increased by 10 per cent on the wages of labor and by 20 per cent on the income of capitalists. Let it be further assumed that each is successful in increasing its income by enough to compensate for the higher taxes and that this increase of income is passed on in higher prices. The situation after the income tax increase is now as follows:

$66.67—labor cost
12.50—capital cost (including normal profits)
22.62—all government costs*
11.31—all other costs

$113.10

The price of the product to laborers has increased by 13.1 per cent, or 2.0 "points" more than their wages. The price of the

*It is assumed that other costs increase by the average percentage increase of production costs, which is 13.1 per cent.

product to capitalists has also increased by 13.1 per cent, but this is 11.9 "points" less than their income increase. The net result under these conditions—where both the capitalist and the worker are able to shift an increase of the income tax through higher prices, where the percentage tax increase is greater for the capitalist than for the worker, and where the total income is spent for the inflated goods and services—is that the owner of labor bears a portion of the burden of the capitalist's taxes in addition to his own.

If it is assumed that the same amount of money is spent on goods after the income tax increase as before and that the same quantity of goods and services is produced (full employment), then if the prices of some goods rise because of the income tax increase, the prices of other goods must fall. It was shown that goods and services with an inelastic demand and an elastic supply are most likely to have higher prices and that those with an elastic demand and an inelastic supply are most likely to have lower prices.

Tax Capitalization

A very fascinating aspect of the incidence of taxation refers to the burden of a tax levied on income from property that cannot be shifted in higher prices of the services arising from the property. The property tax is this type of tax although it does not directly use income from property as the base. It is a tax on income because the value of property is set by the price the property would bring on the market, and this price is determined by the income which the property would produce.

Tax capitalization is the term used to designate this type of tax shifting. For purposes of explanation, let us assume that a piece of property sells for $10,000 where the gross annual income from the property is $1,400. Further let us assume that $200 of this gross income are necessary expenses in producing the income and that another $200 are the property taxes payable each year. The annual net income from the property under these conditions is $1,000; and if the property's market value is $10,000, it means that the market values this type of property at ten times its net income. The tax authorities now decide to increase the taxes assessed on the property by $100 annually. If nothing else is changed, the net income from the property is now $900, and the capitalized value of this return is $9,000.

Under these simplified conditions the burden of the increased tax is borne entirely by the owner of the property at the time the tax is increased. The next buyer of the property would pay only $9,000 for it, and the previous owner will suffer a $1,000 capital loss. The rate of return on the investment will remain at 10 per cent.

This same relationship between the capital value of an asset and its net return after taxes exists in the case of a common stock or a saleable annuity. And just as capital values are sharply decreased, the amount depending on the rate of capitalization, when a tax increase cannot be shifted in higher product prices, so capital values are sharply increased when the tax is decreased if competition or other factors have not forced a decrease of the income arising from the asset.

THE ACHIEVEMENT OF DESIRABLE PRICES

REVENUE raising actions related to prices are of two basic types. The first type is the effect on the price of a particular good, such as tobacco, of collecting a tax on the manufacture and sale of tobacco products. The second type is the effect on the general level of prices of raising revenues. The analysis of this second effect, of raising revenues, is closely related to conventional types of monetary analyses. It differs in that the tools used are fiscal and not monetary, and it is similar in that the economic impact works itself out through monetary channels. This similarity to monetary analyses is true, of course, of a host of economic analyses.

Effect of Taxes on the Prices of Particular Commodities

The United States tax system has for many years included special levies upon particular products. In most cases the special high tax has been levied because the consumption of the article was not considered necessary for good health, and because a tax placed upon the item would bring in substantial revenues. The outstanding examples of this type of tax levy are the Federal, state, and even local taxes on alcoholic beverages and tobacco products. During World War II, very high special Federal retail excise taxes were placed also upon jewelry, furs, toilet preparations, and luggage. These taxes were finally substantially reduced in 1954.

Gasoline is another commonly consumed commodity that has had its price greatly raised by the levy of special taxes. In this case, the state taxes are the most important and they have been levied largely because gasoline consumption has been considered a good measure of the benefits received from highway construction. The funds collected from the application of this tax usually do not go into general revenue, as do most of the revenues of the other special commodity taxes; instead they are largely set aside for expenditure upon highways. However, the Federal gasoline tax of 2 cents per gallon is not levied as a use tax, and the revenues collected are not segregated.

The communication, electric-utility, automobile, and amusement industries have also been selected for additional tax burdens. The levy of special taxes upon industries that provide necessary production services has a particularly undesirable effect upon prices. Prices to the consumer are likely to be increasd by considerably more than the tax because of the common trade practice of percentage markups based on cost, which in these cases would include the tax.* In the case of a retail sales tax, the base is greater as a result of markups and therefore a tax of a lower rate will bring in the same revenues as a higher-rate manufacturing tax.

Probable Effects on Prices of Special Commodity Taxes

The revenues from the taxes on alcoholic beverages have become tremendous. It is estimated that Federal and state tax collections were over $3 billion in 1954. The cynical advice "Put the taxes on the vices for they have the broadest shoulders" continues to be acceptable revenue policy. The quantity of consumption of alcoholic beverages is very sensitive to changes in prosperity and an abundance of purchasing power. Beer consumption is a possible exception to this generalization. High taxes on alcoholic beverages increase prices of legal sales until the difference between manufacture cost alone and cost plus tax is great enough to overcome the risks of illegal manufacture. Money collected in liquor taxes is generally purchasing power that would have been saved or used to bid up prices of other

*An example of the result would be:

    Before tax:

Cost to manufacturer	$10	—markup 10%
Cost to wholesaler	$11	—markup 5%
Cost to retailer	$11.55	—markup 20%
Cost to consumer	$13.86	

    After tax of $1 on manufacturer:

Cost to manufacturer	$11	—markup 10%
Cost to wholesaler	$12.10	—markup 5%
Cost to retailer	$12.71	—markup 20%
Cost to consumer.	$15.25	

A tax of $1 per unit has raised the price to the consumer by $1.39.

luxury goods. Only the tax upon beer is likely to reduce the money available for the purchase of necessities and thus to tend to reduce their price and to have an important deflationary effect.

The tax on tobacco products is largely a cigarette tax. Since 1919, cigarette consumption has continued to increase (with the exception of a slight drop from 1931-1933), despite several Federal tax increases and the introduction of state taxes. The direct Federal and state excise taxes are typically 50 per cent of the price of a package of cigarettes.* Cigarette prices have not increased as much as the tax. This relationship exists because the great increase in volume has made possible a considerable reduction in manufacturer, wholesaler, and retailer margins. Cigarette-consumption data indicate that cigarettes have become a necessity for their users. This is borne out by grocery store managers, who say that a frequent practice is to buy cigarettes first and food afterwards. Low prices on cigarettes have replaced low prices on sugar and flour as leaders to bring shoppers into stores.†

High taxes on cigarettes undoubtedly reduce the quantity of money available to be spent on other goods. In a period of inflation, these taxes tend to reduce prices of food, shelter, and clothing by draining off purchasing power that would otherwise be brought to bear on these prices. During a period of deflation, these taxes result in a reduction of expenditure for goods and services badly needed to maintain their prices.‡

The best information available shows that the special Federal luxury taxes on jewelry, furs, toilet preparations, and luggage were not all luxury taxes. At least they were not luxury taxes in the sense that the persons in the upper income brackets spent a larger portion of their income for these products than people in the lower brackets. Information obtained in the family-expenditures study of 1941 showed that all income brackets between $500 and $5,000 spent about the same portion of their income on jewelry and toilet preparations; however, the higher income classes spent a larger portion of their income on furs

---

*The Federal tax is 8 cents a package of twenty, and the typical state assesses an additional 2 or 3 cents.

†The per-capita consumption of cigarettes in 1929 was 977; by 1939 it had risen to 1,318, and in 1946 it was 2,324.

‡The Division of Tax Research, Treasury Department, made available in February, 1948, an excellent study titled *Federal Excise Taxes on Tobacco*.

and luggage. Undoubtedly, a certain quantity of toilet preparations and jewelry is considered a necessity.*

Although gasoline taxes have been levied since 1919 at continually higher rates, the price of gasoline including the tax declined until the postwar period. The price of gasoline in 1919 was 25.47 cents, when its direct tax burden was but 0.06 of a cent; in 1945, when the tax burden was on an average 6 cents, the price was about 21 cents including tax. Between 1945 and 1954, the price of gasoline rose more rapidly than the tax burden, making the tax a smaller percentage of the price.

The gasoline-tax collections are largely made directly available for road construction and repair. The gasoline tax, by financing an improved road program, has undoubtedly reduced general prices through decreased costs of transportation. However, the natural question to ask is: Couldn't the road-construction program have been financed in another manner that would not have placed quite such a heavy burden upon the quantity of purchasing power available for other goods and services? Actually, during the depression of the 1930's much road construction was financed with revenues from other sources. The Federal government plans to spend much more on roads than it collects from the assessment of the 2 cent tax on the gasoline used to propel vehicles over the public roads of the nation. The portion of gasoline taxes collected on gasoline used for commercial purposes is undoubtedly passed through the economy and results in price rises considerably greater than the revenues obtained by government.

The existing market and production conditions must be very unusual if a sales or manufacturer's tax on a particular product does not raise the product's price. A special commodity tax on one of two close substitutes—for example, margarine or butter —will not only increase the price of the taxed product but also the price of the close substitute. A commodity tax upon a product that is produced largely from the utilization of the nation's natural resources—for example, gasoline—is less likely to be passed on in higher prices than a commodity whose cost arises nearly entirely from the payment of ordinary market-rate wages.

*The Heller Committee for Research in Social Economics of the University of California included expenditures for toilet preparations in their "Restricted Quantity and Cost Budget for Maintenance of Families or Children." The budget also included expenditure for tobacco products (pipe tobacco, however, rather than cigarettes). These budgets were developed to determine relief-expenditure requirements. Therefore, it would seem that some products called luxuries are actually necessities.

However, even in the case of the price of gasoline, the amount paid to the natural-resource owner is a very small portion of the total retail price of the product.

A commodity tax levied upon a product that is customarily sold under luxury conditions—that is, with wide margins of profit and handled by many middlemen—is less apt to bring about a price rise than a tax levied upon a product sold under very competitive conditions. Also, a sales tax or a special excise levy collected when a prevailing buyer's market exists is less likely to result in higher prices.*

Co-ordination of Fiscal and Direct Controls

Some attempts were made during World War II to restrict the use of scarce materials by the assessment of taxes. The special taxes on tires and leather goods are examples. Generally, this method of obtaining additional revenue and also restricting the use of materials in short supply was permitted to remain fallow during the war years. If this theory of obtaining revenue were combined with the ration system it could become a very effective price-control tool.

The portion of the supply of goods obtained by the exchange of ration coupons would be tax free. This exemption would allow individuals living on a minimum budget to obtain their necessaries without paying the tax and would therefore prevent a rise in minimum cost-of-living indices. The same good (specially marked as taxable and ration-free) could be purchased without a ration coupon by the payment of a much higher price that would include a high tax. This procedure would have increased government revenues, kept trade in legitimate channels, and in this manner maintained a larger portion of the market economy and at the same time developed deflationary pressures. The administrative problems of a scheme of this sort would be great but not insurmountable.

Effect of Taxes on the General Level of Prices

Since the establishment of the Federal Reserve System in the United States, it has been generally assumed that the responsibility for providing stable prices rested upon banking and monetary policy. In turn, banking and monetary policy were to be determined with little consideration for government fiscal activities. However, stable prices have not been provided, and

*John F. Due, *The Theory of Incidence of Sales Taxation*, pp. 194-197.

also banking and monetary policy have been effected by government fiscal activities.

Because of this rather widely accepted priority of banking in the field of price-stability policy, public-finance courses have conventionally neglected to analyze government revenues and expenditures in relation to their effect on the price level. However, the actual relationship makes the maintenance of an acceptable price stability an important goal of fiscal policy. Professor Abbott, who is rather pessimistic concerning the ability of fiscal policy to accomplish many of the goals set for it, believes that fiscal policy should be definitely concerned with the provision of an acceptable price stability and also that this goal can be largely accomplished at the present stage of the development of Federal government techniques.* The surprising fact is not that price policy is now included within the scope of fiscal policy, but rather that until very recently it was assumed that government revenues and expenditures did not affect price levels.

Professor Abbott states that fiscal policy should set as its objective: "the provision of a monetary unit the value of which is not subject to wide variation, nor to political manipulation, nor to the threat of political manipulation."† This goal for price stability has been advocated for some time by monetary economists. *The new development is that the goal is now understood to be largely attainable through fiscal policy.*

The maintenance of a stable monetary unit in terms of purchasing power is usually considered to be the first requirement for the development of a rational economic program. Fiscal policy must have as a principal goal the prevention of the depreciation or the appreciation of the value of the monetary unit. Price-stability activity must be related to a base which is accepted by the community as being desirable and accepted by fiscal authorities as being attainable and not contradictory in its effect upon other important aims of fiscal policy. In other words, price trends are not good or bad in themselves Prices are "good" and "bad" only in terms of how they affect economic activity.

The goal of stable price levels does not necessarily require that the purchasing power of money remain constant. It is also true, however, that any monetary unit to be acceptable must possess a great deal of stability, particularly when large portions

*Charles Cortez Abbott, *Management of the Federal Debt* (New York, McGraw-Hill, 1946).

†Charles C. Abbott, *Management of the Federal Debt*, p. 173.

of savings are in investments stated in a certain number of monetary units. Also, the savings held in this manner are savings accounts, insurance, and government bonds, all popular with persons in the low and middle income brackets. If the desirability of maintaining a stable price level is outweighed by other desirable goals of fiscal policy, the goal of maintaining an acceptable price level requires that the purchasing power of the unit be changed. Such a conflict could arise, for example, in regard to the desirability of levying high income taxes, which would take away purchasing power that was being used to bid up prices and would decrease the value of the monetary unit. At the same time, these high tax rates would reduce the attractiveness of new investments and thus retard the development of new production needed to stabilize the value of the monetary unit. Investment is stimulated by rising prices, but rising prices mean inflation— the reduction of the value of the monetary unit. An additional factor to be considered is that investments made during a rapid price rise are selected less carefully and are likely to be less productive and therefore relatively inefficient in reducing inflationary pressure.

Problems in Eliminating Inflation and Deflation (the Two-Headed Dragon)

Today, a government revenue program can affect general economic conditions much more than it could in 1929. This change has arisen because of the great relative increase of the public economy and also because of the development of the science of economics and the increased quantity of economic statistical data.* The way in which the government collects or does not collect $75.2 billion from a gross national product of $365 (1953) will obviously have a much greater effect than the manner in which it collected $11.3 billion from a gross national product of $103.8 (1929).

Desirable fiscal policy to prevent a fall in prices will be quite different from the type of fiscal policy recommended to prevent an increase in prices. Fiscal-policy recommendations must be constantly re-examined to steer the nation's economy in the "middle course between inflation and unemployment."†

The year 1954 in the United States has been a period during which it was desirable that fiscal policy be aimed primarily at

---

*Depressions are costly affairs. It has been estimated that the depression of 1929 to 1941 cost the businessmen of the United States over $300,000,000,000 in lost sales. Taken from Randolph E. Paul, *Taxation for Prosperity.*

†Alvin H. Hansen, *Economic Policy and Full Employment*, p. 248.

the prevention of the development of a depression. During the period of World War II, inflation was an ever-present menace; the citizens were well aware of the danger and supported government programs aimed at reducing it. After the conclusion of the war, the realization of harm from inflation was less evident and, in addition, the danger of deflation began to appear. Thus, intelligent fiscal policy during the postwar period has had to be two-headed, one head facing inflation and the other facing deflation. Because of the very different problems, the two programs must also be very different. This fact has led to frequent charges of inconsistency and confusion. These charges of inconsistency and confusion arise from either a lack of understanding of the problem of maintaining economic stability or a desire to gain a political advantage from creating a misinterpretation.

The problem of pursuing the narrow winding path between inflation and deflation is to a great extent political and psychological. The main political problem lies in placing sufficient power in an agency that can act quickly when conditions appear to be approaching either inflation or deflation. Another political problem stems from the psychological influence of a boom period when public opinion is very much opposed to government action that will disrupt what seems to be a new era. However, after a deflation period has set in, public opinion aids government activities to raise prices and increase the amount of economic activity. The business community, which to a large extent determines the ability of government to act, enjoys a boom period but does not enjoy a deflation period. Yet if the boom period which businessmen enjoy is allowed to continue upward, it will create the conditions for the deflation period which they dislike.* In a democracy, it is very doubtful whether any agency of the government will ever be given sufficient power to act decisively to prevent a boom or a depression whenever one or the other *appears* to be developing.

Another problem of maintaining correct general price levels arises from the lack of adequate current statistical data and techniques to determine accurately what is developing in the economy.

---

*See Alvin H. Hansen, "Cost Functions and Full Employment," *American Economic Review*, vol. 37, Sept., 1947. If boom periods are expected to continue, the profits arising during the period would not be great because capital would soon cease to be the scarce factor. The high profits of the boom period have been the main cause of the assumed instability. These high profits during the period that the boom was becoming stabilized could be eliminated by excess-profits taxes or price controls.

The data are particularly meager in regard to the expenditure and saving plans of individuals and business firms.* Certainly any intelligent action that might be decided upon to keep the economy in the middle ground between deflation and inflation can be determined only on the basis of adequate information.

Functional Finance

A type of fiscal policy aimed at stable prices has been stated by Professor Boulding as the "adjustable tax plan." Professor Boulding describes the plan as being usually preferable to expenditure in that it can be more readily adjusted. Briefly, the plan is that "the rate of tax should depend on the movement of money income during the past month."† Thus, if money income has risen during the past month beyond an amount designated, the rate of tax in the next month should be increased in order to prevent inflation. The plan of Professor Lerner called "Functional Finance" also includes the idea of fluctuating tax rates. "The Government . . . will tax individuals, or a certain class of individuals, when it believes it to be socially desirable that they should not be so rich or should not spend so much. It will tax particular forms of spending (on whiskey for example) as a means of decreasing them. It will tax more generally as a means of cutting down total spending, when this is necessary to prevent excessive total demand and inflation. Taxation is important not as a means of raising money but as a means of cutting down private spending."‡

In order to rid the mind of the concept that governments must assess taxes to obtain funds required for expenditure and therefore must abandon a tax policy consistent with the requirements for stable price levels, Professor Boulding suggests that we assume the government has no expenses. "Then the tax rate would fluctuate between positive and negative levels, accordingly as inflation or deflation threatened."§ When the analysis is made upon this basis, it is seen that even though there were no government revenue requirements the tax system would still be continued as a very useful tool of economic and social control.

*See Max F. Millikan *Income Stabilization for a Developing Democracy* (New Haven, Yale University Press, 1953) pp. 169–211. This chapter was written by Everett E. Hagen.

†Kenneth E. Boulding, *The Economics of Peace* (New York, Prentice-Hall, 1945), pp. 161, 162.

‡Abba P. Lerner, *The Economics of Control* (New York, Macmillan, 1944), p. 308.

§K. E. Boulding, *The Economics of Peace*, p. 165.

Both Professors Lerner and Boulding point out with considerable vigor that their plans for adjusting tax rates do not necessitate a huge government debt. For example, changes in the tax system to increase the taxes upon the rich and decrease them upon the poor will increase the income stream available for the purchase of consumer goods but may not decrease government tax revenues; in fact, tax receipts may increase. If the system is suffering from an over-all shortage of money, taxes would be lowered, and the government would obtain funds by the direct printing of money; this, also, would not increase the debt. Furthermore, if the government obtained funds from borrowing during periods of an abundance of liquid funds, it could repay these loans during a period when there was a shortage of funds in the hands of individuals; thus the debt would not continue to climb year after year. Borrowing under the adjustable-tax plan is accomplished to decrease the quantity of money in the hands of individuals. Government borrowing from the commercial banks to increase the quantity of money in the hands of individuals would be discontinued. Governments would increase the quantity of money by printing directly.*

The World War II Record

Inflation danger is always greatest during a period of war. It is then that large additional quantities of money reach consumers but that the quantity of goods for consumer purchase tends to decrease. A period of war is also the time when the revenue and expenditure of government become an increased portion of total economic activity.

The control of inflation during the period of actual hostilities has proven easier than during the postwar period. It is possible for governments to impose strict direct controls during the actual shooting war, but it is very difficult to maintain these restrictions during the period of reconstruction. For example, in the United States on the day following Japan's surrender, the controls over man power were dropped; within a few weeks many price, priority, and production controls were lifted; by the end of 1945 rationing of all commodities other than sugar had been removed; and by the beginning of 1947 nearly all wartime direct controls were gone.

*Some of the problems involved in financing government expenditures from sources other than tax receipts are discussed in *Deficits and Depression* by Dan Throop Smith (New York, Wiley, 1936).

Tax activities of the Federal government played a secondary but co-operative role in the effort to prevent price rises during the war period. Also, much government borrowing was attempted in a manner that would decrease the inflationary pressure. Credit and monetary controls of the war period played a relatively minor part in inflation control. In general, credit was extended so as to raise rather than lower prices.

The excess-profits tax was raised three times during World War II, and the final rate was 85.5 per cent.* This tax on profits made it politically and therefore practically possible to use severe direct economic controls effectively. Also, this tax combined with the regular Federal corporate-profits tax reduced substantially the dividends paid to individuals by corporations and the accumulations of corporate reserves. Both of these effects reduced the inflationary pressures.

The Korean War Record

The outbreak of the Korean War on June 26, 1950 signaled an inflationary pull, the likes of which this country has seldom experienced. The pull was strong enough to raise the consumer price index from 172 in July 1950 to 182 in January 1951. This rise of over ten points in six months approached the price increases of 1946 after rationing and price controls were eliminated.

It has been traditionally assumed that under conditions such as these, monetary controls, because they merely require administrative decisions, will be the quicker while fiscal controls will be initiated more slowly because in most instances they require legislative action. But this did not turn out to be the way events evolved in 1950 and 1951. By December 1950 the House Committee on Ways and Means had approved an excess profits tax bill. During the same five-month period the credit outstanding of the Federal Reserve System increased by $2 billion. Part of this increase of Federal Reserve credit was seasonal but much of it fed the flames of inflation.

The Excess Profits Tax Act of 1950 was retroactive to July 1, 1950. The ordinary corporate income tax was also increased, and this, too, was made retroactive.

The Revenue Act of 1951 increased the tax rates by 11 per cent on the first taxable income bracket, i.e., taxable incomes up

---

*The tax was 95 per cent, but a postwar credit of 10 per cent was included. This was a type of compulsory saving.

to $2,000; by about 11¾ per cent on income brackets up to
$26,000; and by about 9 per cent on all brackets above $26,000.
Corporate income taxes were raised again in this revenue act, and
the rate for medium- and large-sized corporations became 52
per cent. This made possible a marginal rate of 82 per cent on
the profits of corporations subject to the excess profits tax.

In addition, the Revenue Act of 1951 increased the excise tax
rate on alcoholic beverages, cigarettes, gasoline, and automobiles
and related products, and placed new taxes on diesel fuel oil,
wagering, fountain pens, mechanical pencils, and cigarette and
cigar lighters.

Many of these Korean War tax increases linger on. The
individual income tax scheduled rates have been decreased to
the level before the war, and because of additional exemptions,
the effective rates are below what they were then. The excess
profits tax was allowed to die at the end of 1953, but the 52 per
cent corporate profit tax rates were continued through 1955.
Also, the big revenue raisers of the new and higher excise taxes
enacted in 1951 were continued through 1955, although many
excise tax increases of the World War II period and a few of the
Korean War period were decreased in 1954.

Fiscal action was prompt at the outbreak of the Korean War
—much more prompt that it had been in the World War II
period. The tax increases enacted are estimated to have raised
about $9 billion of additional revenues annually. Because of this
effective (measured in terms of previous war period experience)
action, the Federal budget was approximately balanced for the
first two years of the Korean War period, but as planned war
expenditures reached their peak in the fiscal years 1953 and
1954 and new taxes were not enacted, the Federal budget became
badly out of balance on the deficit side.

The Korean War experience points up the rather general
acceptance of the importance of a proper fiscal policy if prices
are to be kept in line during a war period. The experience also
shows that despite a quite adequate fiscal program, prices will
rise when buyers hear the "bugles of war."

Again in 1954 when price trends were downward, many
elements of the economy clammered for lower taxes as a relief
measure. Their demands for lower taxes used both of the logical
bases available to support their request. They contended, first,
that lower taxes would increase purchases because potential

buyers would be richer, and second, that lower excise taxes would increase the sales of particular goods or increase the profits from the sales of particular goods.* The excise tax cuts of April, 1954 generally resulted in price reductions; and in some cases the price reductions were greater than the tax cut, indicating that the original tax was pyramided on the basis of percentage markups. The price of theater tickets was a rather general exception to this rule. Even though the excise tax on theater tickets was cut, many theaters continued to charge the same admission price, which included the higher tax, charged before the tax cut.†

Spendings Tax

During World War II and again during the Korean War, a spendings tax was recommended in the United States as a method of discouraging consumption and raising revenue without placing a heavier burden on the low income recipients. The tax was not adopted; however, the possibility that it might be adopted in the future is not ruled out, for it has received strong support from labor groups and from manufacturers of products likely to be selected to bear the higher special excise taxes.‡

The spendings tax works like this:

It would be collected through the use of tax returns supplementary to the regular individual income tax. The taxpayer would add up the additions to his savings such as larger security holdings, purchases of land, more money in the bank, and the like. This amount would be deducted from his income for the year, and the remaining income would be the expenditures subject to the tax. If the taxpayer had reduced his savings, the amount of the reduction would be added to his expenditures. Investment for business expansion or medical expenditures would be considered as savings.

*See J. K. Hall, "Excise Tax Incidence and the Postwar Economy," *American Economic Review Supplement*, March, 1942, pp. 83–101.

†For some other price policies, see "The Effect of the 1954 Reduction in Federal Excise Taxes Upon the List Prices of Electrical Appliances—A Case Study," by John F. Due, *National Tax Journal*, September, 1954, pp. 222–226.

‡See Milton Friedman, "The Spendings Tax as a Wartime Fiscal Measure," *American Economic Review*, March, 1943, pp. 50–62; and Kenyon E. Poole, "The Spendings Tax: Problems of Administration and Equity," *American Economic Review*, March, 1943, pp. 62–73.

A tax of this sort could provide for an exemption of a minimum amount of expenditures. It is also capable of utilizing graduated rates similar to those of the individual income tax.*

The weakness of the tax arises from problems of administration. The tax requires a continual check on changes of taxpayer savings. The tax would have to provide for some sort of adjustment between persons renting their homes and those occupying homes they own. Also a satisfactory method of handling installment purchases and purchases of a large quantity of durable goods in one year would have to be worked out. But these problems are not insurmountable. If the tax were introduced as a substitute for most of our excise taxes during a period of peace the administrative problem could be solved then, and the tax would be a smoothly running mechanism ready for use if war erupted. It is during a war that the tax would be most useful.

Purchase Tax

The purchase tax was devised in Great Britain during World War II and continues to be used there. In a way it is a combination of a luxury excise tax and a tax to conserve scarce raw materials. It is levied at the wholesale level at extremely high rates on selected commodities.

The high rates of the tax apply to style clothing and furniture but not to the "utility" type of clothing and furniture developed in Great Britain. The items taxed are divided into three categories and for a considerable time the rates were $33\frac{1}{3}$, $66\frac{2}{3}$, and 100 per cent. The top rate applies to jewelry and silverware; the middle rate to household appliances, motor cars, and the like; and the bottom rate to household goods. To prevent pyramiding of the tax, the British law restricts markups on account of the tax to the amount of the tax.

The purchase tax is a practical method of gearing the excise tax system to a war economy with its shortage and its need for keeping the cost of living of workers relatively stable.†

*The plan proposed by the Treasury in 1942 consisted of two parts, a flat-rate tax plus a graduated surtax. The flat-rate tax of 10 per cent was applicable to spendings in excess of $500 for a single person, $1,000 for a married couple, and $250 for each dependent. The surtax was to be levied at graduated rates ranging from 10 to 75 per cent on spendings in excess of exemptions, which were twice as high as those under the flat-rate tax. The flat-rate tax was in the nature of a compulsory loan. *Annual Report of the Secretary of the Treasury for the Fiscal Year Ended June 30, 1943*, pp. 410–420.

†See "The Purchase Tax and Fiscal Policy," by Arnold M. Soloway, *National Tax Journal*, December, 1951, pp. 304–314.

Compulsory Lending

Compulsory lending is a fiscal device that lies halfway between taxation and voluntary lending. Like a tax, it must be paid at a rate applied to a base established by legislation. Like a loan, the amount paid in, and perhaps also the interest earned on the amount paid in, will be returned to the lender-taxpayer at some future date.

The aim of compulsory lending is to decrease the purchasing power of workers during a war-inflationary period without destroying their willingness to work harder for longer hours. The device was highly recommended in 1940 by J. M. Keynes in his book, *How to Pay for the War*, and it was made a part of the British Finance Act of 1941. Canada followed with its compulsory lending program in 1942, and the United States' income-victory tax included the idea in 1942.

The United States experience was extremely limited, and the postwar credits accumulated were converted into current tax offsets after a little more than a year. The Canadian effort was more extensive than that of the United States, both in terms of the portion of government receipts affected and the length of time during which the law was in effect. The British experience was by far the most extensive. The amounts involved in Great Britain were about 13 per cent of total individual income tax collections during the 1941-1946 period.

Most of the support for a compulsory lending scheme was given by those who believed that a great shortage of purchasing power and a severe deflation would occur in the immediate post World War II period. But because there has not been a postwar shortage of purchasing power, Great Britain has been able to pay back only a small portion of its compulsory lending accumulation. Repayments there have been limited to those having credits who have reached retirement age.

An examination of the World War II experience shows that the procedure was difficult to administer, largely because exemptions were permitted to those who were already engaged in as extensive a savings program as they could carry. Also, it does not seem to have had a stimulating effect on the willingness of laborers to work. Finally, the postwar world did not need the purchasing power accumulated.*

*See Walter W. Heller, "Compulsory Lending: The World War II Experience," *National Tax Journal*, June, 1951, pp. 116–128.

THE ACHIEVEMENT OF A
DESIRABLE CONSUMPTION LEVEL

IF resources are to be most efficiently used, the consumption level must be high enough to give laborers the goods and services needed to bring forth the greatest possible labor effectiveness. This would necessitate (1) a minimum consumption level—that is, adequate housing, food, clothing, education, medical care, and recreation—and (2) savings sufficient to assure the introduction and wide use of the most efficient machines and techniques. In a capitalistic society, these achievement goals require that the holder of savings must be induced to risk them in a new venture, and savings must not be so great that consumption loses its ability to encourage new investment. However, it is possible for consumption to be high enough to avoid oversaving and yet not great enough to support maximum labor effectiveness. This would be true if the additional goods and services that could be purchased with the earnings arising from increased labor activity were insufficient to stimulate the increase. This was perhaps the actual situation in England until very recently; it arose from the rationing of many consumption goods and the resulting reduction in the ability of money to command goods and services. The difficulty can be alleviated by payment of both money and ration coupons to certain groups of workers.

The whole problem of getting the correct level of consumption is closely related to income distribution, which is discussed in relation to government revenues on pp. 116-129 and in relation to expenditures on pp. 159-166. Government revenues affect consumption directly by reducing purchasing power in the hands of individuals and indirectly through effecting the distribution of income. Consumption from a given national income is also affected by interest rates, distribution of savings, availability of consumption goods during a previous period, population composition, and provision for social security; a number of other relationships perhaps also have an important effect. The quantity of personal savings in the United States between 1946 and 1947 shows the importance of these miscellaneous factors in affecting consumption. The tax system between 1946 and 1947 did not change a great deal, the distribution of income was approximately the same, and the total personal income of the period rose from $177.7 billion to $190.5 billion; but the personal savings in 1947 were $8 billion less than in 1946. Thus the percentage of personal income consumed increased.

Saving and Consumption Relationships

The variations arising from different methods of obtaining revenue are closely related to the portion of income saved in the different income brackets and the portion of revenue raised that is obtained from the different income brackets. If the government obtains its revenues without reducing the revenue available to individuals—for example, borrowing from commercial banks or printing money—the raising of revenue by the government does not in itself decrease consumption or saving activity of individuals.

Table 5-1, given below, contains data of savings made within the different income brackets. The table shows that in 1944, when the United States was benefiting from price controls, high wages, and full employment, 30.9 per cent of the families were within income brackets with no net savings. Additional taxes

TABLE 5–1. Average money income, expenditures, and savings of families and single persons in cities, by income class, 1944*.

Annual income after personal taxes	Expenditures for current consumption	Net savings or deficit	Per cent of families in each class
Under $500	$ 594	−$320	4.2
$500 to $1,000	939	− 206	7.7
$1,000 to $1,500	1,317	− 126	7.1
$1,500 to $2,000	1,690	− 3	11.9
$2,000 to $2,500	1,946	213	13.9
$2,500 to $3,000	2,375	236	13.2
$3,000 to $4,000	2,816	538	19.9
$4,000 to $5,000	3,428	767	9.6
$5,000 and over	4,324	2,856	12.5

Source: *Monthly Labor Review*, January, 1946.

*The savings arising in the middle income brackets are overstated in this study. The overstatement arose from considering all mortgage-principle payments as savings and not reducing them by depreciation taking place during the year.

collected from these brackets would increase their deficits or reduce private consumption by very nearly the full amount of the taxes collected. The portion of individual income saved varies directly with size of income and size of asset holdings. However, individuals with uncertain incomes such as farmers and small businessmen have a higher propensity to save than those receiving an assured income. Also rural dwellers and white-collar workers are more likely to save than are urban laborers.

By obtaining its funds in different ways, the government can have a varying effect upon the private consumption levels.* If revenues are obtained by the levy of taxes that are paid largely by persons in the low income brackets who are city dwellers and nonwhite-collar workers, private consumption expenditures will be decreased by nearly the full amount (if unemployment develops, consumption will be decreased by more) of the revenues obtained. If revenues are obtained by taxes collected largely from the members of the upper income brackets, consumption will be decreased by considerably less than the amount of the revenues obtained. This difference arises because most savings are made by individuals in the upper income brackets and because saving levels rather than consumption levels will be changed when the tax burden is increased. If the government obtained its funds from taxes upon businesses or by borrowing from individuals or business firms, the resulting reduction in private consumption would be even less. If the government borrowed from commercial banks or printed money, and full employment did not exist, the amount of private consumption would surely expand. Government receipt of revenues from the sale of basic commodities would also, under most conditions, expand the quantity of private consumption.

How Taxes Directly Affect Consumption

An increase of the tax burden in itself reduces the quantity of funds available for consumption and saving. The desire to maintain consumption levels is greater than the desire to maintain saving levels, thus savings will be decreased in all income brackets but the decrease will be most important where net savings arise; in the lower income brackets there will be an immediate reduction of consumption by very nearly the full amount of the tax. If the tax is general and brings about a reduction of total quantity of money bidding for goods and services of all kinds, the general price level will tend to decline so that the regular quantity of consumption can take place with the reduced quantity of money; this tendency would be particularly strong in the case of a sales tax with the revenues utilized to repay public debt held by commercial banks. Recent studies have shown there is considerable variation of savings within

---

*In this analysis it is usually assumed that funds obtained by a government do not affect government expenditure. See Chapter 7 for the general impact of government expenditures upon the consumption level.

income brackets.* Therefore, the effect on consumption and savings will vary, depending on which groups within an income bracket are affected.

How Commodity Sales Directly Affect Consumption

The sale of commodities by the government increases the quantity of goods and decreases the purchasing power in the hands of individuals. The direct effect is deflationary, and consumption of the commodities sold will increase. Government action of this type is limited, of course, by the quantities of commodities possessed. The Ever-Normal Granary Plan adopted by the United States in 1938, after the bumper crop of 1937, is aimed at the equalization of the supply of farm products between good and bad years. The plan, which is financed by the Commodity Credit Corporation, attempts to accomplish this aim through storage and sale from storage. A sale of large supplies of farm commodities held by the Federal government at the outbreak of World War II made it unnecessary to ration bread in the United States and increased the consumption level of our allies.

The sale of commodities by the Federal government also increases the revenue of the government. If the commodities have been originally purchased with borrowed funds, their sale will merely reduce the quantity of money existing in the community and increase the quantity of commodities. If the products have been purchased with funds obtained from taxes, their sale makes possible a reduction of taxes and increased consumption at constant prices. Also, if the commodities are sold for a price higher than their purchase price, the sale would be very likely to become a basis for decreased taxes, whether the original funds had been obtained by borrowing or tax receipts. If it is considered undesirable to reduce government debt, the money obtained from the sale of commodities would always be available for additional expenditure or a tax reduction. Any of the alternative actions would stimulate consumption.

The Interest Rate

The rate of interest, which is sometimes called the price paid for holding assets as cash, is in addition to this a price which affects the portion of income that will be consumed and the portion that will be invested (saved). It is undoubtedly true

*The studies of Consumer Finances by the Board of Governors of the Federal Reserve System in 1946 and 1954 referred to on p. 71.

that the rate of interest can be established in a modern state by the central banking authorities. In the United States this would mean that the Federal Reserve System can establish the interest rate—at least the interest rate on assets with a high degree of moneyness.

The central banking system can decrease the interest rate under a given set of conditions by increasing commercial bank reserves, and it can increase the interest rate by decreasing the money supply. However, the interest rate can also be affected by the use that is made of current income with the money supply remaining relatively neutral. If a large portion of national income is saved (small portion consumed) and invested, the interest rate will fall; if only a small portion of national income is saved, the interest rate will rise—again, the rather unreal assumption is made that nothing else changes. It is this second way of changing the rate of interest—changing the portion of national income saved (consumed)—that government revenues and particularly taxes can affect the interest rate.

It has been assumed by most economists that a high rate of interest stimulates savings and decreases investment; this, of course, would make the interest rate important in determining the amount of consumption and economic activity.

However, a British study concludes that "the effect of variations in the rate of interest on business savings seems to have been so small as to be negligible."[*]

Apparently savings and investment are closely related to profits and money wages, as well as to the capitalized value of earnings, which is determined by the interest rate. If interest rates increase, the capitalized value of earnings decreases sharply; if interest rates decrease, the capitalized value of earnings increases sharply.[‡] Money-wage levels are important because when they go up costs of capital goods in the future will be higher; in addition, high wages will mean an active demand for goods produced. Emphasis upon the importance of the long-term rate arises because it is to a great extent an independent variable and because it does affect investment; perhaps it is largely in its effect upon investment that the rate of interest affects savings.

If the government obtained its funds from persons in the

*E. A. Radice, *Savings in Great Britain, 1922-1935* (London, Oxford University Press, 1939), p. 78.

‡The capitalized value of earnings is calculated by dividing earnings by the prevailing rate of interest.

upper income brackets through either taxation or borrowing, the rate of interest would tend to increase. The same tendency would exist if funds were obtained by borrowing from the commercial banks. This tendency for interest rates to increase with the latter type of government revenue-raising would be much greater if excess commercial-bank reserves did not exist. The tendency of interest rates to rise as a result of obtaining revenues from savings or through borrowing from commercial banks counteracts slightly the direct expansionary effect on consumption of obtaining revenues from these sources.

The government, through the levy of taxes upon persons in the high income brackets, also reduces the net return on investments. This relationship arises because a large portion of the income of the wealthy is obtained from the ownership of property. A high tax upon corporate profits would have the same effect upon the return on investment.* This would mean that investments that had seemed to offer a sufficient financial inducement prior to the levy of the tax were no longer considered desirable. (It is doubtful whether, under even the most favorable conditions, it would be possible to shift the full amount of a corporate income tax.) We have here, therefore, two indirect effects of obtaining revenues from persons in the higher income brackets. The first effect is to increase interest rates and the quantity of savings, and the second effect is to require a higher return on investment.

The higher rates of interest would tend to stimulate the amount of saving but would tend to reduce the amount of investment. This undesirable impact on the balance between saving and investment plans could have a very detrimental effect on the total activity of the economy and, therefore, on the amount of total consumption.

The Effects of Government Sale of Gold

The purchase and sale of gold has usually been a monetary operation and not a fiscal activity of government. The purchase and the sale of gold usually do not directly increase or decrease government revenues or expenditures. An exception to this was the sterilization of gold by the Federal Treasury late in 1937. The Treasury at this time spent about $1,400 million of

---

*During World War II, corporate tax rates increased greatly but net profits after taxes did not decrease; rather, they increased by 125 to 150 per cent. The expiration of the excess profits tax in 1954 helped to hold up corporate profits during a period of recession.

government revenues for the acquisition of gold. However, in 1938 the quantity of business activity decreased and it was considered desirable fiscal and monetary policy to desterilize the gold. Thus, late in 1937 expenditures were made for the purchase of gold, and early in 1938 revenues were obtained from the sale of gold.

The reserves of the Federal Reserve System and the entire private banking system are based upon the quantity of gold held by the United States Treasury. If the government began the sale of gold, the amount of credit which commercial banks could extend would be reduced. This reduction would be particularly sharp if the reserves required by law for the Federal Reserve Banks were completely utilized. Such a restriction in credit would reduce business activity and, as a consequence, would lay the basis for a serious depression and a reduction in consumption. This unusual effect of the sale of this commodity by the government arises from the unique position that the commodity gold holds in our banking and monetary system.*

The difference between the sale of gold and the sale of commodities such as wheat and cotton is that the sale of wheat and cotton would also lay the basis for the reduction of debt or the reduction of taxes. The reduction of taxes would be stimulating to the private economy, particularly if the taxes were being collected largely from the low income brackets. This stimulation does not arise from the sale of gold, nor does it arise when the Federal Reserve System sells securities on the open market.

The sale of gold by the government would also tend to raise interest rates through its reduction of the reserves of commercial banks. This reduction in the reserves of commercial banks arising from the sale of gold has an effect on consumption similar to the decrease in the quantity of money in the hands of individuals arising from the government sale of wheat and cotton.

The Use of Taxes to Control a Consumer Boom

The booms developed during a period of war are closely related to consumption expenditures and could be called consumer booms. The booms developed during periods of peace are likely to be closely related to investment expenditures and could be called investment booms.

*An interesting discussion of the effects of gold is given by Raymond Mikesell in an article titled "Gold Sales as an Anti-Inflationary Device," *Review of Economic Statistics*, vol. 28, no. 2, May, 1946, pp. 105–108.

The control of a consumer boom requires that taxes be aimed at reducing the quantity of purchasing power being used to bid up prices, while increasing· the portion of the total resources of the nation that is allocated to the provision of additional production facilities. High excise or spending taxes closely correlated with an efficient rationing program are best suited to achieve this goal.

An effect similar to a spendings tax can be obtained by placing a higher tax upon corporate distributed profits than upon profits not distributed. This is done by placing extra taxes on corporate profits distributed and lower taxes on corporate profits used to expand production. Such a relationship partially exists in 1954, with corporate income subject to additional taxation if distributed. Under the Federal income-tax laws of 1955, if corporate profits are used to expand the business the tax rate is 52 per cent, while if they are distributed as dividends the tax rate is 52 per cent plus the individual income-tax rate applicable to the bracket in which the receiver of corporate dividends falls.*

Rachet Effect

The economic relationship referred to by the term "rachet effect" or "rachet formula"† is the tendency of the level of consumption not to fall as low in a depression period ·following the most recent boom period as it fell in the depression period following the previous boom period. This tendency results in the consumption level in successive depression periods providing a higher platform from which the next boom can spring.

It seems that consumption is maintained because during successive boom periods, consumers become accustomed to successively higher standards of living; and during successive depression periods, they are willing to enter into considerable dissaving in their attempts to maintain it.

The over-all effect of this tendency is to add stability to the economy.

*One of the better recent tax studies is *Taxes and the Budget* by the Research and Policy Committee of the Committee for Economic Development (November, 1947). This study recommends a stabilizing budget policy. Briefly, the program is as follows: Set tax rates to balance the budget and provide a surplus for debt retirement at an agreed high level of employment and national income. Having set these rates, leave them alone unless there is some major change in national policy or condition of national life.

†See James S. Dusenberry, *Income, Saving, and the Theory of Consumer Behavior* (Cambridge, Mass., Harvard University Press, 1949), pp. 114–116.

CONCLUSION

THE level of taxation and the types of taxes collected are now generally recognized to be very important in establishing the general price level and the prices of particular goods and services. Recent actions of the Federal government to control inflation and deflation (the general level of prices) have placed a major portion of the burden on changes of tax rates and the introduction and elimination of taxes. The achievement record appears to have been sufficiently good to justify continued emphasis.

Taxes raising the same amount of total revenue from a given national income may have a varying effect on consumption. This relationship exists because one type of tax may collect nearly all its revenues from income or funds that would have been spent for consumption if they had not been paid in as taxes, whereas the revenues collected by another tax may come largely from income or funds that would have been used for investment. Because of this possibility, plus the ability with available income data to determine in a general way which type of private expenditure (consumption or investment) will be affected by government tax collections, policy makers can recommend taxes to raise a given amount of revenue that will have the desired effect on consumption or on investment.

QUESTIONS AND PROBLEMS

1. What is meant by built-in revenue flexibility? What are the principal advantages of this type of revenue flexibility?

2. Define shifting and incidence of taxes. Explain why a market transaction is necessary for a tax to be shifted. Explain why the existence of a buyers' or sellers' market is important in determining how a tax is shifted.

3. Explain the relationships that must be considered to understand the possibilities of shifting the individual income tax.

4. It is generally said that the corporate income tax is more likely to be shifted than the individual income tax. Develop arguments for and against this point of view.

5. Briefly outline the ideas of Professors Boulding and Lerner regarding the correlation of government revenue sources with the needs of the economy.

6. Explain in your own words how taxes affect the general level of prices.

7. How can excise taxes affect the portion of national income spent for consumption and investment?

CHAPTER 6

Revenues in Relation to Employment and Income Distribution

CHAPTER 5 considered the relation of government revenues to prices and consumption. This chapter continues with the analysis of government revenues in relation to employment and income distribution. Again the analyses will be largely in terms of taxes, and the ones selected for consideration here are Federal taxes.

THE ACHIEVEMENT OF A DESIRABLE EMPLOYMENT LEVEL

THE emphasis on Federal revenue sources is justified by two facts: (1) the Federal government possesses a much greater freedom of revenues source, and (2) the important fact that the Federal government raises the great preponderance of revenues.

In this section, taxes are considered nearly entirely in relation to their influence upon full employment through their effect on the aggregate demand of the private economy.

The aggregate demand of the private economy consists of total private consumption expenditures plus total private investment expenditures.

General Effects of Taxes on Investment Expenditure

The consideration of taxes in relation to their effect upon private investment expenditure requires attention to the following points: (1) The effect upon savings available for investment. This relates largely to the accumulations of the rich and the use that corporations make of their profits and reserves. (2) The effect upon return obtained from an investment. This relates to the way in which taxes of various types affect interest, dividend, and profit payments, as well as capital gains. (3) The relationship between tax burdens borne by private and public

107

enterprise. The opportunities of private investment in those industries in which there is public competition will be reduced if the public enterprises receive tax favors.

The encouragement of private investment is important, but it must also be remembered that every boom period that arose, other than those occurring during a period of hostilities, came to an end largely as a result of a relative over-expansion of all types of private investment. There were not too many homes or too many hospitals or too many resort hotels to meet the requirements of the advertised American standard of living, but there were too many of them in relation to the purchasing power available in the hands of the people who were supposed to utilize these facilities. It is largely true, also, that the reason private investors require an opportunity to make large returns is the uncertainty whether purchasing power in the hands of the consumers will be great enough to buy at a sufficient price the goods or utilities produced from the investment. In a private economy, higher prices and capacity production produce the higher returns which become the incentive for increased investment. However, the dividend and interest payments would not have to be as great if investors were certain of them.

Another powerful reason for business investment in buildings and machines results from competition. It does not require that consumer expenditures be expanded but rather that there is the possibility that they can be diverted from competitors. Such investment will be large under conditions of active competition and rapid technical development. The fact that the investment is made will cause consumer demand to increase through the multiplier effect; that is, the investment is not made because the total consumer demand has already increased. In other words, this type of business investment, which is very important in our economy, is made because of the possibility of getting a larger portion of the market and not because the market has expanded.

Accelerated Amortization

Taxation can either encourage or discourage competitive investment, depending on the provision made in the corporate income tax law for the deduction of depreciation allowances.*

*For a summary of treatment of depreciation, see "Depreciation in the Tax Laws and Practices of the United States, Australia, Canada, Great Britain, New Zealand, and South Africa," by Raymond E. Manning, *National Tax Journal*, June, 1948, pp. 154–174.

Because the future is always difficult to forecast and because the further into the future a forecast is attempted, the greater the uncertainty, business firms are encouraged to invest if they are permitted to deduct rapidly the cost of machines used in the productive process.

It has always been recognized as legitimate to deduct the cost of a machine over the expected period of its useableness in arriving at taxable income. Investment is encouraged if the rate of depreciation deduction is accelerated because (1) the planning period of corporations is shortened and (2) the portion of the cost of the machine which the government pays (the corporate income tax rate, which at this time is 52 per cent) is received by the corporation more quickly. In the purchase of a machine, for example, the corporation's cash reserve can be more quickly replenished, or if it borrowed money, its loan can be more quickly repaid. In either case, the business firm is encouraged to invest sooner in another machine because of the rapid amortization.

During World War II and again during the Korean War, special legislation was passed providing for rapid amortization of investment judged necessary for the war effort.* This legislation is still in effect on investment judged necessary for the national defense. It may permit complete write-off of investment within five years.

The Revenue Act of 1954 made provision for more rapid amortization of all investment as a regular part of the Internal Revenue Code. It was considered an important fiscal development aimed at avoiding additional unemployment in 1955. Under the old straight-line procedure, a machine with an estimated life of twenty years would be 19 per cent depreciated by the end of the fourth year; whereas under the sum-of-the-years-digits method provided for in 1954, it would be over 33 per cent depreciated by the end of the fourth year.

Capital Gains

Another technical aspect of our income tax law closely related to the amount of investment is the treatment of capital gains. A capital gain usually arises when a security or real

---

*The Second Revenue Act of 1940 provided rapid amortization (accelerated depreciation) on capital equipment purchased under the conditions of a necessity certificate granted by the government. The Revenue Act of 1950 again added rapid amortization to the Internal Revenue Code. See "The Impact of Accelerated Depreciation," by R. W. Lindholm, *National Tax Journal*, June, 1951, pp. 180–186.

estate is sold at a price greater than its original cost. Because our income tax law taxes a capital gain only when it is realized (this is the only practical administrative procedure, for it would be very difficult to value each taxpayer's assets every year), the taxpayer can avoid paying a tax by not selling. Also, when he sells in one particular year he may realize an increase in value which may have been accruing for many years or he may realize an inflationary price increase; it thus seems unjust to tax all his gain in one year and put him in a much higher income tax bracket for that year. On the other hand, if a person dies owning property which has increased in value, this increase is never taxed as ordinary income or as a capital gain. It does, however, form a part of the value of the estate and is taxed under the estate and inheritance taxes; but this would also be the case if it had been subject to ordinary income or capital gains taxes.*

Considerable evidence has been gathered to show that a low tax on capital gains, and particularly a low rate tax on capital gains held over six months, encourages business investment and that a high rate, of course, discourages investment.†

The desirability of a low tax rate on long-term capital gains both as a matter of justice and as having a desirable effect on the operation of our economy has been recognized by Congress. Capital gains from assets held over six month (long-term capital gains) at the taxpayer's option either are included in income at 50 per cent of the amount of the gain or are taxed at a flat rate of 25 per cent. This treatment is provided for capital gains of individuals and corporations. Under the law, therefore, an individual could be in an income bracket in which additional ordinary income would be taxed at an 80 per cent rate but long-term capital gains would be taxed at only 25 per cent. Likewise, a medium- or large-sized corporation with its net income taxed at 52 per cent could enjoy a long-term capital gain income and pay only a 25 per cent tax rate on it.

Low capital gains taxes encourage realization of investment gains. The result is an active securities market. This in turn makes it easier for corporations and businesses of all types to raise the funds needed for additional investment. Also, capital

---

*For a summary of United States treatment, see "Legislative History of Treatment of Capital Gains Under the Federal Income Tax, 1913–1948," by Anita Wells, *National Tax Journal*, March, 1949, pp. 12–32.

†J. K. Butters, L. E. Thompson, and L. L. Bollinger, *Effects of Taxation on Investment by Individuals* (Boston, Harvard University Graduate School of Business Administration, 1953); and R. W. Lindholm, *Taxation of the Trucking Industry* (Columbus, Ohio, The Ohio State University Bureau of Business Research, 1951).

gains taxes which are lower than taxes on ordinary income encourage wealthy persons and corporations to invest funds in new and untried enterprises because the earnings, if any, would result in capital gains taxable at the low rate. In fact, a high tax rate on individual incomes might actually encourage investment if the tax rate on capital gains is low. The investment stimulating effect of a low capital gains tax is dependent upon a high tax on ordinary income.* In this respect, the low capital gains tax is similar to rapid amortization, for the investment stimulation in both cases arises out of the existence of high income taxes.

Loss Carry Back and Carry Forward Provisions

Although, generally speaking, the income tax laws tax income realized each year, there has for many years been an attempt to do some income averaging. Businesses with widely fluctuating income particularly gain from an ability to apply losses of one year to gains of other years. Therefore, when the corporate income tax law is liberal in its provision for the carrying back and forward of losses, it is encouraging investment in industries which are likely to have widely fluctuating incomes as well as new businesses which will experience losses while establishing themselves in the market. The 1954 law is more liberal than legislation of the past; it permits a two-year carry back of losses and a five-year carry forward of losses, thus providing an eight-year period over which losses may be spread.†

Tax-exempt Securities

The special provisions of the income tax laws presented above stimulate investment in the private economy. The exemption from the income taxes of the Federal government of interest received by holders of state and local government securities (called municipals) stimulates investment in the public economy. And it may cause some transfer of investment from the private economy to the public economy. But because all large investments of state and local governments, other than in utilities, are

*For a detailed discussion of all aspects of capital gains taxation, see L. H. Seltzer, *The Nature and Tax Treatment of Capital Gains* (New York, National Bureau of Economic Research, 1951).

†State and local governments occasionally use exemption from property taxes for a period of time as an inducement to new industrial investment. This reduces the cost of establishing a new firm and tends to expand total investment as well as attract industry away from established areas to new locations.

not appropriate for private investment, the result of the tax exemption is almost entirely a stimulant to additional investment.*

The tax exemption of municipals permits these levels of government to borrow funds required to build a road or a school at an interest rate considerably below that which they would have to pay if the interest paid were taxable income. For example, a commercial bank holding a long-term Federal government security receives about $2.50 interest each year for each $100 invested; of the $2.50, about $1.25 must be paid in income taxes. Thus, the bank could hold a municipal which pays in interest only $1.25 for each $100 invested and receive about the same net return as on the Federal government security. This relationship permits state and local governments to market their debt at lower interest rates, with the result that, with a given amount paid in taxes, a larger bond issue can be floated and needed investment can be made, which might have been delayed if the interest had been taxable.

General Effects of Taxes on Consumption Expenditure

The analysis of the effect of taxes on purchasing power requires consideration of the effects of the revenue measure on (1) individuals with varying propensities to consume and (2) prices of consumption goods.

Taxation aimed at maintaining a high level of consumption must, under the existing distribution of income (see Table 4-3, p. 72), be progressive. The data available indicate the tax burden borne by the low income levels in the United States to be entirely too high in 1954. Consumption can be increased most readily by tax measures if the tax burden of those possessing a high propensity to consume is reduced. This requires a lowering of the taxes paid by the recipients of small incomes. The Temporary National Economic Committee study of tax burdens in the United States and the study completed by Tibor Barna of tax burdens in England show the burden of the different excise taxes to be particularly heavy on the low-income receivers.† These

*Because state and local government expenditures are not classified in the national income accounts as investment, their expenditures for schools, highways, and bridges would be added to their expenditures for teacher salaries and upkeep of prisons as a portion of the total expenditures of government.

†Temporary National Economic Committee, Investigation of Concentration of Economic Power, Monograph No. 3; Helen Tarasov, *Who Pays the Taxes?*, Monograph No. 3 (Washington, U. S. Government Printing Office, 1940), p. 6; and *Redistribution of Incomes* by Tibor Barna (Oxford, Clarendon Press, 1945), p. 188.

same studies show the burden of the income taxes and the estate taxes to be relatively heavy upon the recipients of large annual incomes. If private consumption expenditures are likely to lag, the inexorable conclusion is that the relative importance of excise taxes should be decreased and that of estate, property, and income taxes increased. (See Table 6-1, p. 118.)

Undistributed Corporate Profits Tax

It was generally believed in the mid-1930's that a tax which would increase the portion of corporate earnings distributed to stockholders would stimulate national income, and particularly the consumption portion of national income. In line with this thinking President Roosevelt in his message to Congress on March 3, 1936 recommended the adoption of an undistributed profit tax.* Such a tax would have applied only to the profits of corporations not distributed as dividends. In this way the double taxation of corporate earnings would have been eliminated. The tax was never completely adopted, but it was experimented with for several years. It disappeared completely in 1939.

Undoubtedly an undistributed corporate profits tax could be made workable, and it would certainly result in reduced savings, for all withheld corporate earnings are savings, whereas many stockholders would spend a portion or all their additional dividends on consumption.

Savings Tax

Under our tax system, not only is income taxed but also the portion of income that is spent for consumption is very likely to be taxed again as the goods purchased bear various excise and sales taxes. In addition, the prices of many goods include portions of other taxes paid by the producers and distributors of the goods. On the other hand, the income that is saved is not subject to other taxes. Out of this relationship between repeated taxation of income that is spent and single taxation of income that is saved arises the justice of an additional tax on savings. In addition, a tax on savings is seen as a method of increasing consumption by making saving less desirable.

A savings tax has never been introduced, but the application of the general property tax to intangibles can result in an incidence similar to a savings tax. However, the tax on intangibles

*Alfred G. Buehler, *The Undistributed Profits Tax* (New York, McGraw-Hill, 1937); and R. W. Lindholm, *The Corporate Franchise As a Basis of Taxation* (Austin, Texas, The University of Texas Press, 1944).

is not generally enforced, and in many states its rates are so low that its effectiveness is not sufficient to provide the results which could be expected if a savings tax were collected.

Miscellaneous Ways of Stimulating Consumption

Methods to stimulate consumption expenditures similar to those introduced to encourage investment expenditures while high income taxes and many excise and sales taxes remain in force have been used only sparingly, but there are untapped possibilities in this area.

The provision for the deduction of interest paid on installment purchases and housing mortgages from the taxable income of the taxpayer is one way that the income tax law has been changed to encourage consumer spending. It is true that expenditures for housing are classified as an investment for national income accounting purposes, but the decision to spend or not to spend in this area is usually basically a consumer-type decision.

Another example relating to consumer spending for housing is the special capital gains provision adopted by Congress in 1951. Under this provision, an owner who sells his home is not subject on this sale to capital gains taxation if he spends the amount received for another home within a period of a year and a half.

Also, the individual income tax permits the deduction from taxable income of the cost of special clothing and equipment required to earn an income, which encourages consumer expenditures in this limited area.

Opportunities for expanding special stimulants to consumer expenditure within a framework of high income taxes are wide. Three possibilities that come to mind are summarized below:

1. Increase the exemptions for dependents either by raising the personal exemption above the $600 level or by allowing the deduction of a specified amount of tax for each dependent. The latter procedure would permit a more liberal allowance for persons in the lower income brackets while increasing the amount of tax collected from those in the higher income brackets. For example, under the present system, if the lowest income-tax rate is 20 per cent and the highest is 80 per cent, the low income-tax payer saves $120 of tax for each dependent and the high income-tax payer saves $480 of tax for each dependent.

2. Permit the deduction from the income tax liability up to some maximum amount, say $500, of all Federal excise taxes

paid. It would be desirable to treat state excise taxes in this same way instead of permitting their deduction from income as the present law allows. Placing this provision in the income tax law would increase the progressiveness of the tax and would make it easier to adjust the economic burden of excise taxes to meet current needs.

3. Increase estate and inheritance taxes. This would encourage the income earner to spend his income for consumption and discourage the delay of expenditure generally.

Taxing Idle Money to Provide Full Employment

Always in a depression there appears to be a shortage of money. The obvious action is either to increase the amount of money or to force the holders of money to spend. Those persons opposed to an unbalanced Federal budget have recommended programs aimed at directly increasing the velocity at which money circulates.

During the period of the middle 1930's, considerable popular support was obtained for tax plans aimed at increasing the circulation of money. The advocates of plans to tax cash balances thought that, by levying the special tax, pressure would be placed upon persons to transfer funds into investments or to use the money to purchase consumer goods.

Unutilized spending power is always held by relatively wealthy individuals and business firms. If these holders of liquid assets could be induced to spend by the levy of a tax, economic activity would be expanded. It was believed that the levy of such a tax would stimulate additional investment or induce "consumer spending by the rich above the customary levels." However, it is doubtful that these expected results would have been realized if the program had been actually adopted.

At least some of the excess deposits might have been used to purchase private and public investments held at that time by commercial banks. This would have resulted in a decrease in the quantity of money and certainly only a very slight increase in the velocity. To the extent that this latter result would arise, the levy of a tax upon cash hoards would not have accomplished its purpose. The desire to place funds in investments rather than in cash will reduce the rate of interest. The old theory was that this would increase investment by reducing the cost of money; just as important a result is that, when interest rates are low, individuals are less likely to assume the risk of investment. This reduced inducement to invest arises because the loss of income from holding funds as cash or idle deposits has decreased. The additional income arising from investment of funds is not enough to compensate for the additional risk. However, despite the danger of the falling interest rate making liquidity more desirable, the general stimulating effect of a tax on savings is important and actually provides a part of the desirability of income and estate taxes. Also, a tax upon liquidity provides a stimulation of investment similar to a rise in interest rates without the disadvantage of increased costs to borrowers.

THE ACHIEVEMENT OF A DESIRABLE INCOME DISTRIBUTION

THE incentives of a capitalistic economy are largely determined by the manner in which income is distributed. Income distribution also has a great effect on the portion of national income spent for consumption and the portion saved or invested. Income distribution is determined by the prices paid for various types of resources—for example, labor or cotton—and by the quantity of the resource controlled by particular individuals. The actual income distribution determined by the interplay of market forces is, to a great extent, determined by the ability of individuals and groups to produce cheap and sell high. However, this efficiency or ingenuity, which is rightly so highly valued in the United States, is not the only determiner of income distribution. Inheritance and fortuitous circumstances are also important in determining the existing inequality of income distribution.

The Relationship of Goal to Government Revenues

The assumption underlying fiscal policy is that the income distribution achieved through prevailing patterns of prices and existing ownership of resources does *not* provide the most desirable distribution of income. Also, a necessary part of the achievement of the goal is the existence of some standards other than relative price that may be applied to determine efficiency of resource use. (The discussion of minimum personal budgets and quantity of savings on pages 68-72 provided a basis for a different income distribution.) The present income distribution must be considered most desirable if the relative prices paid resource owners, which is reflected in income distribution, is considered correct.* Finally, to have the goal related to government rev-

*With the exception that unequal income distribution due to existing unequal resource ownership need not be justified on this basis.

enues, it is necessary that its achievement be closely associated with the manner in which governments obtain their funds.

The collection of government revenues affects income distribution among individuals (for example, the rich and the poor), producer groups (for example, farmers and manufacturers), and income types (for example, profits and wages). The change is largely made in two distinct, general ways: (1) The collection of revenues through taxes or loans or sale of commodities can directly reduce the net assets and/or liquidity of assets of individuals and firms. (2) The collection of revenues on particular types of income or particular commodities can discourage certain economic activities relative to others. The second reaction to revenue collection is partially an effect of the original impact of a reduction in net assets and/or liquid assets.

The levy of high taxes on the poor and low taxes on the rich would reduce the relative quantity of net assets available to the poor and increase the quantity of net assets available to the rich. At least this would be the case if the tax levy did not bring forth an even greater relative change in government expenditures in the opposite direction. High taxes on the rich and low taxes on the poor would have the reverse effect. This is the most important type of income redistribution and is called *vertical redistribution*.

The Effect of Tax Levies on Income Distribution

Vertical Redistribution of Income. Much economic theorizing has been concerned with the problem of changing the existing level of individual incomes. The Malthusian theory of population combined with the Ricardian theory of tax incidence left little doubt that it would be impossible to improve the position of the low-income groups by lightening their load of taxation. The incomes received by laborers would always be at subsistence level, whether the taxes were light or heavy. A decrease in the cost of subsistence would cause an increase in the number of laborers until their incomes were again down to the subsistence level. This would be the case because population (laborers) according to Malthus and Ricardo, would increase more rapidly than the food supply (susbsistence).

Vilfredo Pareto (1848-1923) developed* what has become known as the "Pareto law of income distribution," which concluded that relative inequality of income distribution could not

*In the *Cours d'economie politique* (1896-1897), by Vilfredo Pareto.

be changed because it represented the unequal distribution of human abilities. The relationships "proved" by the data gathered by Pareto to provide a statistical basis for his law have nearly completely disappeared. The logical foundation that incomes are distributed on the basis of ability was always weak.

It is doubtful that any useful purpose was served by the past theorizing regarding the possibility of changing income distribution through taxation. Fortunately it is possible today to do more. The results of studies aimed at answering the question, "Can taxation change income distribution?" offer reliable data on this subject.

An excellent study examining the effect of British taxes upon the distribution of British income in 1937 is available.* The general conclusion of the study is that the British taxes in 1937 did reduce the inequality of the income distribution.† The data included in Table 6-1, given below, shows the proportion of the income of different individual income brackets that was taken in taxation in the United States in the year 1938-1939 and in Great Britain in 1937.‡ All British taxes took about 17 per cent of

TABLE 6–1. Taxes as proportion of income in Great Britain (1937) and in the United States (1938–1939).

United States income classes	Proportion of income taken in taxes, %	British income classes	Proportion of income taken in taxes, %
Under $500	21.9	Under $500	16.8
$500–$1,000	18.0	$500–$1,000	18.1
$1,000–$1,500	17.3		
$1,500–$2,000	17.8	$1,000–$2,000	20.0
$2,000–$3,000	17.5		
$3,000–$5,000	17.6	$2,000–$4,000	27.4
$5,000–$10,000	17.9	$4,000–$8,000	33.8
$10,000–$15,000	25.5		
$15,000–$20,000	31.7	$8,000–$40,000	44.5
$20,000 and over	37.8	$40,000 and over	71.8

Source: United States data taken from Temporary National Economic Committee Monograph No. 3, *Who Pays the Taxes?*, p. 6. This was written by Helen Tarasov under the general supervision of Gerhard Colm. The British data are taken from Table 49, p. 187, of Tibor Barna's study *Redistribution of Incomes*.

*Tibor Barna, *Redistribution of Incomes*.
†Tibor Barna, *Redistribution of Incomes*, p. 188.
‡The British data are for the calendar year 1937, and the United States data are for the year 1938–39. The differences in the incidence assumptions are not sufficiently great to destroy the comparability of the data. Problems in allocating tax burdens to different income brackets are formidable. See discussions of R. A. Musgrave, Rufus S. Tucker, Haskell P. Wald and L. Frane in the 1951 and 1952 issues of the *National Tax Journal*.

the income of persons having an annual income below $500 and approximately 72 per cent of incomes above $40,000. This varies considerably from the tax burden in the United States, where 22 per cent of the income below $500 was collected in taxes and 38 per cent of the annual incomes above $20,000 was taken in taxes. The British tax system before World War II provided for a considerably greater income redistribution than the tax system of the United States.

The comparison of the entire schedule of proportions of income of the different income brackets taken in taxes shows a considerable variation between Great Britain and the United States. In Great Britain, the percentage of income paid as taxes shows a continued increase from the lowest brackets to the highest, while in the United States the percentage of income paid in taxes is less for the middle income brackets than for the very lowest. The British tax system is progressive throughout all income brackets, while the United States tax system is regressive in the lowest income brackets, approximately proportional in the middle income brackets and progressive in the highest income brackets. However, the tax systems of both nations reduce the portion of the total national income available to the members of the high income brackets and increase the portion available to members of the lower income brackets.

Redistribution of Income by Type

The kind of income redistribution that has been largely the subject of our analysis here has been between the different income brackets or vertical redistribution. There is also redistribution of income between different types or categories of income. Government revenues obtained in different ways have a varying effect upon income obtained as wages, pensions, interest, rent, dividends, and profits.

Because most of the income obtained in the lower income brackets comes from wages and a large portion of the income obtained in the upper income brackets comes from property, a progressive tax system would place a lighter burden on wages than upon interest, rent, and profits. Different types of income also bear varying tax burdens in addition to differences in tax burden due to size of income.

The study previously referred to of the effect of British taxes in 1937 contains an estimate of the quantity of redistribution of income of different types of categories provided by the

British tax system. The summary of the findings is given in Table 6-2, below. The amount of redistribution by income types is not so great as that between income brackets. The situation in the United States would be similar to that existing in Great Britain, with proper consideration taken of the greater progressivity of the British system. A possible exception would be the taxation of social income, which is largely exempt from the income (direct) tax burden in the United States but is subject to these taxes in Great Britain.

TABLE 6–2. Taxes as proportion of different income types in Great Britain (1937).

Type of income	Per cent taken as Taxes
Rent, profits, and interest:	
Actual	34
Imputed	40
Salaries	22
Wages	18
Social income	16

Source: Tibor Barna, *Redistribution of Incomes*, p. 193.

The recent increase in the tax burden on income obtained from property ownership, particularly profit income, has been the subject of considerable speculation and analysis. The higher burdens have been considered desirable because they reduced savings that were thought to be too great for investment opportunities, and to be undesirable because they reduced the return from risky investments and therefore decreased the quantity of venture capital. Finally, the increased tax burden on property income has been considered as a mere incidental arising from the necessity for an income distribution sufficiently equal to preserve the economic basis required for democracy.

Comparatively low taxes upon income obtained from productive activity under conditions approaching competition and relatively high taxes upon income obtained without productive activity or as a result of monopoly would foster increased efficiency of resource use. Efficient resource use requires that taxes upon wages and return upon competitive investments be decreased. It means, also, that taxes upon inheritances, windfalls, and return upon monopoly investments should be increased.

Redistribution of Income by Source

The total national income of a nation arises from the nation's different industries. A tax burden varying from industry to industry can affect the national income and the income arising from a particular industry. If the taxes are high upon agriculture, for example, the returns paid on capital and labor used in the agricultural industry would decrease, and thus there would be a decrease in the income arising from that industry. Gradually, the amount of capital and labor in agriculture would decrease, which would force up the return per unit of producing factors. However, resources do not flow readily from one industry to another; therefore, a change in the tax burden changes the immediate return that the factors receive in a particular industry.

The redistribution of income by source does not necessarily mean a change in the vertical distribution of income or a change in the relative portions of different types of income, but it does influence the quantity of resources used in different industries and the return per unit of producing factors. Only very meager data are available for comparing the tax burden of various industries. Also, the determination of incidence and effects of taxes on business is particularly difficult.*

In 1938, Dun & Bradstreet completed a study of relative tax burdens of manufacturing, wholesaling, and retailing and also the tax burdens of the different industry groups within these three broad classifications.† The most useful basis of comparing the tax burden borne by different industries is that of total tax paid as a percentage of value of services rendered. Table 6-3, given on p. 122, shows that in 1938 there was considerable variation between industries. The very high taxes paid by the distilleries, breweries, petroleum refiners, and tobocco-product manufacturers reflect the very high excise and manufacturing taxes assessed on the products of these industries. The taxes paid by other industries vary within the range set by the low of 2.18 per cent of value of services rendered by wholesalers of dairy and poultry products to the high of 18.56 per cent of canning and other food manufacturing. (This high rate arose largely

*One recent study of this type is *The Public Finance of Domestic Air Transportation*, by Richard W. Lindholm, Bureau of Business Research, Ohio State University, 1948.

†The study is based on questionnaires completed by 27,000 business firms. The study is for the calendar year 1938, when only $5 billion were paid in taxes by or through all commercial enterprises. In the year ended June 30, 1954, the Federal corporation tax liability alone totaled $17.2 billion.

from special taxes on margarine.) The manufacturers of automobiles and transportation and agricultural machinery were also high taxpayers, paying 15.66 per cent and 15.56 per cent respectively of the value of services rendered.

TABLE 6–3. Taxes paid by business (1938) as percentages of value of services rendered.

Business	Tax	Business	Tax
Manufacturing—total......	12.43	Nonferrous metal products	6.95
Meat packing...........	4.55	Distilleries and wineries ..	70.07
Flour and feed milling....	6.87	Breweries..............	53.41
Canning and other food		Petroleum refining.......	40.49
manufacturing........	18.56	Tobacco products.......	72.66
Clothing	4.56	Wholesaling—total........	17.11
Lumber and planing mill		Dairy and poultry pro-	
products	6.88	ducts.................	2.18
Furniture.............	6.66	Alcoholic beverages......	47.72
Industrial chemicals.....	6.67	Petroleum and petroleum	
Iron and steel..........	11.35	products	32.47
Automobiles	15.66	Lumber and fuel	12.18
Other transportation.....	15.56	Retailing—total..........	7.73

Source: *A Survey of Taxes Paid by Business in 1938*, Dun & Bradstreet, Inc. (New York, 1939), table 10, p. 29.

The relative tax burden upon different commodities partly indicate the tax burden of industries making, selling, or using these products.* As an example, the special taxes upon truck bodies, truck parts, truck tires, and gasoline certainly place additional tax burdens upon the trucking industry. Also, the taxation of these products places an additional tax burden upon the producers of automobile parts, tires, and gasoline. Other examples of commodities that have been selected for special taxation are the so-called luxury items † such as tobacco, alcoholic beverages, jewelry, toilet articles, and leather goods. The general sales tax in many states places an additional tax burden upon those industries producing goods in relation to those producing services, owing to the common practice of exempting services from the state general sales taxes.

*The T.N.E.C. study, *Who Pays the Taxes?*, gives the relative tax burden by industry as a per cent of income produced in 1938–39. The burden varies from 25.7 per cent in the case of utilities to 3.8 per cent in the case of construction. See p. 22, table 5, of the study.

†See pages 83–87 for an analysis of luxury taxes.

The Effect of Government Revenues on the Fundamental Causes of Income Distribution

Government fiscal activities will always change the distribution of income. The previous changes in income distribution arising from fiscal activity were largely accidental. Taxes and expenditures were made because of their desirability—that is, the existing revenue system plus the politically and socially acceptable changes decided the manner in which funds were raised. The effects of these two sets of conditions determined the income redistribution arising from government fiscal activity. For example, these determiners decided that fiscal activities would have a considerably greater effect upon income distribution in Great Britain than in the United States.*

The redistribution of income attempted in both the United States and Great Britain has been in the nature of a palliative rather than a cure. Redistribution of income activities has not attempted to get at the fundamental reasons for maldistribution of income. Briefly, the most important reasons are (1) the unequal distribution of capital ownership, (2) too large a portion of national income paid to capital owners, and (3) unequal opportunity for acquiring skills and adequate nutrition and medical care. These basic causes of unequal income distribution can be affected by government revenue-raising and expenditure activities.

Estimates of the Distribution of Capital Ownership. The importance of capital in creating the unequal distribution of income is clearly shown in the table given below. Table 6-4 contains data of wage income and dividend and interest income of selected income brackets. The data were obtained from the Federal individual income-tax returns for 1945.

The data provided in Table 6-4 do not give a complete picture of the relative importance of income obtained as a result of ability and productive activity and of income due to possession of property. However, it does offer a sufficiently accurate idea of the relationship between the two types of income to show the great relative importance of capital income in the high-bracket

*See the study made by Charles Stauffacher of redistribution through fiscal activities in the United States and the study by Tibor Barna of the redistributive effects of fiscal activities in Great Britain.

TABLE 6–4. Relationship in the United States of interest and dividends to wage payments for calendar year 1945.

Selected adjusted gross income classes	Salaries and wages (in thousands)	Ratio of salaries and wages to total adjusted gross income, %	Dividends and interest (in thousands)	Ratio of dividends and interest to total adjusted gross income, %
$1,000 to $1,250	$3,356,289	83.1676	$ 57,041	1.4135
$2,000 to $2,250	6,246,287	88.9485	73,960	1.0532
$4,000 to $4,500	1,629,488	23.6399	90,289	1.3099
$10,000 to $11,000	431,315	39.4210	85,186	7.7858
$20,000 to $25,000	564,235	30.4381	200,835	10.8342
$50,000 to $60,000	176,973	24.1925	111,128	15.1914
$100,000 to $150,000	108,853	16.4564	141,410	21.3783
$500,000 to $750,000	6,519	5.6883	36,969	32.2583
$2,000,000 to $3,000,000	153	0.9104	5,734	34.1188

Source: *Statistics of Income for 1945*, Part 1.

incomes and the relative unimportance of income from this source in the lower brackets.*

The Temporary National Economic Committee's study of *Concentration and Composition of Individual Incomes, 1918-1937*, also shows that a large portion of the income received by individuals in the high income brackets arose from property ownership.† It is of interest in relation to the oversavings theory of economic depression that the study's findings indicate that there is a greater concentration of income, and therefore the likelihood of much greater savings, during periods of prosperity than during periods of depression.

The concentration of property ownership is considerably greater than that of income receipts. Large portions of the population of all countries of the world are practically property-less, but all individuals must receive an income sufficient to provide the necessities for life. This concentration of the control of the economic system through concentration of property ownership and control has been frequently condemned, but little information is available regarding the actual distribution of property ownership. The data on page 124, which showed that a large portion of the income obtained by individuals in the highest income brackets came from property ownership, are also proof of the unequal distribution of property ownership.

The concentration of wealth in the United States is shown in a general but striking fashion by the list‡ of American corpora-

---

*Other types of property income not included are rents and royalties, sales and exchange of capital assets, income from estates and trusts, and business income from professions and partnerships. Also, a portion of dividend and interest income arises because of either present or previous productive activity of the recipient.

†T.N.E.C. Monograph No. 4, by Adolph J. Goldenthal, pp. 18, 39.

‡Morgan-First National: American Radiator & Standard Sanitary Corp., General Electric Co., Baldwin Locomotive Works, Continental Oil Co., Kennecott Copper Corp., National Biscuit Co., Phelps Dodge Corp., Pullman, Inc., United States Steel Corp.

du Pont: General Motors Corp., du Pont (E. I.) de Nemours Co., Inc., United States Rubber Co.

Cleveland financial group: Goodyear Tire & Rubber Co., Inland Steel Co., Interlake Iron Corp., Republic Steel Corp., Wheeling Steel Corp., Youngstown Sheet & Tube Co.

Mellon: Aluminum Co. of America, American Rolling Mill Co., Crucible Steel Co. of America, Gulf Oil Corp., Jones & Laughlin Steel Corp., Koppers Co., Pittsburgh Plate Glass Co., Westinghouse Electric & Manufacturing Co.

Rockefeller: Atlantic Refining Co., Socony Vacuum Oil Co., Inc., Standard Oil Co. of California, Standard Oil Co. of Indiana, Standard Oil Co. of New Jersey.

Source: *Economic Concentration and World War II*, Senate Document 206, 79th Congress, 2d Session (Washington, U. S. Government Printing Office, 1946), p. 347.

tions controlled by the five interest groups: Morgan-First National, Mellon, Rockefeller, du Pont, and the Cleveland financial group. The five groups control 31 of the 250 largest American corporations. "The facilities of these 31 corporations total 18.2 billion dollars, or 30 per cent of the Nation's usable manufacturing facilities."*

Actually, the determination of the total wealth of a nation is a very difficult matter and any estimate of it is subject to a wide margin of error. None of the estimates of wealth in the United States has been sufficiently detailed to permit its accurate distribution by brackets in the same manner as income. Table 6-5, given below, summarizes the findings of different wealth studies.

TABLE 6-5. Principal findings of major wealth studies of the United States.

Studies	Percentage distribution	Period
Massachusetts Labor Bureau..	2% of pop. own 48% of total	1873
Thomas G. Shearman.........	1% of pop. own 70% of total	1889
George K. Holmes............	10% of pop. own 75% of total	1890
Charles B. Spahr.............	1% of pop. own 55% of total	1896
Willford I. King..............	2% of pop. own 59% of total	1900
Willford I. King..............	2% of pop. own 40% of total	1921
Federal Trade Commission	1% of pop. own 59% of total	1922
Robert R. Doane.............	1% of pop. own 20% of total	1932

Source: *The Anatomy of American Wealth*, by Robert R. Doane (New York, Harper, 1940), p. 32.

The data, of course, do not provide a complete distribution of wealth but appear to give an indication of great concentration of wealth holdings for at least the past seventy-five years.

The study of wealth completed by the Federal Trade Commission is the most complete attempted in the United States. The study is now over twenty years old. It was based on probate records and therefore gives wealth distribution only at time of death. The study showed that, in 1923, 11.1 per cent of the population possessed only 0.2 per cent of the private wealth of the nation and that only 0.3 per cent of the population possessed 17.9 per cent of the total private wealth.†

Economic Concentration and World War II, p. 42.

†*National Wealth and Income*, 69th Congress, 1st Session, Senate Document No. 126 (Washington, U.S. Government Printing Office, 1926), p. 59.

A study recently completed provides a comparison of income and property or estate concentration in England. These data are given in Table 6-6. Examination of the table shows that the

TABLE 6-6. The distribution of personal incomes and estates in England, 1937.

Income distribution		Estates distribution	
Cumulative per cent of persons	Cumulative per cent of income	Cumulative per cent of persons	Cumulative per cent of estates
0.01	2.3	0.01	9.8
0.05	4.3	0.06	18.3
0.6	13.4	0.5	39.0
1.6	19.2	1.3	54.7
4.2	26.9	2.5	65.8
14.4	41.9	8.4	83.9
30.6	56.9	16.1	90.7
54.0	72.2	31.0	95.8
100.0	100.0	100.0	100.0

Source: Tibor Barna, *Redistribution of Incomes*, p. 68.

1937 conditions in England and those appearing to prevail in the United States (see Table 6-4 and 6-5) are not greatly dissimilar; 46 per cent of the population received only 28 per cent of the income, which is bad enough; but the situation in property distribution is much worse, with 69 per cent of the population possessing only 4.2 per cent of the total quantity of property.

The Reduction of the Concentration of Capital Ownership. The maldistribution of income created by the concentration of capital ownership can be most efficiently corrected by getting at the cause, namely, the reduction of the concentration of property ownership. The collection of government revenues can have an effect upon the concentration of wealth ownership.

The most efficient revenue devices for the reduction of property-ownership concentration are the estate, inheritance, gift, and property taxes. For greatest efficiency, these taxes must be properly correlated with each other and also with the income tax. The efficiency of these taxes is based upon their ability to reduce property ownership concentration without destroying the incentive to produce. However, if only the reduction of concentration of property ownership is considered, the revenue measures to use would be the income tax and the capital levy. They would be favored because of their greater speed in accomplishing the purpose.

Congress, however, believes death taxes are undesirable. The Revenue Act of 1948 decreased estate taxes in the United States. Prior to 1948, a net estate (after deduction of funeral expenses, debts, taxes, etc.) of $500,000 left to a wife would have borne a tax of $116,500. Since 1948 the tax has been only about $45,300.

The right to pass property accumulated during life to particular individuals is a basic cause of maldistribution of property ownership and income. This right is guaranteed by legislation and is made possible largely through government action. The government can and does levy a tax on this kind of property transfer. The taxes levied when these transfers are made after death are called estate and inheritance taxes, and, if made while alive, gift taxes. Theoretically these taxes could be levied at such high rates that all possession of wealth through inheritance would disappear. Actually, modest-sized estates are exempt, and the assessed rates upon larger estates are much lower than they may appear to be. That a lower applicable rate than the statute rate exists, arises because of the many ways in which the tax base (size of taxable estate) can be reduced. If estate-, inheritance-, and gift-tax rates are increased and the typical loopholes for avoidance removed, the concentration of property ownership would be reduced; and as a result the vertical distribution of income would be made more proportional.* It is generally agreed that the collection of death taxes has a less undesirable effect on productive activity than any other tax.†

Reduction of the concentration of property ownership is also accomplished by high individual and corporate income taxes. If an individual's income is reduced, the probabilities are very great that accumulations will also be reduced. The principal disadvantages of this method over the use of death taxes are that the incentive to produce and earn a larger income is reduced, and the reduction of profits decreases the quantity of new investments. Thus reduced property accumulation will be partly attained through the reduction of the national income. This is undesirable and unnecessary. The same aim can be achieved and the harmful effects largely avoided through the levy of effective

*The tax brings in about 1.5 per cent of total Federal revenues, and the different state death taxes bring in about the same percentage of total state revenues.

†See *Economics of Public Finance* by Edward D. Allen and O. H. Brownlee (New York, Prentice-Hall, 1947), chapter XVII.

high-rate death taxes. In this case the productive activity of the decedent is completed, and the productive activity of heirs is likely to be increased.

Concentration of property ownership is increased by the levy of regressive taxes. During the eighteenth century, when the Western European nations were suffering from a shortage of savings, this might have been a desirable policy; but the dangers of ownership concentration outweigh any possible gain from expanded savings in the twentieth century in the United States.

An effective way of preventing concentration of property ownership is the elimination of large incomes arising from market domination caused by control of essential raw materials, patents, and trade marks. This control by private individuals can be replaced by government control. However, the political problems arising from a great extension of public control are tremendous and in many cases may be greater than the economic problems arising from private control. Taxation can· decrease income arising from monopoly control by encouraging new and additional firms in the area. Inducement of this type on the revenue-gathering side would be in the form of tax reductions for new and small firms, taxation of excess profits, and special taxation of unused capacity. On the expenditure side, inducements would be in the form of subsidies paid to producers of new products, government-financed research, and government investments in certain areas.

Revenue raising activity has, however, been discussed most frequently in regard to its effects on vertical income distribution. This emphasis is justified by the effectiveness of government revenue collection in changing the vertical distribution of income and by the vital importance of income-distribution changes. Revenue collections can do the most adequate job of changing income distribution if they change the distribution of wealth holdings, and this change can be effected most advantageously at the time wealth is transferred from one living person to another as a gift (*inter vivos*, that is, between living persons) or at death.

CONCLUSION

WRITERS of tax legislation have been quite ingenious in developing loop-holes in the high income tax rates applicable to the wealthy and to corporations to reduce the tendency of these taxes to discourage investment. Less effort has been put forth to prevent the tax system from reducing the expenditures of low income receivers for necessary consumer goods. Developments in both areas are practical tax procedures to be used when stimulation is needed to keep aggregate demand sufficiently high to maintain the customary level of employment in the private economy.

QUESTIONS AND PROBLEMS

1. Why do high income taxes discourage investment?

2. Why might there be additional investment even though the demand for consumer goods is not expected to increase? How can this type of investment be encouraged?

3. Explain how the provision for accelerated amortization, taxation of capital gains and the loss carry back and forward provisions of our corporate income tax encourage investment.

4. Give the reasons why you favor or oppose the exemption of the interest of "municipals" from the Federal income taxes.

5. What is an undistributed corporate profits tax? Why is its use likely to increase consumption?

6. What information would you have to have to determine if income saved is taxed as heavily as income spent? How would each bit of information be used to determine relative tax burdens borne by savings and consumption?

7. How effective have tax programs been in changing vertical income distribution? Do you think that vertical redistribution of income through taxation is desirable? Why?

8. Explain how the distribution of wealth affects the distribution of income. Do you believe that taxes should be used to make more equal the distribution of wealth? Why?

CHAPTER 7

Expenditures in Relation to Prices and Consumption

CHAPTERS 5 and 6 considered the effects of taxes on the selected goals of fiscal policy. This chapter is concerned with how government expenditures can be used to affect prices and consumption.

The consideration of expenditures by themselves is a continuation of the basic assumption of our analyses that expenditure determination is separate from taxes and debt management decisions. It can be shown that this separation does not always exist, and in terms of an efficient use of resources, it can be argued that it should not exist.* However, the separation of government expenditures from revenues can be justified. First of all, at the Federal level there are no important exceptions to the rule that expenditures are independent of revenue sources. Second, public finance and public administration officials have for years opposed tying expenditures to particular revenue sources. Third, in the public economy it usually does not make good economic sense to relate expenditures to a particular revenue whereas this is seldom true in the private economy. Finally, the separation of expenditures from revenues makes it easier to distinguish the impact of each and therefore makes possible more precise economic analyses.

The use of government expenditures to affect economic conditions is better established than the conscious use of revenues. In all cases, however, it is necessarily true that what is spent must previously be raised. The greater emphasis upon expenditures has perhaps arisen from their greater political popularity. Public interest in a prospective expenditure can be

---

*See "Government Expenditure: Significant Issues of Definition," by C. Lowell Harriss, *The Journal of Finance*, December, 1954, p. 361.

aroused much more easily than public interest in most revenue programs. This is the case because the beneficial results arising from an expenditure are likely to be much more concrete than those arising from a change of revenue source. Also, it has been typical for legislatures to decide upon expenditures first and then to determine the means of obtaining the required revenues.

Built-in Expenditure Flexibility

Some of the expenditures of government decline during prosperity and increase during depression without the initiation of new government action. Expenditures of this type have a stabilizing effect on the level of aggregate demand and are said to possess a desirable built-in flexibility. Unemployment compensation payments and the expenditures arising from the farm-price parity program are examples of government expenditures having this feature.

The Federal and state unemployment-compensation legislation results in an increase of government expenditure during depression and unemployment. The legislation is written in such a manner that unemployment-benefit payments increase when the number of unemployed rises. Another example of this type of legislation is the Federal farm-price-parity program. When agricultural prices begin to fall, it is also true that the economy is generally in need of additional government expenditure. It is precisely at this time that the Federal farm-price-parity program provides for an automatic increase of government expenditure.

The built-in flexibility of the unemployment-benefit payments has been reduced by the introduction in all states of a type of what is called the experience-rating method of determining the unemployment-compensation tax rate.* Briefly, this scheme provides that individual employer-contribution rates are varied from the standard rate because of the employer's experience with the risk of unemployment and the condition of his account with the state unemployment fund. This has the effect of increasing unemployment-tax rates during a period of depression and unemployment and decreasing them during a period of prosperity and full employment. The experience-rating schemes have reduced the net impact of the desirable flexibility of unemployment benefit payments.

*U.S. Department of Labor, Unemployment Insurance Service, *Comparison of State Unemployment Insurance Laws*, (Washington, U.S. Government Printing Office, 1954).

THE ACHIEVEMENT OF DESIRABLE PRICES

The General Effects of Expenditure on Prices

A government expenditure increasing investment will change existing price patterns in a different manner than a government expenditure increasing consumption. An expenditure by the government providing additional productive facilities—for example, additional investment in electric-power development—will decrease the relative price of electricity. The relative price decrease will arise because the supply of electric power has been increased beyond that required to meet the effective demands at the old higher prices. Government expenditure that expands consumption will tend to increase prices of certain products for which the demand is expanded. This increase in the relative prices of particular products would tend to decrease as additional private investment, stimulated by these prices, increases the production facilities. Prices can be made permanently higher if additional government programs are undertaken to prevent the increase of production.

During the 1930's, government expenditure was made to decrease the quantity of production of certain agricultural products and also to increase the quantity of consumption. Both of these expenditure programs had the effect of increasing the relative prices of agricultural products.

Payments were made to farmers if they would reduce the area planted in certain crops and would increase their soil conservation activity. These expenditures would tend to raise prices in the short run and decrease them over the long run. Farm prices would be increased in the short run because the supply of agricultural commodities would be decreased through restriction of plantings. (The demand for most agricultural products is quite inelastic.) Farm prices, however, would be reduced in the long run because the quantity of soil suitable for raising crops tomorrow would would be increased by soil conservation activity today.

An amendment to the Agricultural Adjustment Act in 1935 provided that 30 per cent of the gross customs collections should be spent to increase the consumption of agricultural products. The first program to stimulate demand was that which provided for direct purchase of food for relief. The largest amount was spent for this program during 1934-1935 ($149,339,000). Since July, 1939, the School Lunch Program has been in effect as a method of providing a market for farm products. This program is also very important in assuring an adequate diet to develop strong healthy citizens capable of maximum productive effort. In May, 1939, a Food Stamp Program was developed for families on relief; the program was abandoned on March 31, 1943, when the demands arising from the war had eliminated all surplus agricultural products.

Actually, the Food Stamp Program was not more than a large-scale experiment ($10,000,000 a month); however, the experiment showed that this type of program possessed great possibilities in the maintenance of suitable agricultural prices without waste. Under the scheme developed, relief families would purchase from their local retailer the quantity of orange stamps equal to their normal food purchases. The purchase of these orange stamps entitled the individual to blue stamps equal to one-half the value of the orange stamps. The orange stamps could be used to purchase any type of food desired. The blue stamps could only be used to purchase those commodities which had been designated by the Secretary of Agriculture as surplus. The nub of the plan was to assure that additional purchases of surplus foods would not decrease the sales of other types of foods.

The low electricity-rate schedules announced by the Tennessee Valley Authority in September, 1933, had an important relationship to the general reduction of electric-power rates which followed. The rates announced by T.V.A. were based on the old American idea that it is financially sounder to sell a large number of units at a low price than a few units at a high price. This idea has proven to be largely sound in the production and sale of electricity as it had previously proven to be largely correct in the other great American mass-production industries. The reduction in costs that has arisen to a great extent from government activity has made it possible for private companies to reduce prices and expand profits. In addition, the private electric-appliance companies in the Southeast, where the influence of T.V.A. is the greatest, became the largest sellers of electrical appliances in the nation.

The Effects of Expenditures on Prices during Different Phases of the Business Cycle

An increase of government expenditure during a period of great unemployment may have little effect on prices but have a great influence on quantity of production. The result would be reversed if government expenditures were expanded during a period of overemployment. This difference in the effect forms a large part of the basis for the recommendation that government expenditures should be increased during depression and reduced during prosperity.

Violent fluctuations of prices of certain basic raw materials —for example, wheat and cotton—have added to the difficulties of maintaining a high level of productivity. Government expenditure through purchasing these products during periods of super-abundance and making them available during periods of greater relative need can increase the stability of basic commodity prices. The government parity-price program in agriculture provides for this type of government expenditure activity.

Basic farm prices can be kept at generally agreed desirable levels by a wholehearted realistic government program. This type of program would necessarily include at least the following concepts: (1) Provision must be made for storage from good years to lean years. This storage must be only to level out production fluctuations and storage of products must not rise because of a weakened demand for the product or because of an increase in average annual production. (2) Funds of the government must be available to equalize demand. During periods of depression, consumption of food must be stimulated by the establishment of aggressive minimum-diet programs. Also, funds must be available to aid in the rapid transfer of agriculture production factors from agriculture to other industries and from one type of agricultural product to another in order to meet the shifting demand for farm products.

The stabilizing of the price paid labor would go far to prevent violent fluctuations of economic activity. The government has partially provided a minimum base through its social-security program. For example, payments under the Unemployment Insurance plan, the Old-Age and Survivors Insurance (O.A.S.I.) program, and the Old Age Assistance (O.A.A.) programs tend to prevent the decline of wages to extremely low levels.

The average family benefit paid by the Federal government under the Old-Age and Survivors Insurance legislation was about $90 a month (1954). Although this sum is still inadequate, with subsistence-living costing $200 a month, it is a considerable expansion from the 1945 average of $40. The benefits received under the O.A.S.I. arise largely because of equal contributions made by employees and employers totaling 4 per cent of the first $4,200 of annual salary. The Old-Age Assistance program makes payments from general revenues of the Federal government with the states matching Federal funds. In most states O.A.A. benefits are paid only to those aged who can show a need; a poverty oath is required in many states. The monthly benefits per person under this program averaged $51 in 1954. In 1954, $1,650 million was paid out under the O.A.A. program and $3,500 million under O.A.S.I. If the worker is not aged and employed in an industry covered by unemployment insurance, he will receive unemployment benefits for a maximum of 16 to 26½ weeks, depending upon the state in which he resides, with 26 weeks being the most common maximum length. The maximum weekly benefit averages $24 a week. This average payment of about $624 will help to maintain purchasing power during a brief period of unemployment and will prevent wages from going below this level. The payments for unemployment benefits are limited, which is also partly true of O.A.S.I. benefits, by the size of the trust fund set aside for their payment. In 1954, the Unemployment Insurance Trust Fund totaled $8.2 billion and the O.A.S.I. fund totaled $16.5 billion.

The minimum-wage program is an example of the government's use of police power to prevent wage fluctuations. The offering of wages at particular levels under the Works Progress Administration program during the depression of the 1930's also prevented the further fall of wages. The "52-20 program" of payment of unemployment aid to veterans of World War II and the $676 maximum paid to veterans since 1950 are also expenditures that prevented wage decreases. The provision of education by the government and the opportunity to join the Armed Forces are other types of government expenditure that have an important effect in stabilizing wage levels. All of these government expenditures are useful in preventing very low wage rates and therefore helpful in laying the basis for more intelligent private production planning. All of them taken together, however, are still insufficient to prevent serious fluctuations in the price paid labor.

The government could prevent wages falling below a certain level by offering to hire all persons at a set minimum wage. This commitment would not only prevent wages from fluctuating widely but would also provide economic and social security and maintain purchasing power. The discussion of different types of expenditure on pages 154-158 and 179-189 indicates ways the government could efficiently employ varying numbers of laborers.

Effects of Expenditures on Prices during War

World War II government activity provides excellent examples in the use of government expenditure to prevent high prices. Payments to the agriculture industry to induce the production of certain scarce products was one example. Providing expanded plant facilities for synthetic rubber and aluminum are other examples. In these instances, production was expanded more quickly and beyond that level determined by market prices. Also, high prices to the consumer were avoided by the payment of subsidies—for example, the prices of milk and some meat products were lower to the consumer than the actual cost of production. This type of activity, which was largely developed during World War II, can also be used during times of peace.

During World War I, the prices of agricultural commodities were prevented from increasing only through stimulation of production (supply) by the use of guaranteed prices. During World War II, subsidy payments (combined with rationing) were used to decrease the price of agricultural products to the consumer and were also used to stimulate producer activity.

The payment of subsidies to enable the farmers to obtain high prices for their products—and thus to stimulate production and, at the same time, to make the products produced available to consumers at low prices and thus to encourage high consumption and reduce the likelihood of inflation—was quite successful. The program was similar to the food-stamp plan but adjusted to the very different economic conditions. Both programs have the effect of improving the diet and therefore the health of the lower income groups; the subsidy during World War II was combined with a rationing arrangement to prevent short supplies of subsidized foods. The war program, by keeping the price of food down, prevented a rise in the cost-of-living indices which made possible effective wage controls that provided the foundation for the entire war price-control program.

The details of these various programs cannot be included here, but a few thumb-nail sketches are informative. The production of peanuts was stimulated by two types of subsidies; one providing a subsidy to peanuts used for the production of oil, and the other to peanuts for edible purposes. The beef-cattle-feeding subsidy program provided for the payment of 50 cents per 100 pounds, live weight, to cattle feeders when eligible cattle were sold for slaughter. The flaxseed program included the novel provision of a payment of $5 for each acre seeded in flaxseed.

The war program for subsidy payments to roll back prices was largely limited to hogs, beef, and dairy products. The payments were quite substantial, especially on dairy products. Agricultural subsidy payments were the greatest in 1946, totaling $845 million; $544 million of this total were payments to milk producers.

The payment of subsidies mentioned above helped forestall general increases in wages. Much higher wages would have been demanded and obtained if costs of living had not been held down. Also, government expenditures were necessary to provide the rather effective price-control and scarce-raw-material-allocation programs of World War II which further helped to prevent the rise of particular prices and the general rise of wages.

Government expenditure can effectively prevent high wages in particular areas. This possibility was demonstrated during World War II. To do this, the government spends money to (1) train laborers to perform specialized activities, (2) move them where they are needed, and (3) provide housing for them at their new jobs.

Government expenditure can be used effectively to eliminate high prices for necessary imported consumption and raw material goods. The war-developed program of stock-piling demonstrated the efficiency of this type of project. Also, in order to prevent foreign cartels or monopolies from obtaining high prices in the United States market, government expenditure can be used for constructing stand-by industries and for research in developing domestic substitutes.

It was feared that farm prices would drop immediately after World War II; realization has been postponed by tremendous European relief programs, by the Korean War demands, and by direct farm price support activity. The very high parity-price payments (of 90 to 95 per cent), provided during the war on most agricultural products, were continued until 1954 when modest adjustments were made. The Commodity Credit Corporation has been given additional grants by Congress when more funds have been needed to finance the purchase of farm products that drop below their parity price. These are rather elaborate preparations to prevent the reoccurrence of the sharp drop in agricultural prices that took place at the end of World War I and the agricultural depression that continued throughout the prosperity of the 1920's. The weakness of the plan is that little provision has been made for production control or for subsidizing consumption, and therefore the problem of surpluses has arisen.

The use of fiscal tools by the Federal government in maintaining prices of agricultural products possesses the possibility of expansion into other areas. For example, the government could offer to purchase the excess production of the steel and textile mills. A portion of this production could be stored for periods of increased demand such as during a war or an investment boom. The price offered by the government for surplus production should be gradually decreased. This would cause a gradual transfer of resources away from the production of the product. In this manner, the price system could still be used to control the type and quantity of production, but the inefficient use of resources arising from unemployment could be largely avoided.

Government Expenditure for Yardstick Plants

Government expenditure to construct yardstick plants or to provide additional capacity in an area of monopoly is a particularly desirable method of reducing prices through prevention of monopoly exploitation. It might also be a method of stimulating production through an increase of prices in other areas. Actually this was very nearly the existing situation when the Federal government became active in the power industry in the 1930's.* The success of government construction in the power industry during the 1930's, and in the aluminum and other industries during World War II, points to this as being another type of government expenditure that can be very effective in increasing the efficiency of the price system in the allocation of resources.

All of these programs intelligently developed and adequately financed can largely prevent price maladjustments. These activities do not mean an expansion of the public economy at the expense of the private but, rather, efficient government collaboration with the private economy. Many of the difficulties encountered by the private economy in efficiently utilizing resources have arisen from bottlenecks and monopoly that government expenditures of the type described above would help eliminate.

Government Purchase of Gold

The purchase of gold by the Federal government is neither a budgetary expenditure nor a revenue-raising activity. However, the purchase of gold has a definite effect upon the general price

*The Federal Trade Commission presented data indicating that by 1932 eight utility holding companies controlled over 70 per cent of the electric-power industry. Also, the construction industry was severely depressed, and it was believed that the erection of great dams would have a very stimulating effect on this industry and the rest of the economy.

level. This repercussion would be particularly great when bank reserves were being fully utilized.

The purchase of the commodity gold, because of its position in the monetary system, has a much greater effect on the general price level than the purchase of most other commodities. Under present legislation, the government can purchase unlimited quantities of gold without the necessity of raising additional funds either through borrowing or taxation. Gold not only provides the money necessary for its purchase but also, by becoming a part of the reserves of the banking system, makes possible an additional secondary expansion of the money supply of the nation.

The large-scale purchase of gold by the Federal government has enabled foreign countries to buy additional quantities of our goods. By payment for United States exports through the sale of gold rather than the sale of goods, foreign trade has laid the basis for lower prices. The increase in gold holdings expands the quantity of money in the United States and decreases the quantity of goods available for domestic sale. Because this has been true, the purchase of gold has worked toward a rising price level through both an expansion of demand for goods and a decrease in their supply.

The purchase of commodities such as wheat or cotton with funds borrowed from the commercial banks also reduces quantity of goods and increases quantity of money. If the excess reserves created by the purchase of the gold are desired for expansion of bank loans, the effect of gold purchases on prices would always be greater than the purchase of these other commodities. Of course, gold always has the advantage that it is purchased without expanding the debt, while the expansion of commercial bank loans to the government for the purchase of other commodities may decrease the amount of lending to private borrowers.

Interest Expenditure

The interest expenditure of the government has an important effect on the price paid for money. The Federal government debt is so great ($278 billion in 1955) that the interest rates paid on this debt influence the general market interest rates. Although the Federal government by its interest policy can affect the general interest rates, it can actually determine interest rates only by directly affecting the relationship between the supplies of loanable funds and the demand for these funds. This relationship can be changed somewhat through government revenue and expenditure policy. For example government revenues can lower interest rates by decreasing the demand for loans by increasing the taxes on profits; and government expenditures to reduce the amount of government securities held by the private economy would have the same effect.*

General Level of Government Expenditures and Prices

On occasion economists of considerable renown have stated it to be their conviction that if taxes and expenditures (they have assumed a balanced budget) rose above a certain established per cent of national income, the result would be inflation.

In the 18th and 19th centuries, 15 per cent was given as the maximum share of national income which the government could utilize if inflation was to be avoided. In the post-World War II period the maximum has been set at 25 per cent of national income. The chief advocate of this economic limit for government taxes and expenditures has been Colin Clark, a well-known Australian economist.†

The portion of national income allocated to United States governments is about 25 per cent. Therefore, according to the Colin Clark thesis, the level must not be increased, or at least should not be increased more rapidly than national income, if continuing inflation is to be avoided.

Clark supports his thesis with references to historical examples of inflation and to a political relationship which he believes exists between taxes and inflation. The political relationship which he describes is that when taxes rise above 25 per cent, people prefer inflation to taxes. The result is that a government's efforts to use more than 25 per cent of the total product of the economy would be thwarted by price increases.

The economic reason given for the price increases is that the employer's normal resistance to higher wages, inefficiency, and waste would be weakened as a result of the high taxes. In January of 1952 the Joint Committee on the Economic Report examined Clark's economic explanation for the limit set in relation to the portion of national income which the government could utilize and yet avoid inflation. They were unable to discover

*See Chapter 10 for analyses of the impact of debt management.
†Colin Clark: "Public Finance and Changes in the Value of Money," *Economic Journal*, December, 1945, pp. 371–389; and "The Danger Point in Taxes," *Harper's Magazine*, December, 1950, pp. 67–69.

statistical proof for the thesis. However, Professor Buehler and other economists testified at the 'hearings of the Committee that they believed that a limit of the sort Colin Clark described did exist but that it was considerably above 25 per cent in the United States. In their opinion, the following factors affect the upper economic limit of the public economy, (1) the type of tax system, (2) the purpose of the expenditures, (3) the speed with which taxes and expenditures are increased, and (4) the average per capita income of the nation. It was mentioned previously that in the United States there is a tendency for government to utilize about one-fourth of national income.

THE ACHIEVEMENT OF A
DESIRABLE CONSUMPTION LEVEL

The General Effects of Expenditures on Consumption

Government expenditures are frequently categorized as follows: (1) investment, (2) consumption, (3) increase in individual net worth, and (4) debt repayment.

The first type, investment expenditure, relates to the use of government funds to finance construction such as highways, dams, and public building. Expenditure by the government to subsidize private investment would also be classified as government investment expenditure. Examples of these would be Federal Housing Administration loans, Reconstruction Finance Corporation loans, and Export-Import Bank loans. These investment expenditures increase consumption indirectly, through the provision of additional employment and the reduction of costs of production. Also, government investments—for example, highways—provide stimulation to private investment which will also stimulate employment and increase consumption.

Government investment expenditure can have a very stimulating effect on both investment and consumption expenditure of the private economy. The example provided by government investment in highways is outstanding in its tremendous stimulation of consumption expenditure. A major portion of the budget of a typical American family consists of expenditures required to purchase, maintain, and operate the family automobile. The enjoyment of this consumption expenditure results largely from the great government expenditure upon highways. The Federal government alone spent $1 billion on highways during 1947 and 1948, and half again as much was provided during 1949 and 1950 and expectations are that many times this amount will be spent in 1956 and 1957.

When the Federal government during the 1930's began to contemplate investment in the electric-power industry, the private power producers presented the argument that their $15 billion industry was providing all the electric power that the nation could effectively use. Government activity, plus the growth of general economic activity, expanded consumption of electric power so that at present the private investment is completely utilized, as is the additional investment of $8 billion of government funds. Government investment is particularly efficient in the expansion of consumption if it results in the reduction of the cost of a good or service the consumption of which can be greatly increased—for example, travel, and power and light.

The second type of expenditure, government consumption expenditure, includes government expenditure for the provision of education, health, social security, housing, and the like. In making these expenditures, the government determines types of consumption through the provision of funds for their financing. From 1928 to 1938, government expenditure of this type increased rapidly in the United States and the nations of Western Europe. Advocates of socialized consumption believe the consumption of a population can be increased more efficiently in this manner than is possible through investment or the direct provision of funds to individuals.*

It is estimated that in 1953 all levels of government spent $10,000 million for the provision of education, $3,000 million for public health, and $800 million for public housing and community facilities. Since 1953, the expenditures in all three of these areas have expanded.

In the case of government consumption, the government provides the actual service or good enjoyed; the individual becomes eligible for enjoyment only if he meets certain requirements aimed at increasing the efficiency with which the good or service is distributed. For example, to benefit from most education services offered by the government, it is necessary to meet certain entrance requirements—that is, age, last grade completed, and perhaps a certain scholastic average.

The third type of expenditure is the direct increase of individual income or net worth. Examples of this type of expenditure are the payment of pensions, veteran benefits, poor

*Sir William Beveridge, *Full Employment in a Free Society*, p. 185.

relief, and the like. The funds spent in this manner are in most cases made available to persons in the lower income brackets. As has been previously pointed out, the people in these income brackets possess a high propensity to consume. Therefore, a large portion of this additional income will be spent immediately for consumption goods. This method of increasing consumption through government expenditure has been criticized as being less efficient than that of direct government consumption. The main reason for this criticism is that individuals in the lower income brackets, often because of lack of opportunity to purchase more desirable goods and services, spend the receipts in a manner which does not materially increase their well being. Sir William Beveridge, the famous British economist, has stated that Great Britain is not sufficiently wealthy to provide for a large amount of consumption increase in this manner. In the United States, however, this method of increasing consumption expenditure has been considered the more desirable. The reason for this difference of attitude is that increased consumption can take place in this manner with a smaller amount of government control and that, because the United States is rich, the resulting waste of resources can be more easily absorbed.

Economists sometimes point out that a subsidy or the free provision of a good or service by the government (the Beveridge program) is a less efficient type of government expenditure than an outright grant of money to those who would otherwise receive the subsidized or free good or service. They justify their belief on the position that a consumer enjoys a greater increase in his satisfaction when the government provides him with a money payment which he is able to distribute as he pleases among the variety of consumer goods available than when the government spends the same amount to furnish him a certain good free or at a greatly reduced price.* In other words, they argue that efficiency of consumption is highest when costs of goods are the same to all people and that resources are used most efficiently in production when the selling price of each item marketed is sufficient to cover the costs of all resources used in its production. This sort of argument is valid under the assumption that the decisions of the market bring forth the most efficient types of consumption and production. But, as has been stated a number of times, fiscal policy has developed because this assumption seems unrealistic.

*For example, Tibor Scitovsky, *Welfare and Competition* (Chicago, Richard D. Irwin, 1951), pp. 64–66.

The final type of government expenditure is that which changes the type of asset held by individuals. The most common expenditure of this type is the repayment of government debt. Another example is the purchase of commodities from individuals. Debt-reduction payments would be made largely to persons in the upper income brackets, where the propensity to consume is small and therefore where a given quantity of government expenditure would have a reduced effect on consumption. The relative stimulation of consumption arising from the purchase of commodities would be determined by the income level of the holders of the commodities. If the commodities purchased by the government were farm products produced on a typical American farm, the income of farmers would be increased and the price to consumers would tend to rise unless a consumer subsidy were involved. An expenditure of this type would have an indefinite direct effect on total consumption and in addition would possess uncertain possibilities of expanding consumption indirectly by maintaining the solvency of important industries—for example, agriculture.

It is clear that all government expenditure is related to consumption. A government expenditure alone very seldom has a repressive effect on consumption. However, a government expenditure could reduce consumption if the manner of obtaining money spent reduces private expenditure more than public is increased. An example of this sort of relationship would be government expenditure of funds to repay the government debt from receipts obtained by the levy of a tax on goods consumed by persons in the lower income brackets.

The Desirability of Government Consumption

The previous discussion pointed out that a method of increasing consumption is for the government to provide and finance certain types of consumption services. Also, this method of increasing consumption is very likely to increase the efficiency with which the resources of the nation are utilized. The price system undervalues certain types of services and goods. This undervaluation arises because part of the utilities or benefits arising from the good or service is not directly available to the individual. The best example of this is in the field of education. A portion of the benefit that is derived from education accrues directly to the individual in an increase in enjoyment of life and an increase in earning power. However, a large portion of the benefit of education accrues to society in a more intelligent and productive citizenry. Because of this lack of individual benefit, this second type of benefit flowing from education will not be given its proper value by the price system. It is quite proper that the government should make funds available so the price paid for education will be commensurate with the total benefit arising from the activity. Through the provision of consumption goods and services, the government can make it possible for persons with low incomes to obtain benefits through co-operative activity which they would not have been able to obtain if each received a small amount of additional funds from the government. As an example, the provision of a play-ground in an area makes it possible for a child to play off the streets, while a small increase in the income of each family would not make it possible to provide small individual backyards.* Another advantage of government-provided consumption is that it can be expanded in a more orderly fashion than private con-sumption.

A disadvantage of the provision of goods and services by the government arises from a tendency of the activity to reduce the incentive to individual effort. If all the requirements of life are furnished on the basis of being able to fill out a form showing need, the lack of goods as an inducement to effort has been largely removed. This type of an argument is based to a great extent upon the position that the quantity and type of goods and services considered to be necessary for the good life remain constant. The provision of a certain group of goods and services by the government may have been considered all that a person could possibly expect fifty years ago, but today the same group would surely fall far short of what nearly every person desires and is willing to work and scheme to obtain.

The Relationship between Consumption Stimulation and Prosperity

During the period prior to World War II, the economies of Western Europe and the United States found it difficult to maintain a sufficiently high level of consumption. The level of consumption is not sufficiently high if at a particular level of income the savings arising are greater than the investment opportunities. The way to decrease savings or expand investment,

*This additional benefit arising to individuals from having the government rather than themselves spend the money would be called the "announcement effect of expenditure" if the terminology of Professor Pigou (in *A Study in Public Finance*, London, Macmillan, 1928, p. 73) is used.

and by so doing bring about a balance between savings and investment, is to expand consumption.

The technological developments of the years 1928-1938 were, on the average, capital-reducing rather than capital-consuming; also, population growth had diminished. Thus, at a time when savings were large and increasing, the demand for investments became relatively smaller. One available method of re-establishing the correct balance between investments and savings and removing a very important cause of economic fluctuations is to increase government expenditure for consumption. The goverment could expand consumption by expenditure for the direct provision of consumption, provision of more funds for persons in the low income brackets, and guaranteeing complete social security to every citizen. This latter type of action would increase consumption directly, and also through the reduction of rainy-day and old-age savings. A considerable portion of the drive of individuals to accumulate a nest egg would disappear if the emergencies of life were provided through government expenditure.*   Total consumption of the economy is greatly dependent upon consumer income expectations. Government consumption expenditures can be maintained during periods of recession through the borrowing of funds from commercial banks or through the actual printing of additional quantities of money. As a result, government consumption expenditure is likely to be more stable than private consumption expenditure. This fact would tend to bring about an increased stability in the economy, as the relative importance of government expenditure increases.

The acceleration principle points out that small changes in consumption greatly affect total economic activity. Government-provided consumption possesses to a great degree the advantage of stability.

The Relative Desirability of Investment and Consumption Expenditure

Government investment and consumption expenditures cannot be completely segregated. What has been called government consumption also necessarily requires government investment —for example, government provisions for public health or education also require considerable government investment in buildings. The problem of correct terminology also arises from

*Alvin H. Hansen, *Economic Policy and Full Employment*, p. 201.

the tendency to consider investment only if a material object is created as a result of the expenditure. Undoubtedly, expenditure on educational instruction and the attention of a nurse or a doctor are investment expenditures also. The investment in these cases is the creation of a more healthy and intelligent population. However, the typical government expenditure that is considered an investment result in the construction of a material object that will provide services over a period of time. Money spent in this fashion is believed to assure a higher standard of living in the future than an expenditure that does not result in a fairly permanent material object. It is very doubtful if there is any general meaning to this type of differentiation, but there is a meaning in specific instances. For example, a government expenditure providing a bonus that is spent for liquor and nightclub entertainment would be less likely to increase the scale of living in the future than a similar quantity of funds spent to construct an electric power dam or to provide soil conservation.

The meaningful differentiation between consumption and investment is based on the relative stimulating effect on the future scale of living of the community. In most instances, the construction of a building, dam, or road provides the basis for a relatively great expansion of the scale of living. In addition to physical improvements, expenditures to improve the health and educational levels of a nation always provide the basis for a relatively great expansion and would, on this basis of judgment, be investment expenditure despite the fact that the construction of permanent material objects was relatively unimportant. The effect of an expenditure on national income is not determined by whether it bears the label "consumption" or "investment," but by its effect on the total quantity of goods and services produced.

CONCLUSION

THE analyses of this chapter have shown that government expenditures can be used to cause price declines as well as price increases. Also, both types of price movements arising out of government expenditures were shown to possess the possibility of stimulating the level of economic activity.

There is a deep-seated but unproved belief that if the portion of national income utilized by government becomes too high, it will cause inflation. Until statistical proof is presented to support this belief, it is best to consider it as akin to "old wives' tales."

Through expenditures the government can directly encourage certain selected types of consumption, and in doing so, it frequently increases total consumption and also changes the pattern of consumption. When the government makes expenditures which directly encourage selected types of consumption, it has in some manner decided that the "general welfare" would be improved over and above that provided in the market place if more of the selected good or service were consumed and also (unless stocks of stored goods are to be consumed) if more of the selected good or service were produced.

QUESTIONS AND PROBLEMS

1. What is meant by built-in expenditure flexibility? Do you think it is desirable? What are its advantages and disadvantages?

2. Briefly point out a number of ways in which government expenditure can directly aid in the achievement of desirable prices.

3. In what two principal ways does the government purchase of gold differ from the purchase of other commodities?

4. Give the four general categories of government expenditure.

5. Utilize the four general categories of government expenditure to show how government expenditure may be used to achieve a desirable level of consumption.

6. Briefly compare the advantages and disadvantages of government or social consumption and private consumption.

7. What is meant by the economic limit to the size of the public economy? Why do most economists think this economic limit exists but is indefinite?

CHAPTER 8

Expenditures in Relation to Employment and Income Distribution

CHAPTER 7 considered expenditures in relation to the first two goals of fiscal policy—prices and consumption. This chapter continues the analysis of expenditures and considers them in relation to employment and income distribution.

THE ACHIEVEMENT OF A DESIRABLE EMPLOYMENT LEVEL

THE expenditures of government that are within the three categories, (1) investment, (2) consumption, and (3) increase in individual net worth, are most important in providing a desirable level of employment. Their approximate relative importance is shown by the order of listing. The fourth type of government expenditure, the change in the type of net worth, is less closely related to the provision of employment. This latter type of expenditure can, however, have an important deflationary influence and might be very useful in preventing the continuation of overemployment conditions.

How Expenditures Can Affect Employment

Government expenditure influences employment by providing or not providing an effective demand for goods and services. The increase of government expenditure, with private expenditure remaining constant, will bring forth an expansion of the effective demand for goods and services. This expansion of the effective demand will cause employment to increase. Of course, an expansion of government expenditure that would cause an equal reduction in private expenditure would have very little effect on the total quantity of employment.

150

The Use of Government Investments

The term "government investments" is used here only to refer to the construction by the public economy of permanent physical structures—for example, public buildings, dams, or highways.* The timing of investment expenditure by the government can have a considerable influence on the importance of investment in achieving a desirable level of employment. It is, however, impossible always to make public investments at the time that would be dictated by employment conditions. An example of this condition is the typical postwar situation. In 1948 and 1953, the need for additional public investment was very great, but full employment of labor was already being provided by the private economy.

The construction industry utilizes 10 per cent of national income when prosperous. Government investment can be utilized to prevent declines in its activity. When private demands are utilizing the full facilities of this industry, public investments should be at a minimum but when private demands are no longer willing to employ construction facilities, government investments can be expanded. The desirable economic effects arising from the stabilizing of the construction industry by government investments would be that (1) the whole economy would not be pulled into a depression as a result of unemployment in this area, and (2) the stabilization of the industry would eliminate the need for high wages and profits during the boom period to tide the industry over depressed periods. This result could reduce building costs and increase the amount of private construction.

Government investment can be economically made in areas in which private investment cannot be made. By this statement is meant that an evaluation of the desirable utilities that would become available as a result of the investment is sufficiently great to justify the use of the nation's resources, yet the monetary return is not of the correct nature to enable private individuals to make the investment. Examples of this type of investment are valley developments such as that of T.V.A., investments to provide health and recreation facilities, and the like. Government investment in fields of this type mean that the resources of the nation will be used more efficiently than if

*Any government expenditure aimed at increasing the health and skills of the population is an investment of a type. Also, the government, by providing cheap loan funds and guaranteeing loans to private individuals or groups, is providing additional investment. Both of these types of expenditure recently have expanded rapidly.

reliance were placed only upon investment induced by prospective monetary return.*

The Use of Government Consumption

Government consumption expenditure, as the term is used here, has often been called social consumption. Actually it arises from the people determining through their government that certain types of consumption should be expanded beyond the point possible through individual expenditure. The reasons for government consumption are largely the same as those which justified government investment: namely, (1) that the price system, because social values are over and above individual values, fails to correctly equate price and value, and (2) that the maldistribution of income makes the price offered for certain very necessary goods and services so low that the market system allocates too small a portion of the nation's resources to their production.†

Government consumption expenditures cannot be readily varied to meet the requirements of a desirable level of employment. However, a degree of expansion and contraction related to the swings of the activity of the private economy is possible. For example, the government during a period of unemployment and depression could offer position to doctors and nurses at attractive salaries and offer an increased quantity of preventive medical attention for the entire population. Another example would be the provision of funds to enable good students to acquire advanced training. This would remove these persons from the labor market and provide employment in the training institutions.

The experiment with food stamps during the depression of the 1930's shows that government expenditures could be effectively used to raise the nutrition level of the nation.‡ This type of a program stimulates employment throughout the nation by increasing the prosperity of a vital industry—agriculture; it also increases the efficiency of laborers.

*The undervaluation of certain goods and services by the price system arises partly from the social value which the good provides in addition to its value to the individual. Under these conditions, the individual is able to pay only for the value to him; but this is less than the value of the good to society. Also, undervaluation arises from the maldistribution of income which makes it impossible for large groups of the population to make their desires adequately felt through the price system.

†One basis for judging "too small" would be that it is inadequate to maintain labor at peak efficiency.

‡This plan is discussed in some detail on p. 134. Briefly, the plan provided to low income groups stamps that could be spent at the neighborhood grocery for food.

The Increase of the Individual Net Worth

An individual's net worth is increased by the government (1) if it becomes possible to sell products or services to the government at a higher price than could be obtained in the free market, or (2) if the individual receives a grant or pension of value from the government. The most effective types of increase of net worth in providing additional employment are those made available to the low-income receivers.

Government expenditure of this type does not determine the manner in which funds will be spent, but rather determines the groups which will receive funds. However, to an extent, the determination of groups to receive funds also determines the manner of expenditure. In the past, war veterans and farmers have been most successful in obtaining government grants increasing net worth.

If the government makes funds available to persons within the lower income brackets, there is considerable assurance that the funds will be spent for consumption goods within a very short period of time. This additional expenditure becomes a part of the income stream, increases the gross economic activity of the private economy, and swells the tax receipts of the public economy. The first effect will be to reduce the need for the expansion of the public economy to maintain a favorable level of employment, and the second effect will be to reduce the need for public borrowing.

The Change in the Type of the Individual Net Worth

The change of the type of net worth is largely associated with the repayment of the government debt. However, it would also include government purchase of commodities at the prevailing market price.

The repayment of borrowings obtained from private individuals and groups other than commercial banks gives the additional funds to groups possessing a high propensity to save. The increase in aggregate demand, and thus employment, would be less than if a similar sum were made available to a group representing a cross section of the population such as a war veteran group.*

*The additional funds may induce increased private investment through lower interest rates. The multiplier effect under these conditions could be of such an order that aggregate demand would increase considerably.

General Types of Expenditure Theories Aimed at Full Employment

The theories that rely to a major extent upon expenditure to maintain economic equilibrium have advocated that the government use its fiscal powers largely in a compensatory manner. This has meant that when the private economy is prosperous and able to maintain relatively full employment the public economy would be relatively inactive, and when the private economy is not able to employ a large portion of the factors of production these factors would be employed by the public section of the economy.*

Public Works. The concept that a depression is a temporary maladjustment and that the level of public investment should be determined by private investment is basic to the idea of a cyclically planned public-works program. Advocates of public works recommend that the various levels of government contract for needed public-works projects during the periods of full employment, that they might have them available to employ laborers upon during periods of depression and unemployment. It is assumed that public works can be delayed and that this type of expenditure provides a good counter-cyclical use of government funds. It is obvious that public-expenditure and particularly public-investment-expenditure timing are good common sense. Actually they have been advocated and practiced for centuries.†

Assumptions Briefly Considered. The need for an immediate increase in public facilities is often very great and to delay it very difficult. The need for additional public-institution buildings may be very great, and new and improved highways may be needed immediately, but the nation may also be enjoying full employment. Actually, historically, most public-works expenditures have been made during periods of prosperity. It is during prosperity that the need for additional public works appears the greatest and that financing, at least by state and local governments, is the most readily accomplished.

The basic assumption of public-works expenditure to provide full employment and economic stability is that private invest-

---

*"The Federal government has become increasingly committed to a policy, which future administrations will find difficult to reverse, of initiating active and direct measures to maintain the national income at a high level and to encourage, if not to assure, employment to those able and willing to work." Paul T. Homan and Fritz Machlup, editors, *Financing American Prosperity* (New York, Twentieth Century Fund, 1945), p. 3.

†The pyramids of Egypt were perhaps constructed as an unemployment-relief scheme. C. J. Bullock, *Politics Finance and Consequences* (Cambridge, Mass., Harvard University Press, 1939), pp. 9–10.

ment instability cannot be avoided. This natural instability of private investment is to be compensated by inducing an unnatural instability in public investment. It would appear more desirable to maintain private investment at a constant level and to have public investment also at a constant level. It is doubtful, to say the least, whether it is desirable to subordinate public-investment needs to those of private investment.

Many public-investment requirements expand naturally with private investment—for example, streets, sewers, and transportation. The undertaking of these investments far in advance of private investment requires a higher degree of foresight than can be assumed to be always available.

Public works, as a single means of maintaining desirable employment conditions, have the important shortcoming of requiring considerable time to get under way, and they cannot be conveniently stopped until the project is completed. If the depression should be short, the major portion of the actual expenditures for the public-works program may be made during the period of prosperity following the depression. The concept of pump-priming has accepted the tenets of the planned public-works program but includes additions aimed to eliminate some of its operational defects.

Pump Priming. The weaknesses of a public-works program, the urgent need for increased economic activity, and the development of the science of economics brought about the development of government expenditure activities which have become associated with the expression "pump priming." The believers in pump priming continued to hold that public works were very important, but because of the slowness with which a public-works program provided purchasing power, they recommended that the government make money available immediately to those groups of the population that would spend the sums received with the least hesitance. As the public-works program got under way, the funds made available directly to consumers could be decreased.

The pump-priming theory is postulated upon the belief that a relatively small amount of government expenditure administered at the correct time and in the correct manner will bring about a considerably greater increase in the income flow arising from the private economy.* Government pump priming activity

---

*"Extremists . . . say that we do not need to worry, because we can always create full employment by pumping enough purchasing power into the system. If there is too much demand for labor and materials — that is, inflation — we

would consist of both socialized consumption and investment (public works) expenditures.†

Assumptions Briefly Considered. The pump-priming program is predicated upon the beliefs that depressions are periods of temporary readjustment which can be shortened and the hardship decreased by government expenditures, and also that the private economy is stimulated by government expenditure. In fact, the theory assumes that the difficulty which made it impossible for the private economy to maintain an acceptable level of employment of the factors of production can be rectified by government expenditure.

The assumption of the program which has been criticized most severely is: The expenditure of government funds for a short period will make it possible for the private economy to employ during a relatively long period all the factors of production without the assistance of the income stream made available by the government pump-priming operations. This is also the basic concept of a pump-priming government expenditure program.

The belief that the private economy can provide desirable economic conditions, after having been given a boost by the public economy in the form of added purchasing power, requires the quite untenable assumption that the mere increase of purchasing power has destroyed the basis for the previous development of undesirable economic conditions. A much more acceptable position would be that, after the needed changes in the relationships of different economic factors have been made, a boost of the pump-priming type would restore desirable economic conditions until other serious maladjustments develop; after these maladjustments had been corrected also, another boost would be required.

The idea of pump-priming does not require that the government expenditure be small; rather, the basic requirement of the program is that the portion of government expenditure determined by a desire to increase the income stream should be made for only a short time. The criticism which has often been leveled at previous pump-priming activities has been that

turn the faucet off and cause a contraction. Thus by manipulation of Government expenditures and taxation, continuing full employment is assured, and we do not need to worry about anything else in the economy." From *Report of the Council of Economic Advisers*, December 18, 1946, given in the *Federal Reserve Bulletin*, January, 1947, p. 20.

†The impetus of pump-priming is expected to arise from the operation of the accelerator principle.

government expenditure has been too little and too late. The basic difference between compensatory spending and pump-priming is not one of size of expenditure but rather of duration. It is, as has been previously mentioned, assumed that pump-priming expenditure will be made for only a short period of time; the duration of compensatory expenditure is uncertain.

Compensatory Spending. A program of government compensatory spending developed out of the failure of the pump-priming programs of the 1930's to ignite the spark that would enable the private economy to continue to employ the factors of production without the aid of large government expenditure. The theoretical basis for the necessity of the program was found in the failure of private expenditure (consumption and investment) to be sufficiently great to maintain full employment after it had been attained by either a public or private expenditure stimulus.* (It is generally assumed, under all three theories of government expenditure, that to obtain desirable economic conditions the financing will have to be largely accomplished through government borrowing operations.)

The most common measure of the amount of government compensatory spending needed has been the difference between the amount of saving which is expected from a national income that would represent full utilization of the resources of a nation and the amount of new investment expenditures that are expected to arise. Statistics gathered during the 1930's showed that at various national income levels that represented something other than depression conditions the amount of savings expected exceeded the investment opportunities.† Under these conditions the expenditure stream is insufficient to maintain the existing employment, and underutilization of the factors of production will arise unless the income stream is implemented. This implementation may be brought about through compensatory expenditure by the government.

*"For a century and a half it has been a commonplace of economics that the creation of pecuniary values in production cannot be less than the sale value of what is produced. If the total amount of income so created somehow fails to flow into the market, obviously something must have happened to it. . . . In that event the re-creation of money values by deficit financing up to the amount of purchasing power necessary to absorb the product of industry at full employment would only be a salvage of purchasing power already lost by its former owners and so to the whole community." C. E. Ayres, *The Theory of Economic Progress* (Chapel Hill, University of North Carolina Press, 1944), p. 276.

†Cf. Professor Alvin H. Hansen's testimony opening the Hearings before the *Temporary National Economic Committee, Congress of the United States,* Part 9, "Savings and Investment" (Washington, U.S. Government Printing Office, 1940).

Assumptions Briefly Considered. It is readily seen that a government compensatory-spending program based on the above type of explanation of need could continue indefinitely, and the fact that the program is followed during a number of years does not necessarily reduce the need for its continuance in future years. The program does not provide a corrective for the difficulty that makes it necessary, namely, the excess of savings during periods of full employment over the investment opportunities arising during the same period.*

It was evident during the 1930's and again in 1949 and 1954 that either the reduction in the amount of saving arising from a given national income or the increase in investment opportunities, or both, was necessary to eliminate the necessity for government compensatory spending. Government compensatory spending is the easy way and actually avoids facing the real problem.

Certainly, conditions could change sufficiently to eliminate the problem of oversaving, which has in turn necessitated the casting about for solutions to the problem. The England of Keynes was bothered with excess savings; this is one problem that has not plagued the post World War II British governments. The England of Cripps (1948) required personal saving rates 1½ times as great as in 1938 to prevent dangerous inflation.

Government compensatory expenditures would apparently be most desirable if they increased the purchasing power of those in the lower income brackets.† There is, however, difficulty in working out within our folklore successful means of distributing the funds to these groups.‡

---

*"Ancient Egypt was doubly fortunate, and doubtless owed to this its fabled wealth, in that it possessed two activities, namely, pyramid-building as well as the search for the precious metals, the fruits of which, since they could not serve the needs of man by being consumed, did not stale with abundance. The Middle Ages built cathedrals and sang dirges. Two pyramids, two masses for the dead, are twice as good as one; but not so two railways from London to York." J. M. Keynes, *The General Theory of Employment, Interest, and Money*, p. 131.

†"Total demand can be increased by a redistribution of income from the rich to the poor. Increased taxes on the rich, offset by decreased taxes on the poor or by greater bonuses to the poor, will increase total demand without unbalancing the budget. The rich will decrease their spending very little while the poor will increase their spending by almost the whole of the reduction in their taxes or the increase in their bonuses." Abba P. Lerner, *The Economics of Control*, pp. 319–320.

‡"Consumer credits — in effect, money — be provided by the government and distributed gratis to workers in the low income groups regardless of whether they are unemployed, whenever the ratio of unemployment reaches a certain specified figure." J. E. Meade quoted by H. Gordon Hayes, *Spending, Saving, and Employment* (New York, Knopf, 1945), pp. 207–208.

THE ACHIEVEMENT OF A
DESIRABLE INCOME DISTRIBUTION

The General Effects of Expenditures on Income Distribution

THE four general types of government expenditure—(1) investment, (2) consumption, (3) increase in individual net worth, and (4) change in type of net worth—can equalize income distribution most effectively through the provision of more equal opportunities.* The provision of more equal income distribution would arise largely from government consumption and increase in net-worth types of expenditure. The degree of income redistribution that would take place with these types of expenditure would depend to a great extent upon the efficiency of administration and the extent to which the typical individual is stimulated to increase his productive efficiency. An example of poor stimulation would be employment offered entirely on the basis of family position rather than training and ability. An example of bad administration would be an individual unable to use effectively his increase in net worth to improve his productive efficiency. This latter shortcoming would exist if additional good low-priced housing, education, and medical facilities were not available. The increase in individual incomes, under these conditions, would be largely dissipated through bidding up prices of the old and inadequate facilities and the purchase of low-utility goods and services. Rather than using all of its funds to provide individuals directly with additional purchasing power, the government should make extensive prior expenditure aimed at stimulating the production of goods and services needed to expand efficiently the scale of living.

The Ability of Government Expenditures to Change Income Distribution

Vertical Redistribution of Income. Vertical redistribution of income is used here to refer to the change in the portion of national income enjoyed by persons within the different income brackets that arises from government fiscal activity. Part of the income that individuals of the different income brackets receive is made up of government expenditure that increases net worth and government provided goods and services that can be

---

*The three basic causes of unequal vertical income distribution are: (1) unequal distribution of capital ownership, (2) too large a portion of national income paid to capital owners, and (3) unequal opportunity for acquiring skills and adequate nutrition and medical care.

definitely allocated to persons of certain income brackets. Government expenditure of those types can be allocated quite accurately to the different income brackets and, if compared with revenues collected, will largely show the amount of income redistribution arising from public-finance activities. However, a large portion of the expenditure of government, particularly the national government, is indivisible. It is impossible to divide these expenditures among the different income brackets on any acceptable basis. Examples of indivisible expenditures would be the money spent to maintain the court system or military establishment of a nation.

This necessary tentativeness of any data attempting to show the redistribution of income arising from government expenditure has discouraged attempts to measure it statistically. In 1941, a study was made of the redistribution of income in the United States through public finance activity. The study showed in a very summary fashion the net effect on income redistribution of Federal government expenditure from 1930 through 1939.[*]

This study indicates that in 1929 the working classes of the United States paid $781.3 million in taxes and received only $600 million in special benefits. In 1936, the working classes of the United States paid $1,180.5 million in taxes and received benefits of $6,273 million. The year 1936 was unusual because of the large war-pension payments. The conclusion of the study is that considerable redistribution of income took place as a result of public-finance activities. This redistribution arose, however, largely from government deficit-finance activity rather than the assessment of high taxes on some income brackets and large expenditures directly related to other income brackets.[†]

A study of the effects of public-finance activities on the redistribution of incomes in Great Britain shows the results in that country in 1937. If public income or indivisible benefits are allocated in proportion to income above the subsistence level, the British redistribution through government revenue-raising and expenditure is as presented in Table 8-1 given below.[‡] An

[*] "The Effect of Governmental Expenditures and Tax Withdrawals upon Income Distribution, 1930–1939," by Charles Stauffacher, in *Public Policy* (Cambridge, Mass., Graduate School of Public Administration of Harvard University, 1941). The studies of Eugene R. Schlesinger and John H. Adler of taxes and government expenditures in 1938–39 and 1946–47 reached about the same conclusion.

[†] *Ibid.*, p. 260.

[‡] Tibor Barna, *Redistribution of Incomes.* This study distributes public income or indivisible benefits on three bases: (1) in proportion to producers' income, (2) in proportion to income above the subsistence level, that is, progressively in relation to producers' income, and (3) progressively throughout the whole range of incomes.

examination of this table reveals that the proportion of income redistributed changes progressively with income—that is, with the increase of income the gain is reduced, or the loss is increased as a percentage of income.

TABLE 8-1. Redistribution of British income through public finance in 1937.

Income brackets	Redistribution as percent of income
Under $500	+18.7
$500–$1,000	+ 4.0
$1,000–$2,000	+ 0.3
$2,000–$4,000	− 6.7
$4,000–$8,000	−12.6
$8,000–$40,000	−23.8
$40,000 and over	−52.6
Under $1,000	+11.0
Over $1,000	−14.2

Source: Tibor Barna, *Redistribution of Incomes*, table 65, p. 230.

An examination of several United States government expenditures closely related to individual incomes will show how they have affected income distribution.

Social Security Expenditures. The expenditure to be considered first is the Old Age and Survivors Insurance (O.A.S.I.) benefit payments. This is an example of a social-type expenditure financed with a special tax, and only those who have paid the tax are eligible to receive the benefits provided for in the legislation.

O.A.S.I. is financed by the levy of a 4 per cent tax on the first $4,200 of wages in a covered industry. One half of the tax is paid by the employer and one half by the employee. It is quite possible that both the employer and employee, particularly if full employment and a sellers' market exist, shift the tax forward in higher prices of goods and services produced. If this is the situation, the cost of O.A.S.I. is borne by the total population in proportion to the consumption of goods and services produced by covered workers. Under these circumstances, uncovered persons would be expected to be bearing as much of the burden of the cost of O.A.S.I. as covered workers; but they would not be eligible for O.A.S.I benefits, as are covered workers.* Also, although the employer bears 50 per cent of the original impact of the O.A.S.I. tax he may receive none of the direct benefits.

*In 1954 about 50 million of the 65 million employed workers of the nation were completely covered under O.A.S.I.

The primary benefit is very closely related to the amount of O.A.S.I. tax paid. This is the amount paid to a single covered employee. However, a married covered worker who had made the same tax payment would receive half again as much, and in addition a covered worker eligible for benefits would receive one half of his primary benefit for each dependent child under eighteen years of age. A worker eligible for benefits, having a wife and supporting a number of children, would receive considerably greater benefits in relation to payment than a single worker eligible for benefits.* To some extent these additional payments are in relation to need; however, the need basis is a very rough approximation.

For example, a single benefit receiver may be completely dependent upon O.A.S.I. benefits and also be suffering from a chronic ailment requiring regular medical expenditure. The need in this case would be very great. The married worker supporting several grandchildren may have a considerable fortune and the O.A.S.I. benefits are not required for the financing of a very desirable scale of living.

The effects on income distribution of O.A.S.I. are still more important in relation to collection than expenditure, for collections under the program are still about one half greater than expenditures. (About $6.1 billion was collected in 1954 and $4.2 billion spent.)

Education Expenditures. Expenditures for social-welfare purposes bring about the greatest redistribution of income if they are financed through the levy of highly progressive taxes or the increase of the government debt. These methods of finance are more likely to exist on the Federal level than on the state or local level. However, the finance of public education (an annual expenditure of over $10,000 million), largely with funds collected by the application of the local property tax, is an example of a local expenditure which may often have important direct redistributive effects.†

Taxes that have been levied only upon land and at a particular level for a period of time apparently have very little effect upon the vertical distribution of income. They, however, would reduce the total net income arising from land ownership (rent income). The expenditure of these funds for education would benefit the lower and middle income-bracket persons much

---

*The benefit payments to the wife plus the husband's primary benefit may not exceed $200 per month.
†See pp. 41–42, 82–83.

more than the higher income-bracket groups. The net effect of education expenditures financed by the levy of the general property tax assessed largely upon land values is to improve the income distribution; the desirableness of this source of revenue decreases as the portion of total valuation represented by structure costs increases.

The state aid provided for the financing of education and any Federal aid that may be provided in the near future have an additional desirable effect on income distribution. These expenditures are made in such a manner that a certain minimum per-pupil expenditure is made in all geographical areas. The source of the revenue is very likely to be such that the larger portion is obtained in the richer areas—for example, this would be true of a general income or sales tax. The provision of equal education opportunities through state and Federal aid increases the total scale of living of the poorer areas or those areas where the percentage of children to adult population is greater.

Indirect Effects. Public finance also causes an indirect redistribution of income. This is in addition to the direct income-redistribution effects which can be partially measured (as shown by the studies that have been quoted of the results in both the United States and Great Britain). The most important indirect effects arise from the provision of equality of opportunity and the reduction of the concentration of property ownership. The more equal income distribution that arises from additional equating of these two relationships also tends to expand the total national income, which in turn makes possible a relatively greater increase of the income of the lower-bracket individuals with a relatively smaller decrease of the income of upper-bracket individuals.

A secondary indirect income-redistribution effect is that taxes collected directly from the worker to finance a particular social expenditure or any other tax may not be borne by the worker. The existence of a strong labor union, a well-established custom, or a subsistence-wage level may be able to prevent the reduction of take-home pay. If this is the case, a payroll tax to finance social expenditures will be largely borne by unorganized workers and the general population, which would include both the workers receiving benefits and those not receiving benefits. The effect of expanded social security or expanded government activity of any type under these circumstances would be to improve the relative position of persons able to maintain take-home pay and receive benefits. The members of these groups would be both high- and low-income receivers.

Redistribution of Income by Type and Source. Government expenditure can redistribute income by type through (1) the increase of social income and (2) the decrease of property income. The increase of social income results directly from government expenditures to alleviate privation and to raise the scale of living of the aged and the unfortunate. Since the Social Security legislation of 1935, this type of income has become much greater in absolute and relative importance.

Also, since the inauguration of the Federal social-security program in 1935, the number of persons receiving assistance of this type from the government has continually increased. In 1954, over $\frac{1}{2}$ million persons were receiving Old-Age Assistance benefits; $3\frac{1}{2}$ million were receiving Old-Age and Survivors Insurance; $1\frac{1}{2}$ million were receiving unemployment benefits, $1\frac{1}{2}$ million dependent children were receiving aid; and $\frac{1}{5}$ million blind were recipients of benefits.

Government investment in the power industry and the provision during World War II of additional aluminum-, steel-, and automobile-production facilities have tended to reduce the relative income arising from property. The development of atomic energy to the place where it can be used to provide a large portion of the nation's power requirements will reduce the returns to persons owning coal and oil properties. In fact, all government expenditure to reduce monopoly decreases the relative portion of the national income paid to owners of property. It is also true that government expenditure made to increase the productivity of the nation—for example, expenditure on agriculture experimentation—decreases the portion of national income paid to owners of property.

Cheap-Money Policy. The active efforts of the Federal government in providing funds at low rates of interest to farmers, businessmen, and home builders has decreased the income from property ownership. Also, the general cheap-money policy which the Treasury and the Federal Reserve System have pursued has decreased relative property income.

The relative portion of the national income going to owners of property increases with the expansion of the quantity of capital goods required in the use of the most efficient production methods.* The relative portion of the national income going to moneylenders also increases if the quantity of capital is relatively

*National income here is used as defined on p. 21.

less abundant than labor. In 1929, with approximate full employment, net interest income was 7.3 per cent of national income; in 1933, with large quantities of unemployment, it was 12.5 per cent of national income. By 1940, net interest was 7.6 per cent of national income; and by 1953 it had gone down to 2.7 per cent. The first cause of the rise in the portion of national income going to property (development of capital-consuming machines) cannot and should not be greatly changed by public-finance activities. It is possible, however, for public-finance activity to reduce the relative scarcity and therefore the portion of national income obtained from property if (1) additional production facilities were constructed by the government or made possible through government loans, and (2) the productivity of property were expanded through experimental and developmental expenditure. This latter type of expenditure reduces property return because monopoly is decreased.

The increase in the national debt and the rise of government interest expenditure is, of course, a direct expansion of income to property owners, the owners of United States government bonds, as a result of government expenditure. If it is assumed that if the money had not been borrowed by the government it would have been borrowed by private individuals and groups, the increase of the government debt decreases the portion of national income paid to property owners. The reduction arises from the lower average rate of interest paid by the government on borrowed funds. If, however, it is assumed that the government could have obtained its funds just as efficiently by directly printing more money as by borrowing, the expenditure of interest by the government must be considered a net increase in the portion of income arising from property.

Government expenditure has both increased and decreased the portion of national income obtained from property ownership. On balance it would appear, however, that government expenditure activity decreasing relative income from property outweighs that tending to increase it.

Agricultural Expenditures. The best example of government expenditure redistributing income by source has been the Federal activity in agriculture. The government, through expenditure aimed at increasing soil fertility, removing surplus crops from the market, and aiding in the marketing of crops, has increased the portion of the national income arising from agriculture. Another excellent example of government expenditure expanding a particular source of income is the government subsidy of the different means of transportation. Government expenditure for war expands the portion of the national income arising from agriculture and the iron- and steel-fabricating industries, but reduces the portion arising from the service industries.

A change in the portion of national income arising from different sources is of particular importance if a large portion of the population of an area earns its income from a certain industry. The government, through the provision of subsidies, can maintain the income of a depressed area while the necessary shifts in population and economic activity take place. The development of atomic energy for commercial use may involve a very considerable program of this type.

All government expenditure is likely to cause a simultaneous income redistribution of all three types—that is, vertical redistribution, redistribution by type, and redistribution by source. Different expenditure, however, varies very greatly in the type and the intensity of the income redistribution created. Certainly the measurement of the direct redistribution arising from government expenditure is very difficult. The importance of the indirect effects of each government expenditure, or even all expenditure, can be approximated only very roughly.

CONCLUSION

IN the past, the effects of government expenditure have been much more apparent in the provision of a desirable level of employment than in the achievement of a desirable income distribution. This ability of government expenditure to directly and rather efficiently eliminate unemployment has been the principal reason for the great popularity of government expenditure as a method of creating and maintaining desirable economic conditions. The unemployment that arises and that has been eliminated by government expenditure was caused by undesirable prices, consumption, and income distribution. Government expenditure in the past has played a relatively less important role in the elimination of these important causes of unemployment.

Government expenditure programs of the future should not be in the form of emergency measures to take care of a serious case of unemployment that has already developed. Government expenditure must be planned and made in such a manner that it aids in the continual efficient use of resources. Also, expenditure activity of this type would avoid most of the criticisms that were made of the government expenditure during the 1930's.

QUESTIONS AND PROBLEMS

1. What are the basic differences between government-expenditure theories included within the concepts (1) public works, (2) compensatory spending, and (3) pump-priming?

2. How have government expenditures been able to effect a desirable income distribution? Distinguish between the effect on vertical redistribution and redistribution by type and source.

3. What are the disadvantages and advantages of government expenditure as compared to government revenues in the accomplishment of fiscal-policy goals? Which fiscal-policy goal do you think is best accomplished by government expenditure? Why?

4. Select a particular type of government expenditure and show how the effects of the expenditure can be changed through different methods of obtaining the funds spent. Also select a particular government revenue and show how the effects can be changed by different types of expenditure. Finally, take this expenditure and this revenue and show how the desirableness of the effects would change depending upon the existing and expected level of economic activity.

5. Government expenditure can have a great effect on prices. Briefly show how expenditure affects the general price level and particular prices. Why is this type of fiscal activity desirable in attaining an efficient use of resources?

6. What are the ways in which government expenditure indirectly affects the distribution of income? Do you believe that democracy and capitalism will be weakened by extensive redistribution of income? Why? What do you believe would be an ideal distribution of income?

7. Do you believe that social security benefits should be financed and distributed in a manner that would directly cause the maximum vertical redistribution of income? Why? What benefit payment and finance scheme would most nearly do what you think should be done?

CHAPTER 9

Administration of Taxes and Expenditures
to Reach Fiscal Policy Goals

INTRODUCTION

THIS chapter will analyze only that portion of public administration directly concerned with the management of expenditure and taxes that is fundamentally related to the achievement of the fiscal-policy goals discussed in the previous chapters.

The effectiveness of fiscal policy in obtaining its legitimate aims will be determined by the type of administration provided. It can be stated on the basis of economic principles that revenues raised in a particular manner, and expenditures made for particular purposes, will bring about certain results; but the realization of the expected reaction will be obtained only if the programs recommended are properly administered.

The basic requirements for effective government action aimed at obtaining and keeping favorable economic conditions are:

1. The establishment of a council of economic experts who have had sufficient experience in the handling of economic data to enable them to give the government expert professional advice on any specific fiscal problem.

2. An accurate forecast of future economic conditions if the government takes no action or if the plans of the moment are carried through.

3. A determination of the type of government action that is desirable to promote the development of more favorable conditions.

4. Provision for quickly changing the manner in which the government obtains its revenues and also a provision for quickly putting into effect an extensive, well-planned expenditure program.

168

5. Sufficient control over political pressures so that program aimed at preventing the development of a boom period can be put into effect as well as a program aimed at preventing a depression (the problem of the two-headed dragon).

In the past, dominant political pressures have often favored government action the reverse of that required to maintain tolerably acceptable economic relationships. For example, during the period after World War I, when profits were adequate and business was prosperous but the accumulated demand developed during the period of the war was being dissipated, the dominant political pressure was for reduced profit and income taxes and reduced government expenditure, rather than for the maintenance of income-tax rates and increased government expenditure. When the depression of the 1930's was at its worst, January, 1933, the administration program of the Federal government called for a Federal sales tax and reduced expenditure with a balanced budget. The program should have provided for a reduction of excise taxes, an increase of expenditure, and a Federal government deficit. It is hoped that recommended economic programs will be a little more intelligent in the future. Recent experience, which includes the elimination of excess-profit taxes for 1946 and the reduction of income, estate, and gift taxes during 1948, is not particularly encouraging. However, it is encouraging that the veto of the tax-reduction bill of 1947 was sustained by Congress, although the 1948 veto was not. President Franklin D. Roosevelt's veto of the Revenue Act of 1943 labeling the tax legislation "not a tax bill but a tax-relief bill providing relief not for the needy but for the greedy" was overridden and became another reason why World War II finance got off to a bad start. However, President Truman's fiscal recommendations at the outbreak of the Korean War were largely adopted, as was President Eisenhower's fiscal program to fight the recession of 1954.

Forecasting

An important part of all administration is forecasting. Forecasting is particularly important in the determination of activity aimed at providing a desirable level of economic activity. Economic forecasting at its best is an uncertain undertaking. A recent example of bad forecasting was the prediction by a group of economists that widespread unemployment would develop during the period of postwar reconversion. An example of good forecasting was the prediction that the removal of O.P.A. would not quickly bring about adjustments that would prevent prices from rising and staying high. It is difficult, except on the basis of hindsight, to determine which forecasts of economic conditions are accurate and which are inaccurate. Yet it is upon economic forecasts that plans aimed at the preservation of a desirable level of economic activity must be made.

After the best economic forecasts are obtained, it is necessary to translate these into desirable executive and legislative action. There is less uncertainty regarding desirable government action to correct a particularly undesirable economic development than there is in forecasting what the economic development will be that will need correcting.

THE EMPLOYMENT ACT OF 1946

FEDERAL legislation passed in 1946 provided for the setting up of a large portion of the administrative machinery required for a successful government fiscal policy directed toward the maintenance of desirable economic conditions. The most important step was the enactment of the Employment Act of 1946.

Provisions of the Act

The Act sets forth the policy of the Federal government to be:

to use all practicable means consistent with its needs and obligations and other essential considerations of national policy, with the assistance and co-operation of industry, agriculture, labor, and state and local governments, to co-ordinate and utilize all its plans, functions, and resources for the purpose of creating and maintaining, in a manner calculated to foster and promote free competitive enterprise and the general welfare, conditions under which there will be afforded useful employment opportunities, including self-employment, for those able, willing, and seeking to work, and to promote maximum employment, production, and purchasing power.

This aim of Federal policy is desirable and is actually a statement of intention to provide full employment and stable economic conditions and to prevent the development of economic crises. The principal weakness of the Employment Act of 1946 is that it does not set down ways in which this responsibility of the Federal government is to be discharged. The Act does, however, make provision for the gathering together into one place (Council of Economic Advisers) the best information available regarding what is happening in the nation's economy.

It also provides for the interpretation of these data and making the interpretation available to the President and Congress for action. This is also done by the Council.

The Employment Act of 1946 does not use the phrase "full employment"; rather the phrase "maximum employment" is substituted. The Murray Bill, which was the basis for the Employment Act of 1946, used the phrase "full employment." The British White Paper which set down the aims of the British government in regard to the provision of economic stability used the phrase "high and stable level of employment." It is perhaps well that the term "full employment" is not used, for it is doubtful that the efficiency of government fiscal-policy tools and democratic methods of allocating labor are as yet sufficiently well understood to eliminate the arising of a considerable quantity of unemployment in a dynamic economic society.*

The Economic Report is a new type of Presidential message. Previously, the Presidential message at the opening of Congress was largely political and dealt only incidentally with economic matters. On January 8, 1947, for the first time in the history of the nation, the President submitted to Congress a "comprehensive picture of the state of the economy and an integrated program for promoting national prosperity and soundness in the year ahead."† Since the first report, midyear and annual reports have been given regularly. In addition, the Council made recommendations regarding the impact on the national economy to be expected from the Economic Co-operation Act of 1948, the Korean War of 1950, and the reduction of defense expenditures in 1953. Only the annual report is required by the Employment Act.

In the preparation of the report, the President has the services of all government departments; the advice of representatives of industry, agriculture, labor, consumers, educational and research institutions, and state and local governments; and the continuous and immediate service of the Council of Economic Advisers.

The Employment Act instructs the President to appoint three well-trained professional economists as members of the Council. The Council has not set up an elaborate organization for the gathering of information but rather has utilized economic

*Professor Alvin Hansen is of the opinion that if not more than 4 to 5 per cent of the labor force of the nation is unemployed conditions of full employment should be considered to exist.

†*The Economic Reports of the President* (New York, Reynal & Hitchcock, 1948), p. vii.

data gathered by the various departments of the government and private agencies. If the Council desires additional or more elaborate data of a particular type, it can obtain this needed assistance from the appropriate government department.

The Employment Act provides for the establishment of a joint Congressional committee called the Joint Committee on the Economic Report. The basic function of this Joint Committee is correlating legislative activity arising from the Economic Report. Also, the Committee is to correlate existing legislation and contemplated legislation in various fields with the recommendations set forth in the Economic Report. This type-of-action recommendation is predicated on the assumption that the recommendation of the report is the basis for the best fiscal policy under existing circumstances. The Committee also has the responsibility of transmitting once a year to Congress its recommendations regarding means of most efficiently carrying out the policy of the Employment Act.

The annual report of the President on the economic state of the nation is divided into four general sections. (1) The report contains a general summary of the existing levels of employment, purchasing power, and production of the nation. This first section also includes an estimate of the level of economic activity required to carry out the provisions of the Act. (2) The report also contains a summary of the expected economic developments during the next year and during the foreseeable future. (3) The third portion deals with the current fiscal policy of the government that is related to the maintenance or the obtaining of desirable levels of employment, purchasing power, and production. (4) The logical concluding portion of the report includes measures for implementing the present fiscal policy with recommendations for additional legislation that the President might consider desirable.

Usefulness of the Act

The Employment Act has already been a very useful administrative addition and has implemented Federal fiscal policy aimed at full utilization of the nation's economic machine. But in order for the machinery to accomplish the aims of the Act, it will be necessary that both the Executive and the Congress have a genuine desire to use the powers of the government to provide economic security. If the President and particularly Congress are of the opinion that the economic well-being of the nation can be best provided by the government doing nothing and in this way permitting the economic forces of the nation to work themselves out, the Act will be of little importance.

If it is assumed that the President and Congress wish to use government action to increase the economic well-being of the people, and this has been a rather settled policy since Alexander Hamilton in 1791 called for a "degree of support from the government." The efficiency of the Act in accomplishing its purpose will depend upon (1) the adequacy of economic data available and (2) the caliber of the personnel of the Council and the Joint Committee.* The fact that the Report is closely tied to the ultimate judgments of the President is certain to make it a report slanted toward the economic philosophy which appears to be the better politics for the President. A desirable reform would perhaps be the submitting of a majority and minority Economic Report. The differences would usually not be great, but this might enable economists to make available to the public what they think is the best policy—with political considerations thrown out the window.

THE ADMINISTRATION OF TAXES

THE effectiveness of the administration of the different taxes is very important in determining the ability of the tax to bring about the correct level of prices, consumption, employment, and income distribution. The method of administration is, of course, a part of tax legislation adopted by the different legislatures. An important cause of the growth of Federal fiscal power has been its efficiency of tax administration.

Flexibility of Tax Rates

Neither Congress nor the state legislatures has seen fit to provide any important degree of administrative discretion in the determination of tax rates. In order for taxes to play the full role of which they are capable in providing the correct level of prices, consumption, employment, and income distribution, it would be necessary to grant an executive group the power to change rates within various broad limits. It would be possible, as previously indicated, to set up certain criteria to be

*See Randolph E. Paul, *Taxation for Prosperity*, pp. 229–236; also Alvin H. Hansen, *Economic Policy and Full Employment*, pp. 106–120.

used as the basis of tax rate changes. Also, legislative provision could indicate the amount which tax rates could be changed if certain conditions arose. These restrictions would assure the legislative bodies that determined principles would not be abandoned, and yet the Executive division would have sufficient freedom for administering the taxes of the nation in the manner best suited to maximize the utilization of the nation's resources.

In 1954, the President could change the tax policy through administrative procedures only to the extent that the executive had been given power to change tariff rates (Reciprocal Trade Agreements Act, 1934) and perhaps by issuing administrative orders that all doubtful cases should be decided either for or against the government. The reductions in tariff rates provided under the Reciprocal Trade Agreements Acts could have and have had a considerable effect on the efficiency of resource allocation in the United States. Tariff reductions would almost certainly increase efficiency of resource use if full employment were maintained. In regard to administrative orders, it is doubtful that a change in official attitude toward an uncertain tax liability could produce any important predictable results.

Effects of New Tax Levies

The Federal government relies primarily upon revenues obtained from the individual and corporate income taxes. Recently, tax bills have been passed at frequent intervals that provided for different effective individual- and corporate-tax rates. Although the rates determined upon, the types of income taxed, and the exemptions provided have important determinable effects upon the development of the economy, the considerations given greatest attention continue to be largely political. The mere frequent passage of new tax bills does not guarantee tax legislation better tailored to the requirements of desirable fiscal policy. For example, the tax-reduction bill passed by Congress in 1947 but vetoed by the President met the economic requirements of desirable tax legislation less accurately than legislation in effect. This was also true when tax legislation was enacted by Congress in 1945 and again in 1948; however, the tax legislation of 1951 and 1954 represented a responsiveness to fiscal needs.

The economy to a great extent becomes adjusted to an old tax and tax rate. The economy requires time to adjust itself to the imposition of new taxes and different rates. It is the situation that exists after these adjustments have been completed that largely determines the long-run effects of a tax. However, the economically disrupting effect of new taxes is important and should be minimized. This disrupting effect should be considered in determining the manner in which new taxes and rates are administered. In some instances it might be desirable to introduce a new tax by degrees. This could be done by making the tax applicable at first only to those sections of the economy which, because of economic resources or method of organization, are well suited to bear the original impact of the tax. This type of procedure was used to some extent in the introduction of social-security taxes.

The effectiveness of new income-tax levies in increasing and decreasing the quantity of purchasing power possessed by individuals has been improved by the introduction during World War II of withholding and quarterly payments under declarations of estimated income. This has meant that within a matter of weeks wage earners received larger pay envelopes as a result of the 1948 and 1954 Federal income-tax reductions, and smaller pay envelopes as quickly as a result of the 1951 income tax increase. This more current payment of Federal income taxes applies to all sections of the economy except agriculture. It would be desirable if it were extended to include this area.

The withholding- and quarterly-payment schemes result in prompt changes of tax payments, but provision is not included for prompt repayment of tax overpayment. As matters stand in 1954, if a man is unemployed for a spell, he gets a claim to a tax refund the next year. The administration problems encountered in a more prompt refund method are very great. It has been recommended that personal exemptions be given as a refund by the government, perhaps on a monthly basis, and taxes withheld on the basis of income without personal exemptions. ("Personal exemptions" refers to the $600 of tax-free income allowed to the taxpayer and for each dependent). Then if a man were unemployed he would receive the personal-exemption payments but would be subject to no taxes. The plan would involve making out millions of small checks and getting them to individuals. The task would be a large one, perhaps too great for the benefits resulting.

State and Local Tax Policy

The ability of the state and local governments to affect economic activity by taxation is greatly limited by the types of taxes which they can administer effectively and by the rates which can be assessed—for example, local governments have difficulty in administering income and death taxes. Each of the different states is to an extent in competition with all other states in obtaining the location of manufacturing industries and also of distribution and management facilities. It has usually been politically impossible for a particular state to initiate a tax program that is greatly different from that existing in other states. This has been the case because of the belief, and proof is lacking, that tax burdens have an important effect upon the location of industries. This factor has been particularly important in regard to state and local taxes levied directly upon business-enterprise profits. A number of states, particularly Mississippi and Tennessee, are active in offering tax inducements to obtain new industries.

THE ADMINISTRATION OF EXPENDITURES*

THE administration of an economic Federal program of expenditure correlated with the needs of society for certain services and goods and the maintenance of a proper level of economic activity would require the establishment of an additional Cabinet post. The duties of this new member of the President's Cabinet can be roughly defined on the basis of the previous analysis of the requirements of an effective program to maintain a desirable level of prices, consumption, employment, and income distribution.

A Secretary of National Welfare

This new Cabinet member might be called the Secretary of National Welfare. It would seem logical that those duties of the Bureau of the Budget which relate to the correlation of the expenditures of the various departments of the Federal government be transferred to the new Secretary. In addition, the new Secretary would have as a portion of his responsibility the working out with industrial leaders of ·plans for expansion and reorganization of industry which would correlate with those of the government. If a sphere of activity in private hands appeared to require expansion and reorganization, it would be the duty of the Secretary to bring about such expansion through the pro-

*The analysis of this section is largely based upon the excellent study of the International Labour Office titled *Public Investment and Full Employment* (Montreal, International Labour Office, 1946).

vision of funds or the use of whatever other means were required. The acceptance of this responsibility by a government department would prevent the use of investment funds in an area of the public economy that, according to all measures of productivity, would be of less value to the community than investment expansion in a segment of the private economy.

The new Secretary should also be responsible for working out advance engineering and finance plans for desirable projects to be actually constructed when the need for the services which they would provide would be best correlated with the type of activity required to maintain the desired level of economic activity. Planning of this type brings with it all of the problems attending the determination of priorities which are discussed in considerable detail in another section,* and the much less difficult problem of providing a reserve shelf which is also discussed in considerable detail in another section.†

The efficient performance of the duties mentioned above as being those properly assigned to the Department of National Welfare necessitate the development of a detailed national plan for the expansion and conservation of the nation's material and human resources.

An examination of these required powers emphasizes the necessity of crossing departmental lines, and of the Secretary being able to place strong pressure upon Congress for the provision of enabling legislation. The new Cabinet post would provide for a new superior member of the executive family. It is very doubtful that such powers as outlined will be extended in an outright grant, but rather that the required activities and co-operation will take place on a more or less voluntary basis. If this were the case, the Secretary of National Welfare would be able to perform the functions of his position with greater or less efficiency, depending upon Congressional and Presidential attitudes toward the administration of economic plans.

Local Administration Problems

The problems of local administration of government expenditures are to a great extent the same as those of central administration. In addition, however, local administration would be greatly concerned with the determination of (1) the projects

*See pp. 183–189.
†See pp. 179–180.

which would fit in best with local conditions, (2) the letting of contracts on an efficient basis, and (3) the problems associated with the acquiring of suitable sites.

The expenditures of all government levels could be made more rapidly if they were executed through force-account projects rather than through the letting of private contracts.* Also, expenditures of higher levels of government could be made more rapidly if lower government levels were not used in the channeling of funds. In the future it is likely that greater expenditures will be made directly by higher government levels, with the work accomplished through force account. The factors that will strongly mitigate against such an administrative procedure are (1) the desire of local and state governments to determine to at least some extent how Federal funds are to be allocated, (2) the contribution by lower governments of a portion of the costs of projects, (3) the desire to maintain considerable decentralization of government and the fear of the development of a strong Federal bureaucracy, and (4) the belief that the letting of private contracts is the capitalistic method of making government investment.

Elaborate advance preparations must be made if government funds are to be spent through the letting of private contracts and local participation in the financing and selecting of projects. This preparation is basic if the expenditures are to be made sufficiently rapid to prevent employment, price, and consumption levels falling considerably below what is desired.

The W.P.A. experience indicated that force-account projects were more efficient in putting men to work, and thus more efficient in implementing the income stream, than private-contract programs. The experience gained from W.P.A. expenditure also indicated that if work is to be done through private contracts with an efficiency approaching that of force-account, it is necessary to do the following things beforehand: (1) all legal and financial complications must be taken care of, (2) all plans and specifications must be prepared, (3) all sites to be used must have been acquired, and (4) it would be desirable if a procedure were worked out for the letting of contracts in advance.

---

*In a force-account project: The public investment is undertaken directly by a public authority, with labor hired, equipment owned, and materials bought by the public authority, as contrasted with work done through a private contractor.

A Local Public-Expenditure Board. State and local administrative boards are needed to direct expenditure programs with fiscal-policy aims. These boards must be bipartisan or nonpartisan. Citizens will have relatively high confidence that boards of this type will make expenditures in the most efficient manner. Every effort must be exerted on the national, state, and local levels to prevent the waste of funds either through the (1) inefficient or dishonest letting of contracts or (2) inefficient or dishonest determination of project priority. In order to prevent the embroilment of regular state and local public-expenditure boards in the heated discussions that are certain to arise with initiation of a project providing utilities previously furnished by private-enterprise or government subsidy grants to certain private industries, it would be desirable if the determination of this type of project were referred to separate boards. This arrangement would prevent the regular boards, which determine most expenditures, becoming involved in these arguments that take a great deal of time and would be certain to create bad feeling and reduce prestige.

A Reserve Shelf*

The principal weakness of government expenditure activities to increase the level of economic activity, during the depression of the 1930's, was the lack of a stock of sufficiently well-planned expenditure projects. A good reserve-shelf program would provide for the development of fully-planned projects in all areas to meet the various requirements of expenditures aimed at the maintenance of prosperity.† It is much easier to maintain prosperity than it is to bring it forth after a depression has set in. It would be desirable to establish a timetable of planned expenditures. Expenditures would be made first in those areas where unemployment was developing. Projects that would quickly require many of the unemployed would be selected first. At the same time, preparations would be speeded for the construction of important larger projects in any area. The selection of all projects would be determined largely by the need for the development and by types of resources unemployed. It is obvious

*"Reserve shelf" means a reserve of planned public-investment projects to be ultimately included in the program of a public authority, but for which no funds are expected to be made available during the period in which the program is laid out.

†See pp. 185–189 for a more complete analysis.

that this is the efficient manner to plan the use of government expenditure to maintain a desirable level of prices, consumption, and employment. However, it cannot be obtained without an administrative program that recognizes that governments, to perform their newly accepted function of maintaining sound economic conditions, must fully plan *beforehand* the steps to be taken in case of a threatening depression or a threatening boom (the two-headed dragon problem again).

The reserve shelf should contain projects that not only possess the characteristic of being able to provide employment quickly, but they must also be easy to terminate—that is, it must be possible to reduce government expenditure quickly when the need is gone. The cost of developing such a reserve shelf is not excessive, and the technical knowledge required for its construction so that it will meet the economic, engineering, and legal requirements is available in the United States.

Difficulty of Creating a Reserve Shelf. Fundamentally, the inability to create an adequate reserve shelf has been political. In the past, the majority of the voters have believed that such a reserve shelf was neither necessary nor even particularly desirable. Also, these existed a good deal of skepticism regarding the technical ability to construct one.

The efficient government planning during World War II has removed many of the doubts of technical ability. The waste of labor power during the 1930's convinced many that thorough planning is a necessary prerequisite of economic government expenditure. The great direct effect of government spending in bringing about a full utilization of the nation's resources was thoroughly demonstrated in the 1937-1938 upswing and downswing and in the pre-World War I and World War II periods. The inability of monetary and banking policy alone to rectify a condition of underemployment was very completely demonstrated during the depression of the 1930's. Also, even the most ardent advocates of government tax revision as a method of providing a desired level of economic activity include additional government expenditures as a part of their program. Opposition to a planned reserve shelf nevertheless continues from those groups who believe that periodic unemployment is desirable to eliminate maladjustments and also from those who believe that we have entered a new era and that the nation will not experience another depression.

Legal Bottlenecks

If the Federal government is going to make use of investment expenditures partly financed and controlled by local government, a great deal of preparatory legal and administrative work must be done. In the 1930's, these legal difficulties sometimes arose from incomplete or confused legislation providing for the expenditure. In addition, delays in getting projects under way arose because of time-consuming procedures that had to be followed in the letting of contracts and in the acquisition of sites.

Enabling Legislation. A legal difficulty encountered during the early period of P.W.A. arose from the failure of the Act to set up plain rules for the determination of the lines of authority. A must of expenditure-enabling legislation is the clear establishment of the manner in which the purpose of the act is to be accomplished. If this is poorly done, much needless delay and confusion will arise and the provision of economic stability, the primary purpose of the original legislation, will be endangered.

State and municipal laws, constitutions, charters, and ordinances provide another legal delay. States and cities should be made aware of the necessity of changing their legal requirements for expenditures upon projects largely financed by the Federal government and related to effective emergency action. Local government debt-limitation laws are an excellent example of this type of legal bottleneck. Another enabling delay on the local level arises from the failure to pass legislation providing for state and/or municipal agencies that can co-operate with the Federal agency.

Contract Letting. Many of the delays encountered in the letting of contracts during the period of the 1930's were of a legal nature. Much of this legal protection was found unnecessary during World War II and was eliminated. The irreducible legal protection desired when contracts are let to private firms is that associated with the advertising for bids, checking the bids submitted, and, if they are considered to be legal bids, awarding the contract. At the very best, the use of private contracts requires a delay to meet the minimum legal safeguards. The problem from the legal side could be solved by letting contracts for certain planned projects a considerable period in advance of the time when construction is desired. The solution of the legal difficulty brings with it administrative problems arising from the need to develop methods of handling changes in cost from the period when the contract was let to the period when the construction takes place.* It would seem that procedures worked out during World War II, when great price changes were taking place within a short period of time, would be practical also in the above type of situation.†

Securing Sites. The legal problems involved in the acquisition of land can be as serious as any other in the quick development óf a project. The problem involved in the purchase of land by a government to be used for the development of a project has been succinctly stated by the United States National Resources Planning Board:

Land acquisition on a large scale, especially if the purposes to be served require blocking in of large contiguous areas, is at best a difficult, complicated, and slow process; and unless it is conducted under competent administration, it can become very costly. It requires individual transactions with large numbers of persons.‡

Legal title to land could be obtained very quickly if the government were indifferent to the price paid. This, however, cannot be the case. In most cases condemnation is the best method of obtaining land by a government in the United States. In most states the power of condemnation is quite broad and adequate, if it can be shown to the satisfaction of the court that the property when acquired will be used for a public purpose. Condemnation can be obtained through either the so-called (1) judicial procedure or the (2) administrative procedure. The judicial procedure includes bringing suit against the owner; then the court determines if the property is to be used for a public purpose and also determines the value of the property. The great objection to the judicial procedure is that it sometimes requires as long as two or three years to obtain title to needed property. The administrative procedure provides that the government agency makes public its intent to take certain properties. This method gives the government practically immediate possession; but if the owners are unwilling to accept what the

---

*The term "general escalation" clause is used to refer to contract provision for increase in price of finished product if raw-material or labor costs increase.

†See John Perry Miller, "Military Procurement in Peacetime," *Harvard Business Review* (Summer, 1947), vol. 25, no. 4, pp. 444–461; and "War Procurement — A New Pattern for Contracts," by David Fain and Richard F. Watt, *Columbia Law Review*, March, 1944, vol. 44, pp. 127–215.

‡National Resources Planning Board, *Public Land Acquisition*, Part I: "Rural Lands" (Washington, U.S. Government Printing Office, June, 1940), p. 6. Taken from *Public Investment and Full Employment* by the International Labour Office.

government offers, they may appeal to the courts, and the government will have to pay whatever the court decides is a fair value. Under the so-called judicial procedure, the government can refuse to purchase the property if it considers the price, as set by the court, too high. The danger of paying too high a price and the delay of court condemnation proceedings can be avoided by advance planning through the purchase of land at opportune times and holding it until needed.*

Public-Expenditure Priorities

The determination of public-expenditure priorities is very definitely a portion of the problem of administering a public-expenditure program. The order in which expenditures should be made can be determined by rating in accordance with (1) the utility which is expected to accrue or (2) the process effects.† Usually projects are chosen on a basis determined by assigning weights to these two factors. If the need for immediate stimulation of employment is very great, the second base would be given greater relative weight; if the need is not so urgent, the first base should certainly be the more important. If government expenditures were completely determined by the second base, however, the total cost to obtain a given increase in economic activity would be minimized. However, an expenditure program of this type would be particularly open to the criticism that government funds were being wasted. It is possible through very careful planning and efficient administration to combine

---

*The practice of municipal purchase of properties is quite common in Europe. Helsinki owned 13,000 acres and Stockholm 21,000 acres at the outbreak of World War II.

†Process effects include the total increase in national income and employment resulting from the process of securing and financing public-investment projects. These effects are classified as primary, secondary, and tertiary.

Primary effects:
  On-site employment (and income)
  Off-site employment (and income)

Secondary effects:
  Multiplier effects on income and employment
  Relation effects on income and employment
  Effects through induced private consumption
  Effects through induced private investment

Tertiary effects:
  Further increases in consumption arising out of secondary increases in investment, and
  Further increases in investment arising out of secondary increases in consumption.

the utility and process-effect bases in such a manner that the expenditures maximize both of them.

Investment Versus Consumption. If a downward trend in economic activity is apparent, the all-important priority consideration is: Will a particular expenditure have important primary, secondary, and tertiary effects and can the expenditure be made quickly so that the stimulation of these process effects will be available immediately? This, in nearly all cases, will mean that the additional fiscal action of government will be of the type labeled "consumption." It will involve the underwriting of consumption by paying subsidies to reduce the price of necessities, by reducing all excise taxes, and by the payment of substantial unemployment benefits. The period of need for the direct increase of purchasing power will be long or short, depending largely upon the completeness with which the reserve shelf of government investments has been planned.

Government expenditures of the consumption type are often considered wasteful and at times are believed to lead to a deterioration of the morale and the skills of the population. As soon as possible, the expenditure of government should be upon projects that are of recognized worth. As quickly as possible, the basis of employment on government projects should be skill and other related factors, rather than need. It is preferable to make direct unemployment payments than to include "projects whose value in themselves is so low as to be almost negligible, but which may be resorted to where a definite amount of relief work has been determined upon and where no better projects can be found."*

Conflict is likely to develop concerning the factors of production to be employed and the projects that have the highest utility value and greatest process effects. Care should be taken that the projects chosen do not require materials in short supply. Also, it is possible that skilled laborers would be unemployed while common labor would be fully employed. It is desirable to immediately make full use of the resources of the skilled-labor pool. There is no reason why skilled laborers, because they have a greater financial ability than unskilled, should have to remain unemployed waiting for the secondary and tertiary effects. The loss to the community is actually considerably

*John Maurice Clark, *Economics of Planning Public Works* (Washington, National Planning Board of the Federal Emergency Administration of Public Works, 1935), p. 58.

greater when skilled laborers remain unemployed than when the unskilled are unable to find employment.

It is sometimes advisable to complete projects completely out of line with any sort of a priority rating system. This would be the case if the completion of a particular project leaves labor and supplies very convenient for the undertaking of this less important project. On occasion it might be desirable to employ within a brief period the largest possible number of persons in a particular area. This would require that projects planned over a period of time be telescoped within a much shorter period. This again would require that high-ranking projects that were not as yet completely planned or that would require too long to complete would be set to one side and replaced by projects possessing a much lower desirability rating.

Provision of Full Employment versus Efficient Use of Resources. The analysis of priority must include the requirements of government expenditure to preserve a desirable level of prices, consumption, and employment with those of the most efficient utilization of the resources of a nation. The attainment and maintenance of one of these goals may reduce the speed with which another goal is reached. However, it is largely possible to obtain and retain a particular level of economic activity and at the same time utilize available resources in a manner that will bring about in the most direct fashion and in the quickest possible time the attainment of a social minimum of the type Beveridge advocates.

The problem of determining the desirability of particular types of investment expenditures is often simplified and placed on a purely engineering basis—that is, the aims, (1) using the resources in a generally recognized useful manner and, at the same time, (2) putting the largest number of persons to work in the quickest possible period of time, are made the sole basis for decisions regarding a certain expenditure. If this is done, it is possible to make quite specific recommendations. The ability to follow even this simplified basis of priority for government expenditures would be a great improvement over the administrative determination of priority used during the depression of the 1930's.*

A good criterion for the speed with which a project utilizes the resources assigned to it is that of determining the number of months required "to absorb say 90 per cent of the total

*Administrative here means the dominance of largely political and emergency considerations.

man-hours" required to complete the project. The projects listed below are arranged in order of the speed with which, in an engineering sense, they can utilize 90 per cent of the total man-hours. The first type of project listed requires the briefest period of time and the last the longest.

> Water mains
> Dredging
> Grading and drainage
> Flying fields
> Concrete paving
> Bituminous paving
> Sewers and sewage systems
> Locks and dams
> Levee construction
> Post offices and similar buildings
> Hospitals
> Schools*

The speed at which a program will be completed is also determined by the size of the project. Projects of great magnitude require a greater amount of time to consume the same quantity of money than do a number of smaller projects. This is, however, considering only the engineering aspects of the problem; the administrative and legal bottlenecks of a number of smaller projects may more than consume the time saved through greater engineering speed.

A study which has been made of the time patterns of a number of projects initiated and completed by the government during the period of the 1930's indicates that speed of investment is determined more by the size of the project than by the type. The smaller projects of about $100,000 apiece were most useful in utilizing unused labor resources.

As a footnote, in a manner of speaking, to this whole matter of government expenditure of various types aimed at providing a desirable level of economic activity, there are the results of both the British and the American studies regarding the mobility of labor. The definite conclusion of these studies is that labor is much more mobile from one type of employment to another than it is from one geographical area to another.† Government

---

*Taken from *Public Investment and Full Employment* by the International Labour Office.

†For example: "Work and Wage Experience of Willow Run Workers," *Monthly Labor Review*, December, 1945, pp. 1–23.

expenditures must be aimed at providing additional employment to the particular geographical area in which unemployment has developed.

Toward a Yardstick for Public Expenditures. The failure of the Reconstruction Finance Corporation expenditures of the 1930's to bring forth any sharp increase in employment was due to the fact that the sole judgment basis for a grant of Federal funds was: Is the proposed project self-liquidating? Under the P.W.A., applications for Federal funds were considered upon a very different basis. Projects were accepted and granted funds on the basis of (1) the social desirability of the proposed projects, (2) the extent of integration with other projects in the same state or in that area, (3) the swiftness with which the project could be gotten under way and completed, (4) their nearness to an existing center of unemployment, and, of course, (5) upon legal, financial, and engineering soundness. Finally, (6) attention was given to the extent to which the project would remove individuals from the relief rolls.

The Subcommittee on Publicly-Financed Construction Projects of the Canadian Advisory Committee on Reconstruction has suggested the following general standards to be used in the evaluation of projects, in addition to the financial, technical, and legal factors:

(1) Will the project increase directly or indirectly the economic or industrial efficiency of the region concerned?

(2) Has the project special relationship to additional works which may be necessary for the readaptation of industrial plant or other facilities of the district from wartime to peacetime uses?

(3) Is the project concerned with amenities which increase productivity or which help to produce a revenue indirectly (such as highways, waterways, pipelines, or other transport facilities, communication facilities, certain conservation or land drainage measures, etc.)?

(4) Is the project concerned with new construction, additional works, or maintenance or repairs deferred owing to the war?

(5) Will the project contribute to the welfare of the community (e.g., in the form of recreational, educational, cultural, public health facilities, etc.)?

(6) (a) To what extent are locally produced materials and equipment available to the project? (b) Will the project compete with existing local industries?

(7) In what other ways, if any, is the project of particular relevance or importance in this particular area?*

*Taken from *Public Investment and Full Employment* by the International Labour Office, pp. 126–127.

These are pertinent questions which must be answered before any government expenditure project should be undertaken.

The test of which expenditure should be made first in the private economy is usually that of the estimated relative profit-ableness. The public economy does not possess quite such a simple yardstick for the determination of relative desirability of expenditure, or, putting it differently, the greater responsibilities of the public economy do not permit it to use such a simple yardstick.

Various individuals working with this problem of the determination of the priority of government expenditures have developed more or less acceptable criteria.

Professor J. M. Clark believes that (1) time required to complete projects, (2) relation of projects to an organized program, (3) amount of maintenance involved, (4) effect on private expenditures, (5) effect on private capital outlays, (6) proportion of outlay going to direct labor, and (7) relation to future self-maintenance of workers should be the principal factors to be considered in the determination of public expenditures.*

Professor Alvin H. Hansen, in writing of the type of project in which public funds should be invested, stresses those projects that are not self-liquidating in a monetary sense but which "in the nature of the case, cannot be undertaken by private enterprise, yet without them we should not be able to take full advantage of the level of productivity made possible by technical progress."† It is also true that a project that meets the above qualification may also be profitable to the government if the multiplier and the marginal tax rate were high, for under these conditions tax receipts may increase enough to cover the expenditure. It is doubtful that public expenditures should ever be determined upon the basis of their direct benefit to the treasury; rather they always should be made on the basis of their benefit to the community.

It has been stated as a generalization that those projects that prevent things from getting worse should be completed before those projects aimed at the improvement of existing conditions. It is doubtful if this sort of a pessimistic attitude would be particularly helpful.

---

*John Maurice Clark, *Economics of Planning Public Works*, pp. 57–59.

†Alvin H. Hansen, *Economic Policy and Full Employment*, p. 191.

A classification that follows the standard of values held by capitalists of Western Christian nations would give the highest priority to projects essential to life, health, and safety and a very close second to those projects essential to economic activity. More near the end of the list would fall those projects essential to social welfare and, finally, those projects essential for cultural and esthetic development. However, because public expenditures and particularly investments, if they provide utilities falling within the first two categories, are likely to compete with private facilities, public investment is often made in the latter categories while some of the essentials for providing the requirements of the first two categories remain unsatisfied. This could be remedied by closer co-operation between the public and the private economy.

The development of methods for the establishment of government-expenditure priorities is a field of fiscal research that has been only partially explored. If government expenditures continue to expand during periods of normal economic activity and are also used as the most important weapon in the government arsenal of antidepression weapons, then certainly well-tested standards to meet every type of situation should be developed to determine project priority.

CONCLUSION

THE experience gained during the 1930's and World War II points toward a large number of ways in which the administration of government fiscal activities may be improved. This experience, of course, was not available during the great depression of the 1930's, and thus many of the mistakes made were excusable; however, the making of similar correctable errors in the future should not be tolerated. Within this category of correctable errors would certainly fall those weaknesses of fiscal activity during the 1930's that arose from failure to have well-planned projects available and from delays in getting an undertaking started because of various legal bottlenecks.

However, future fiscal activity aimed at a desirable level of prices, consumption, employment, and income distribution will continue to be reduced in effectiveness because of fundamental principles of American government organization and the relative undeveloped state of economic forecasting. The Employment Act of 1946 is an important step forward in improving the portion of fiscal-policy administration that is related to the provision of accurate economic information to the President and Congress.

QUESTIONS AND PROBLEMS

1. Outline the basic requirements for an effective administration of fiscal policy aimed at the provision of desirable economic conditions.

2. How is the Employment Act of 1946 related to the administration of fiscal activity?

3. Do you believe the administrative problems of a flexible tax rate are important? Why?

4. Do you believe a Secretary of National Welfare should be established? Defend your opinion.

5. Define the following terms: (1) reserve shelf, (2) force account, (3) administrative procedure, (4) tertiary effects, (5) process effects.

6. Point out the principal legal bottlenecks in the administration of government expenditure and the manner in which they can be largely overcome.

7. What is the basic difficulty in determining priority of public expenditures related to obtaining desirable economic conditions?

8. What are the good points and the bad points of determining priority on the basis of speed of resource utilization?

9. What has been the development of the Council of Economic Advisers as a Federal government agency?

10. Evaluate the problems involved in the administration of fiscal policy during periods of full employment and peace, full employment and war, and unemployment in a political democracy and in a political dictatorship.

CHAPTER 10

Borrowing and Debt Administration in Relation to the Goals of Fiscal Policy

THIS chapter will analyze the economic impact of two different but closely related government fiscal activities. The first part will analyze the economic impact of increasing and decreasing the size of the national debt, in terms of the effect on prices, consumption, employment, and income distribution. The second part will analyze the economic impact of various ways of managing the refunding operations of a given-sized national debt, again, largely in terms of the effect on prices, consumption, employment, and income distribution.

Sources of Government-Borrowed Funds

The Federal government can go into debt in a number of different ways; to a great extent it is possible for it to choose the manner in which debt will be incurred. The choice of type of debt largely involves selecting the lender or the purchaser of government debt. For purposes of the discussion at this time it is convenient to divide the purchasers of government debt into three broad groups:* (1) commercial banks, (2) wealthy individuals and business concerns unable to find a more lucrative place for the investment of their savings, and (3) individuals or business concerns with funds that would have been spent, if the bonds had not been available, for capital goods or consumer goods. These three divisions of government bondholders overlap, and there are many borderline cases that cannot be placed definitely within either group. However, separation is sufficiently

*These three groups do not include the purchase of debt by government itself. For a more comprehensive study of the different types of Federal government debt, see pp. 46–50.

accurate to provide considerable aid in analyzing the effects of government loans on employment levels.

Bonds purchased by the first group, commercial banks, bring about expansion of purchasing power by the full amount of the loan. Bonds purchased by businesses or individuals possessing savings that would not have been used to purchase additional capital goods or consumer goods have practically the same effect as bonds sold to commercial banks. The difference in the effect would be that interest rates—that is, the cost of investment funds—would increase if the excess of savings seeking private investment were reduced; and as a result of this the amount of private investment would tend to decrease. The price of money, like the price of bananas, goes up when the quantity is reduced. The stimulation would also be decreased if the provision of a safe haven for savings in government bonds were to cause a withdrawal of funds invested in private undertakings. The importance of these countereffects of borrowing from savers would vary, but it is doubtful that the variation would be important under normal conditions.

During periods of government propaganda to reduce capital construction and consumption, or because of high costs or scarcities, the third type of holder of government bonds, those who delayed desired expenditure, becomes important. This group becomes a large holder of debt during periods of war or when unusual conditions similar to those arising from war exist. Debt purchased by this group amounts to a transfer of purchasing power similar to that which takes place upon the payment of taxes. The stimulus to additional employment and the increase in the expenditure stream that arise from the increase in government borrowing from the first two groups does not arise from government borrowing from the third group. However, it is possible that borrowing of the third type would result in employment increase if the shift in demand arising from the transfer of purchasing power were to stimulate new investment.*

Government borrowing generates full employment by increasing aggregate effective demand either through public investment, which does not compete with private investment and in fact provides opportunities for additional private investment (for example, builds highways or schools, or cleans out slum areas), or through the subsidizing of consumption by the man in the street by the payment of subsidies or the lowering of direct taxes. The advantage of finance through borrowing is

*The accelerator effect.

that it does not involve curtailed private investment (unless the rate of interest is forced up) and does not reduce (in most cases) the quantity of private consumption.

Measuring the Debt Expansion

The gross national debt (outstanding debt of the Federal government) was but $19 billion at the end of 1932, and national income at that time was but $58 billion, or 3.1 times the national debt.

Both the national debt and national income increased during the nine-year period prior to our entrance into World War II. By the end of 1941, the national debt was $58 billion, and national income $126 billion, or 2.2 times the national debt.

During the World War II period, or from the end of 1941 to the end of 1945, the national debt reached the high level of $278 billion, and national income $214 billion, or 0.76 of the national debt. Both the national debt and national income increased rapidly during this period, but the expansion of national income was much slower than that of the national debt.

The next five years were years of post war readjustment and some retirement of the national debt while national income climbed.* By the end of 1950 which was before the new Korean War borrowing, but not before some income stimulation due to the war, the national debt was $257 billion, and national income $285 billion, or an increase during the five-year period to 1.1 times the national debt.

During the Korean War and the post-Korean War period, the national debt has again climbed, to $278 billion. National income has also increased rapidly during this period, and in 1954 is about $362 billion, or an increase during the four-year period to 1.3 times the national debt. However, the comparison of the present relationship with that of previous years is becoming less meaningful because of the rapid expansion in state and local government debt. New borrowing by state and local governments was $6.5 billion in 1954, which is 20 per cent greater than the record high set by these governments in their 1953 borrowing.

Another way to measure debt expansion is by considering interest payments as a per cent of national income. When this is

*About $10 billion of the reduction of the national debt was possible because funds borrowed to finance the invasion of Japan were not needed as the result of Japan's early surrender.

done, a slightly different relationship is seen to exist. **Table 10-1** summarizes the relation of national debt and interest payments on national debt to national income.

TABLE 10–1. National debt and interest on national debt as per cent of national income (selected years).

Year	National income as per cent of national debt	Interest on national debt as per cent of national income
1932	310	1.2
1941	220	0.9
1945	76	2,3
1950	110	1.9
1954	130	1.8

Sources: *Annual Report of the Secretary of the Treasury on the State of the Finances* (1953); *The Budget of the United States Government* (1955): *National Income, 1954 Edition.*

The interest payments on the national debt of 1954 are only 0.7 of a percentage point more when measured against national income than they were in 1932. Yet since 1932, the national debt has expanded to fight the great depression of the 1930's and to meet the financial requirements of two wars.

Diagram 10-1 summarizes the size of the net public debt of Federal, local, and state governments from 1929 to 1953. It can be seen that neither the state nor the local governments increased their indebtedness during the depression period of the 1930's while the Federal government increased its indebtedness considerably. On the other hand, since the end of World War II, the indebtedness of the Federal government has changed very little while that of the state and local governments has increased rapidly. A compensatory relationship seems to exist between state and local government debt and Federal government debt—when state and local indebtedness is constant or decreasing, Federal indebtedness is increasing, and vice versa.

EFFECT OF FLUCTUATIONS IN SIZE OF DEBT

BORROWING must be recognized as an important method available to government for acquiring a quantity of funds. The decision whether it is a desirable way to obtain funds needed must be based to a great extent upon price considerations.

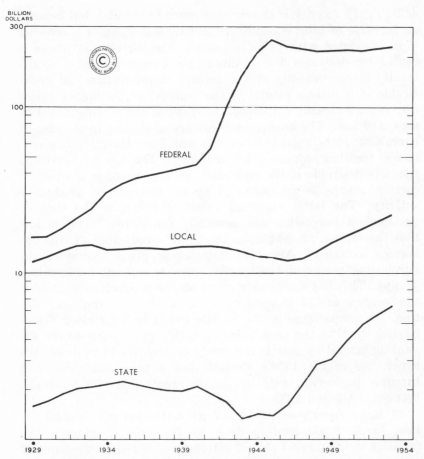

DIAGRAM 10-1. *Net Public Debt, 1929–1953.* SOURCE: *The Conference Board, Road Maps of Industry, No. 987.*

Effect of Borrowing on Prices

The desirability of government borrowing from the banking system is partly determined by the expectations regarding private borrowing. Often large government borrowings of this type produce conditions conducive to expanded private borrowing. The expansion of both public and private borrowings is very likely to bring about a price rise greater than is desirable or is anticipated. It is at this point, or where private borrowing begins to develop, that monetary and banking policy can be most helpful through co-operative action. The action must be aimed at preventing the expansion of money from becoming too great.

When credit expansion is not involved borrowing in itself is deflationary (money is merely exchanged for bonds), but because an increase of total expenditure usually accompanies borrowing it is associated with price increases. The increase in prices is considered desirable if it results in the employment of a significantly larger quantity of the factors of production and undesirable if it merely results in the transfer of, or higher prices for, factors already employed. Borrowing can be considered as a type of tax. The burden or incidence of the tax in the case of borrowing rests upon the persons who have their relative economic position worsened by the levy. The use of borrowed funds is desirable if the worsening of the economic position of certain groups is accompanied by an increase of productive activity. The latter situation exists if prices at the time of government borrowing are generally considered to be so low that the burden of debt upon important production groups has become excessive. Also, the increase of prices decreases the purchasing power of the inactive groups and the unorganized groups. This has a desirable effect on the productive activity if the increase can be stopped before it reaches the jaws of inflation. The experience in the middle 1940's in the United States has shown that the tremendous possible purchasing-power expansion caused by war is not easily controlled. In contrast, the experience of the 1930's showed that a peacetime price rise through borrowing can be readily controlled—for example, between 1937 and 1938.

A large government debt and an active private demand for loan funds would tend to drive up the rate of interest. An increase in the market rate of interest would reduce the value of long-term government bonds and would also increase the interest burden of government debt and intensify the transfer problem. The expenditure of the Federal government for interest in 1954 is about $7 billion annually, and the average rate of interest is less than 2.5 per cent. A doubling of this average rate would increase the interest burden to $14 billion, equal to total Federal expenditures in 1941; it would also reduce the confidence of investors in government securities, for the higher interest rates would markedly reduce the market values of long term government bonds. Under these circumstances, there would be great pressure for the alternative inflation. The rise of interest rates could be prevented by an increase in the quantity of money through reduced restrictions on private credit creation or through direct government action aimed at increasing the quantity of money. Either of these programs under conditions of full employment would raise prices as well as reduce interest rates. The burden of the debt is then transferred to those whose relative purchasing power declines during an inflation—for example, fixed-salary workers, retired pension and annuity recipients, institutions financed by a foundation, and the like. A large government debt tends to increase the desirability of an easy money policy that is likely to mean a degree of inflation or certainly the prevention of deflation.

Relationship Between Borrowing and Wartime Price Rises

The portion of World War II expenditures financed with taxes appears to have been less than would be desirable if postwar inflation were to be avoided. Only about 40 per cent of the cost of the war was obtained from tax receipts. The remaining 60 per cent, or about $190 billion, was obtained by borrowing. Much of this borrowing was done in a way that added to the pressure for higher prices during the war and the postwar period. The savings-bond program, which was the portion of borrowing that had a deflationary effect during the war, resulted in the sale of about $55 billion of bonds between May, 1941, and January, 1946; however, during the same period $10 billion were redeemed. Moreover, the spending of these savings during the postwar period provided a portion of the support of the postwar boom. Over $73 billion of the wartime borrowing was accomplished through the commercial banks and the Federal Reserve Banks. This latter type of borrowing directly increased the size of the monetary stream and was certainly inflationary.

The effects of the great increase in purchasing power through government war finance and the additional increase through the extension of credit to business firms by commercial banks have shown up in the postwar period.* The result has been a tremendous inflationary drive, which has been allowed to largely work its will during the postwar period.

Effect of Borrowing on Consumption and Employment

The impact of government borrowing should be considered to have a two-way stretch effect. Because the government has decided to borrow, the private economy receives income from government expenditures for goods and services. Also because the government has decided to borrow, the private economy is

*Nonbank liquid assets rose from $86 billion in 1940 to $313 billion in 1947, an increase of $227 billion.

not required to transfer funds to the government through the payment of taxes.

Both sides of this two-way stretch will usually increase both consumption and employment. In fact, the increase of either one through the stimulus of government borrowing is likely to be largely dependent upon the other.

If there are factors of production formerly unemployed that become employed because of the expenditure by government of funds borrowed, the quantity of consumption of the nation has expanded as a direct result of this borrowing activity. Under these circumstances, the consumption expenditure of no individual has been directly decreased, while the consumption of the unemployed who are now employed has expanded considerably. Government expenditures financed by borrowing are very likely to bring forth a decline of consumption if completed during periods of full employment. The result under these latter conditions would be inflation and a reduction of the factors of production allocated to the production of consumption goods, and an increase in speculative hoarding of goods.

Inflation that develops from government borrowing during full employment may decrease consumption because (1) wages tend to rise less rapidly than prices during a period of this type, (2) rising prices stimulate investment and the use of an increased portion of the factors of production for capital construction, and (3) rapidly rising prices stimulate hoarding of goods and therefore a reduction of the goods which can be consumed.*

The general basis for favoring deficit government financing is also convincing, and under certain conditions overwhelmingly so. For example, there is little doubt that the use of deficit financing was the desirable government method of providing funds for the full-employment efforts in the United States during the depression of the 1930's. The general conditions that made the use of borrowed funds desirable were: (1) In relation to the income and wealth of the nation, the government debt was small. (2) Investment in the economy was predominantly dependent upon possibilities of private profit; therefore, an increase in the progressive rates of taxes might decrease greatly the incentives for investment. (The policy-makers of a socialist nation would not have to bother with these effects of progressive taxes.) (3) The portion of the national income collected in taxes was not great enough to make a percentage reduction in tax rates

---

*The sale of gold by the government during this period would reduce the quantities of consumption goods held off the market.

significant. (4) Banks and other investment institutions were anxious to find a place to invest their idle funds. (5) The credit of government was very good; this was especially true of the Federal level.

A government policy aimed at full employment financed with borrowings can usually be accomplished with a smaller change in the institutional arrangement and relative power positions of groups within the society. Also, a smaller total outlay is required if the funds are obtained by government borrowing. A dollar raised by taxation will reduce consumption expenditures, investment expenditures, and savings. The portion that each will be decreased is determined by the type of tax used to collect the dollar and the prevailing economic atmosphere. It is very nearly certain, however, that the whole dollar will not be obtained by a reduction in savings. On the other hand, a dollar spent by the government that was obtained by the sale of bonds to commercial banks possessing excess reserves will increase the expenditures of the community by the full amount of the government expenditure.*

Taxation and borrowing, as has been previously mentioned, can also be considered in relation to their effect upon the income stream arising within the private section of the economy. For example, a fiscal policy composed of combining tax reductions with a maintenance of government expenditure would be this type of a program. Under these circumstances, the increased expenditure is expected in the private economy. However, if the government had formerly obtained its revenue from taxes upon current expenditure, the increase in the income stream would arise because funds for government expenditure came from borrowing which did not decrease private expenditure by the amount of their collection. If the tax reductions were made largely upon income received as profits, then the increase in the size of the income stream would be more closely related to a stimulated increase arising from the private section of the economy. If profit possibilities were bright, a considerable increase in private investment would follow. The expectation of this sort of a reaction is dependent upon excess commercial-bank reserves, the possibility of idle savings, and the fact that individuals and firms benefiting will find the inducement sufficiently increased to warrant the risking of their capital.

*An exception would be where the levy of the tax brought forth an increase in consumer expenditures or investment. Consumer expenditures might be increased by a tax if it were expected that a series of tax increases was to be assessed. A tax could increase investments if it were levied only upon large monopolies or upon imports.

The idea that government borrowing could increase the quantity of employment is a recent development. It is, however, difficult to understand why this should have been the case with the many examples of full employment arising from government borrowing during periods of war. Nevertheless, this was the situation when the national leaders began to develop fiscal policy to combat the rising tide of unemployment during the early portion of the 1930's.

In the spring of 1933, with more than 20,000,000 men involuntarily out of employment and with the relief needs of most of the local government units going unfilled, the defeated President Hoover and his Secretary of the Treasury, Ogden Mills, pleaded for a balanced budget. The balanced budget was to be obtained by cutting expenses to the bone and raising additional revenues by the levy of a Federal sales tax. In the light of developments in fiscal policy that have occurred since 1933, it is difficult to imagine that a government could consciously follow this policy of additional deflation during a period when the country was writhing from pain caused by the existing deflation. The strength of the folklore at this period that required this policy is realized when it is recalled that the new president was elected on a platform providing for greater economies than those practiced by President Hoover. The events proved too strong; after a start at government economies, the new administration soon abandoned attempts at budget balancing, and the Federal budget of 1934 provided for expenditures of nearly $10 billion, with about 70 per cent to be raised by borrowing operations. It had been decided, finally, that a patient suffering from loss of blood should not be treated by the withdrawal of more blood but rather should be given a transfusion.

In this unplanned manner, government borrowing was introduced as a fiscal-policy tool to be used in combating unemployment. It took an additional four years after the 1934 budget before deficit spending was definitely related to the bloodletting of oversaving.* A person dies from loss of blood and does not lose blood because he is dying. The same cause-and-effect relationship exists between purchasing power (the blood) and economic activity (the person).

Effect of Borrowing on Income Distribution

The borrowing of funds by the Federal government brings about a change in the type of asset held by individuals and legal

---

*The establishment of this relationship gave birth to the concept of compensatory government expenditures discussed on pp. 157–158.

entities and/or an increase in the total quantity of assets. Because only the relatively rich have assets that can be exchanged for bonds and only the commercial and Federal Reserve Banks can purchase bonds with money manufactured for the purpose, much of the Federal debt is held by these groups. The manner in which the Federal debt is distributed among different owners affects income distribution. Income distribution is affected because the government collects funds for interest payment by the application of the general tax system and makes the expenditure on the basis of the ownership of government debt. Also, debt repayment affects income distribution because the funds for the repayment of debt are largely obtained by collections from current income, and the repayment is merely a change in type of asset and not income. The repayment of debt may also result in the destruction of the money paid in taxes out of current income. This latter result would arise if tax receipts in excess of government purchases of goods` and services were used to retire the debt held by the Federal Reserve Banks or commercial banks (if reserves were abundant).

Holdings of Federal Government Debt and Economic Relationships. Table 10-2, shown below, shows the manner in which the Federal debt was owned at the end of December, 1953, and at the end of December, 1945. The data do not indicate the ownership of debt in the detail which might be desired, but they do provide a basis for considerable analysis.

TABLE 10–2. Ownership of United States government securities, December, 1945, and December, 1953 (par value in millions of dollars).

	Dec. 30, 1953	Dec. 30, 1945
Total amount outstanding.................	275.2	278.7
Held by banks:		
Total.....................................	89.5	115.0
Commercial banks......................	63.6	90.8
Federal Reserve Banks..................	25.9	24.3
Held by nonbank investors:		
Total.....................................	185.7	163.6
Individuals.............................	65.5	64.8
Insurance companies....................	15.8	24.4
Mutual savings banks...................	9.2	10.7
Other corporations and associations........	21.5	30.2
State and local governments.............	12.5	6.5
U.S. Government agencies...............	48.3	27.0
Miscellaneous Investors.................	12.9	9.1

Source: *Treasury Bulletin*, U.S. Treasury Department, May, 1954, p. 28.

The distribution of the debt given in Table 10-2 also shows a considerable difference in the manner in which the debt was held at the end of a war year, December 30, 1945, and on Dec. 30, 1953. Although the National debt at the end of the war was over $3 billion greater than in 1953, the amount held by individuals at this time was over $1 billion less. Also, since the war there has been an absolute decrease in the amount of debt owned by mutual savings banks and a substantial increase in the amount of debt held by United States government agencies. A very important development since the war has been the reduction of the amount of debt held by commercial banks and insurance companies and an increase in the amount of debt held by United States government agencies.*

Debt Ownership by Income Brackets. The Federal debt held by United States government agencies (1954) has been largely purchased by the Old-Age and Survivors Insurance Trust Fund ($2.0 billion), the Unemployment Insurance Trust Fund ($9.2 billion), and the National Service Life Insurance Fund ($6.5 billion). Other large holders of Federal debt are the Federal Deposit Insurance Corporation, government employees' retirement funds, the postal-savings system, and the railroad-retirement account. This $48.3 billion of government debt is therefore owned largely by all employed persons. This portion of the Federal debt is very widely distributed among all income groups. However, the salaries of workers covered by social security are slightly higher than those of uncovered workers. The $12.5 billion of Federal debt owned by local government* represents reserves set aside for employee pension payments or debt repayment. This portion of the debt is largely owned by state and local governments whose citizens have incomes above average.

Federal debt held by mutual savings banks is largely owned by small savers. In December, 1952, the deposits of mutual savings banks totaled $23 billion, and they had more than 15 million depositors. Also, the postal savings banks operated by the Post Office Department receive deposits from only small savers, and the deposits are invested nearly entirely in Federal government bonds. Postal savings banks have over $3 billion of deposits and over 4 million depositors.

*Hedwig Reinhardt, in his article "On the Incidence of Public Debt" in *Social Research*, May, 1945, points out that debt held by banks has a considerably smaller incidence than debt held by individuals and that the burden of the debt is minimized if it remains unfunded (short-term and held by banks). He is thinking largely of the regressive effect of interest payments.

The Federal debt held by insurance companies* ($15.8 billion) and other corporations and associations ($21.5 billion) is largely a part of the assets of persons in the upper income brackets. New savings arising from life-insurance companies have averaged $5 billion a year. Life-insurance companies find it advantageous to invest a portion of these funds in Federal government bonds. Exact data are not available regarding the number of persons and the amount of their holdings in these institutions; however, it can be assumed with considerable certainty that this portion of the Federal debt is largely held by higher-income individuals.† The same generalized statement can be made of the large holdings of Federal bonds by the commercial banks. The bonds held by the Federal Reserve Banks can be considered to be held by all people of the nation.

As a result of a survey conducted by the Board of Governors of the Federal Reserve System, considerable information has been made available regarding the manner in which the Federal debt owned by nonbank individuals is distributed. Table 10-3 presents a summary of these findings.

The data presented in Table 10-3 merely indicate the government debt held directly by individuals and do not include other types of holdings discussed above.

The campaigns to obtain a wide distribution of ownership of government debt were quite successful. In early 1946, 63 per cent of all spending units possessed some Federal government savings bonds; however, by 1954 the percentage had decreased to 37 per cent. A further examination of Table 10-3 reveals that spending units below $3,000 found it very difficult to hold their savings bonds during the postwar period. (About 65 per cent of all spending units received an annual income below $3,000 in 1946.) The percentage of Federal debt held by the lower income brackets was much less in 1954 than it had been in 1946.

Relationship between Debt Ownership and Tax Distribution. The data obtained in this same study of total liquid savings, which is given in Table 4-3 on page 72, show that even when all types of savings accounts are taken into consideration the portion of the Federal debt held by the low-income receivers is quite low.

---

*End of 1953.

†The survey of the Board of Governors of the Federal Reserve System showed that 78% of all families held some life insurance. The life insurance carried by low-income receivers was small; much of this insurance was national service life insurance and therefore does not represent ownership in private insurance-company assets.

TABLE 10–3. United States savings-bond holdings of spending units in early 1954 and 1946, by income groups.

Amounts of savings bonds	All spending units		Percentage distribution of spending units within income groups							
			Under $1,000		$1,000–2,999		$3,000–4,999		$5,000 and over	
	1954	1946	1954	1946	1954	1946	1954	1946	1954	1946
None	63	37	83	69	76	37	62	18	47	9
$1–$499	20	37	12	24	16	45	24	39	23	21
$500–$1,999	11	20	3	6	6	15	10	35	17	40
$2,000 and over	6	6	2	1	2	3	4	8	13	30

Source: *Federal Reserve Bulletin*, July, 1954, p. 699.

The Federal debt, despite high personal incomes and Treasury policy, is still held in such a manner that unless the repayments and carrying charges are made from highly progressive taxes an undesirable redistribution of income will result. The substantial increase in the holdings of debt by United States government agencies since 1945 has been the most important factor in widening the base of ownership of Federal debt. High prices, plus the greater availability of goods, have been the most important factors tending to narrow the portion of Federal debt held by persons in the low income brackets.

Current data of the distribution of Federal taxes between the different income brackets are not available. However, it is certain that all spending units directly pay some taxes to the Federal government; if not the income tax, then the tobacco or some other Federal excise tax. Also, all persons pay Federal taxes indirectly because Federal taxes become a part of the cost of production of all articles—for example, Federal taxes on gasoline, transportation, etc. However some spending units do not own portions of the Federal debt either directly or indirectly.*

The study of the Board of Governors of the Federal Reserve System previously mentioned shows that in 1954, 26 per cent of the spending units possessed no liquid assets—that is, they did not own bonds or stocks nor did they have any savings, checking accounts, or insurance. The same study showed that 63 per cent of all spending units possessed no Federal government bonds. The vast majority of these spending units that did not possess liquid savings or Federal government bonds were in the low income brackets.

Everyone pays Federal taxes, but everyone does not possess a portion of the Federal debt. Also, the persons who do not possess a portion of the Federal debt are in the lower income brackets. Thus the carrying charges of the Federal debt and its repayment are certain to bring about a greater concentration of income in the upper brackets. In 1937, about 40 per cent of all taxes collected in the United States were obtained from persons within income brackets that, in 1954, apparently possessed no government bonds or had only a very small claim to bonds held by the government (see Table 6-1, p. 118).

---

*An exception would be that all persons could be assumed to possess a portion of the debt owned by the Federal government that is not set aside for a particular purpose.

State and Local Government Debt Considerations. The ownership of state and local debt is concentrated in the upper income brackets to an even greater extent than Federal debt or all liquid assets. This greater concentration of ownership arises from the exemption from the Federal income tax of interest income paid on state and local bonds. Because of this tax exemption, state and local governments find it possible to float bond issues at a lower interest cost. These low interest rates are compensated for by the great gain of tax exemption to the persons in the high income brackets; this tax exemption is not of as great value to persons in the lower income bracket, and therefore ownership of state and local bonds tends to be concentrated in the upper income brackets.

State and local debt is today much less important than Federal debt, but it is increasing much more rapidly than the Federal debt. The expansion of state and local debt possesses the undesirable feature of having the possibility of a greater effect upon increasing the concentration of wealth and income than Federal debt. This results because the ownership is concentrated to a greater extent in the hands of the large-income receivers and because the tax system of the states are much less progressive than that of the Federal government.

The tax exemption given interest paid on state and local bonds encourages the purchase of these securities by the rich, which, with the prevailing state and local revenue system, increases the concentration of income. An effect working in the opposite direction, but growing out of this same tax exemption, is that the ability of local governments to obtain funds cheaply encourages the purchase and construction of utilities and other enterprises. Price policy of government-owned and operated enterprises usually favors low-income receivers and reduces the maldistribution of income.

The effect of government debt on income distribution is closely associated with the influence of government debt on prices, consumption, and employment; and most of all with the relationship between government bondholders and government taxpayers. Most of the saving of the nation accomplished by individuals is done by members of the higher income brackets. Therefore, these are the individuals who own Federal bonds either directly, or indirectly through insurance companies and savings banks. However, individuals in the very highest income brackets are more likely to be large owners of common stock and state and municipal bonds.

Another effect of government borrowing related to income distribution is that it will decrease the portion of the economy controlled by private ownership. The reduction of private ownership of basic resources, particularly, reduces the ability of small groups to obtain huge returns through the attainment of varying degrees of monopoly. Also, the rate of return obtained on investment in government bonds is typically less than that received on investments in the private area of the economy. Both of these latter tendencies would reduce the inequality of income distribution.

The government can reduce the income received by capital owners if it decreases the quantity of funds obtained through borrowing and increases the portion obtained through the direct increase of the quantity of money. If the economic conditions are proper for borrowing from the commercial banks, they are also largely correct for the direct increase of the quantity of money.* If deficit financing is carried out through the direct issue of money, the government interest payments are not increased as they would be if the government debt were increased. Therefore, this method of obtaining revenues would further reduce the portion of national income paid to capital owners.

Debt-Repayment Expenditure. If the experience of the past twenty years is an indication of the future, it is not very likely that the national debt will be reduced. However, there have been years when the national debt total has been decreased. Also, some of the effects of debt reduction arise when the new borrowing of the Federal government is less than the increase of the debt held by United States government agencies. When this situation exists, the bookkeeping budget has a surplus or a smaller deficit than the surplus of the cash budget. Debt reduction in both senses or only in the cash sense took place during the postwar period in 1947, 1948, 1949, 1951, and 1952.

Debt repayment expenditures can be made only to those who own government debt that is either callable or maturing. In practice this has not seriously restricted the Treasury when it has wished to make expenditures to reduce the debt holdings of the broad categories of debt ownership given in Table 10-2. The discussion here will be limited to a brief examination of the probable effect of Treasury expenditures to retire the national debt holdings of Federal Reserve Banks, commercial banks, and business corporations.

*See the analysis of government debt on pp. 46–47. The book titled *Financing Full Employment* by John Philip Wernette (Cambridge, Mass., Harvard University Press, 1945) provides an excellent analysis of this problem.

National Debt Owned by Federal Reserve Banks. If the Treasury used its surplus to retire debt held by the Federal Reserve Banks, it would reduce the reserves of commercial banks dollar for dollar with the reduction of commercial bank deposits. Because the commercial banking system is required to keep, and keeps, only a fraction (say 20 per cent) of its deposits as reserves, the dollar-for-dollar reduction of deposits and reserves would cause the commercial banking system to be short of reserves (assuming that excess reserves were at the minimum level). This situation could be met by the commercial banking system either increasing its reserves or decreasing its deposits. It could increase its reserves by borrowing from Federal Reserve Banks or by not purchasing new Federal government securities to replace those owned but maturing.

The commercial banking system is likely to wish to avoid both these methods of relieving its reserve shortage. There is a strong bank-management tradition opposing commercial banks being in debt to the central bank (Federal Reserve Banks in the United States). The commercial banking system may be unwilling to reduce its liquidity, which would result if it cut its holdings of government securities. Therefore, pressure will develop in the management of commercial banks to reduce lending activity. The banks will turn down some loan requests that would have been granted if the Treasury had not used its budget surplus to retire debt owned by the Federal Reserve Banks. The effect of less lending by the commercial banks will be a cut back in spending, particularly investment-type spending.

There is another facet to the Treasury using its revenues to retire debt, and particularly debt owned by the Federal Reserve Banks. The revenues of the Treasury were received from businesses and households who would have used a smaller or larger portion of their funds to purchase goods and services if they had not been required to pay taxes. When the Treasury uses its revenues to retire debt, it is not directly buying goods and services. Therefore, debt retirement reduces the funds bidding for goods and services. As a result, if everything else remains unchanged, Treasury expenditures to retire debt will reduce the national income.

National Debt Owned by Commercial Banks. If the Treasury uses its surplus to retire debt owned by commercial banks, the deposits of the commercial banking system will be reduced. This will cause the system to have free reserves. The management of each commercial bank will make an effort to use these reserves, i.e., make more loans or buy additional securities.

This effort to use these reserves can have a number of results, two of which will be briefly, and necessarily incompletely, summarized:

1. Loans to individuals and businesses would be increased by the amount that the Treasury reduced its debt. This would mean no decrease, and very likely an increase, of expenditures (national income) as a result of the debt retirement.

2. Securities held in commercial bank portfolios would be increased, but because suitable new securities are not available, prices of securities rise and the released reserves are used up in rising security prices. This would, at least in the first round, cause national income to fall by the amount of the debt retirement.

National Debt Not Owned by Banks. Finally, if the Treasury uses its surplus to retire debt owned by non-bank corporations and others, the deposits of those who had held debt increase. The deposit increase of former debt owners is equal to the deposit decrease of those from whom that portion of tax receipts used to retire debt was received. The effect of this on national income depends on how those who paid the taxes would have used their deposits if they had not paid the taxes and how the spending actions of those who now have deposits instead of government securities are changed by this increase in the liquidity of their assets. Neither the deposits nor the reserves of the commercial banking system are directly affected by this type of debt reduction; therefore, possible actions of the banking system need not be considered.

This brief analysis of a Federal government expenditure to retire its debt considers only a few of the economic results. However, the analyses are sufficiently complete to conclude that a Federal government expenditure to retire its debt is very likely to reduce prices, consumption, and employment and to lessen the likelihood that the income distribution will assist in preserving favorable economic conditions.

THE ADMINISTRATION OF THE NATIONAL DEBT

THE very large Federal government debt of $278 billion (1955) makes government debt-administration activity very important. This is a typical postwar experience, but it is even more important this time because the per-capita debt is greater than ever before and also because our dominant position in the world makes it very important that the value of United States government securities be maintained. Also, the debt must be effectively utilized along with other economic relationships to maintain the prosperity of the United States economy. A badly administered debt can weaken the basis of United States prosperity and prestige.

General Relationships

A government can carry a large debt with much greater ease if the value of the unit in which the debt is quoted decreases. As a result, if a large government debt exists there will be a constant pressure (temptation may be a better word) upon government to maintain prices at a high level and to favor a rising general level of prices. If prices should begin to fall, it would be more difficult to obtain in taxes the funds required to make interest payments, debt repayment would become impossible, but refunding of the maturing parts of the debt would be easier.

Under nearly all circumstances when the debt of government is being increased there will be an upward pressure on prices; when the debt is being reduced, a downward pressure is exerted. This relationship is desirable if debt is being increased at a period when the general price level is considered to be too low and decreased when prices are generally believed to be too high.

In the past, debt creation and reduction has not worked too successfully in the stabilization of prices. Debt increase has been frequently determined by a crisis so serious—for example war—that the undesirable effect upon prices has been outweighed by the immediate requirement of quickly marshaling under government control the productive resources of the nation. However, governments have been much less prone to reduce debt, and thus bring about additional deflationary pressure, when the general level of prices has been too low. The act of debt reduction is a much more voluntary act of government than is the act of debt increase. The very fact of falling prices increases the difficulty of bringing about any important debt reduction through the levy of taxes. Debt policy is apt to be fiscally sounder during periods of falling prices than during periods of rising prices.

An important portion of the administration of a government fiscal policy aimed at obtaining desirable economic conditions is related to the manner in which the public debt is divided among the different holders. This, in turn, is to a great extent related to the rate of interest, maturity date, negotiability, and, in the past, to the treatment of interest for income-tax purposes and conversion rights. Also, the ability of the Treasury to sell certain quantities of securities at different prices (rates of interest) is determined by prior preparation of the money market by the Federal Reserve System.

The borrowing policies followed by the Treasury during the World War II period were very successful. Their success was largely the result of the development of government borrowing tools during World War I and the depression period of the 1930's. The Federal Treasury's efficient use of a "cheap money policy" to reduce the rate of interest enabled the Federal government to obtain huge quantities of borrowed funds at low rates of interest without resorting to the pressure methods adopted during World War I.

Because the typical debt obligation runs for a period of time, the effects of the manner in which the government sells its bonds, notes, and certificates must be carefully considered in relation to expected future conditions.* The ability to take into consideration future conditions is a first requirement of desirable fiscal policy as related to debt administration. This requirement means that the expected effects of the various ways in which the debt could be floated must be carefully correlated with the best estimates of future conditions.

Indirect Effects of Debt Management

One writer recently commenting upon the importance of debt management states:

> The way in which the debt is managed, and the success achieved, will directly affect social security, federal grants-in-aid, banking legislation, the conservation program, and many other matters of public policy that the country has been accustomed to determine with little reference to their effects upon federal finances.†

Another analyst of the effects of the debt sees it also important in affecting the private sector of the economy. The church,

*See Donald B. Woodward, "Public Debt and Institutions," *American Economic Review*, vol. 37, May, 1947, pp. 157–191.

†Charles Cortez Abbott, *Management of the Federal Debt*, p. 3.

family, and business organizations will be unavoidably affected by the huge Federal debt—and, according to this analysis, largely undesirably.*

The administration of the debt is accomplished by the Treasury with a good deal of assistance furnished by the Federal Reserve System. It would perhaps be as accurate as most generalizations to say that the most important function of the Federal Reserve System for some time to come will be the role that it plays in aiding the Treasury in its work of administering the Federal debt.

General Debt-Management Policy

The beginning of an effective postwar administration program was established when the Treasury decided to compartmentalize the debt. The various types of issues were deliberately determined in recognition of the existing investment institutions, of the broader needs of the economy, and of the differing needs of the many classes of investors.† Desirable debt administration of the future requires that the existing compartmentalization be continually examined to determine whether it still meets the needs of our institutions, investors, and the broader needs of the economy. Because the various types of issues into which the government debt is divided determine to a great extent the effects, it would be undesirable if any particular distribution should become permanent. If economic conditions change, it would be desirable for the debt to affect the economy differently, also.

At present, the composition of the Federal debt can be changed by the Treasury without first obtaining Congressional approval. Congress only sets the debt ceiling and the conditions included in savings bonds contracts. This situation is quite different from that existing in the levy of taxes. The present Treasury freedom in the administration of the debt if transferred to the tax field would mean that Congress would set the maximum amount that could be raised by taxes and the tax bases, with the treasury setting the tax rates.

This great administrative freedom in debt management brings with it great responsibilities. The Treasury in its administration of debt policy must consider two general points of view regarding desirable aims of a debt policy. One school of thought, which has been associated with the late Professor

*See Donald B. Woodward, "Public Debt and Institutions," pp. 157–191.

†Lawrence H. Seltzer, "The Public Debt — Discussion," *American Economic Review*, vol. 37, May, 1947, p. 193.

Simons of the University of Chicago, holds that the Federal debt should be managed in a way that minimizes its effect on the economy.* The other school of thought favors using the various facets of debt management to the utmost in affecting the economy in the manner desired. It is quite improbable that Federal government, committed as it is to maximize purchasing power by the Employment Act of 1946, will fail to make use of the help that debt-management policies can provide.

Although the way in which the debt will be managed can be largely determined without consulting Congress and although the Treasury officials can theoretically do just about as they wish, the amount of freedom possessed by the Treasury is definitely limited by attitudes toward Federal debt possessed by the contemplated debtholders. In the administration of a tax program, individuals can be forced to co-operate with the provisions of the law; and funds can be obtained from certain individuals and groups whether they do or do not wish to pay. Debt, however, is largely held by persons and artificial entities as a result of a voluntary action.

The insurance companies have found government bonds having a maturity date of over ten years to be particularly desirable. Over two-thirds of the bonds held by insurance companies are of this type. The commercial banks prefer short-term bonds, and about one-half of their holdings are of bonds maturing in less than a year. Individuals like small-denomination, non-marketable, high-interest securities, and four-fifths of the government bonds held by individuals are of this type. These preferences are important in determining the types of issues to offer to obtain sufficient purchasers and also are basic when the administrative problems surrounding debt renewal are considered.†

The Treasury, in order to have the Federal debt broken up into certain types of issues, must convince individuals that they should hold Federal debt in that particular form. In order to accomplish this, the Treasury must convince the prospective holder that government-debt purchase is the best possible use of funds. The ability of the Treasury to do this is determined largely by the terms offered in the debt certificate, that is, terms meeting preferences of prospective buyers. In addition, the

*Henry C. Simons, "On Debt Policy," *The Journal of Political Economy*, vol. 52, no. 4, December, 1944, p. 357.

†Seymour E. Harris, *The National Debt and the New Economics*, Table 38, p. 253.

Treasury may take other types of direct action or it may induce the Federal Reserve System to act in a particular manner. All three of these types of action will also affect commercial-bank policy. The latter two types of Treasury activity are frequently referred to as an easy or tight money policy.

Debt-management policy could be much more influential if there were no government goals related to debt other than making effective use of it as a fiscal-policy tool aimed at maintaining the proper level of economic activity. There is, however, no prospect that such will ever be the case.

A Treasury policy aimed at getting a substantially larger portion of the debt into the hands of small savers would require a large increase in the interest rate of the debt and strict restrictions against the purchase of government issues by high-income-bracket individuals and business concerns. This policy, however, would not be sufficient to transfer a significant portion of the debt to the masses. In addition, it might be necessary to increase incomes of large groups and restrict the quantity of goods which they could purchase. Obviously, this latter development is outside the administrative powers possessed by the Treasury, and certainly Congress would never pass high minimum-wage legislation or commodity-rationing legislation just to make possible the distribution of the Federal debt among a larger number of persons. The best the Treasury will be able to do is to make different types of issues attractive within rather definite limits to the different segments of the economy.

BASIC DEBT-MANAGEMENT PROBLEM

WHEN the country is enjoying boom conditions, and there is fear that prices will rise too high, the Treasury would like to use its refunding operations (securities issued to replace those maturing) to sell long-term securities to income receivers and private owners of liquid assets. But this is the very time when there are many profitable opportunities for private investment, and the rather meager returns to be expected from a government security are not attractive. Further, a government security does not provide protection against loss of purchasing power during a price rise. Therefore, the efforts of the Treasury to sell savings bonds to individuals, and long-term bonds to insurance companies, mutual savings banks, savings and loan associations, and the like are likely to have little success. During the upswing of the business cycle, these groups are more likely to be attempting to reduce their holdings of governments rather than attempting to increase them.

On the other hand, when the economy is on the downward side of the business cycle, income receivers and asset holders find an investment in governments attractive. But this is the period when the Treasury would prefer that more of the national debt be held with credit created by the commercial banking system. And it would also prefer that individuals, insurance companies, mutual savings banks, savings and loan associations, and the like invest their funds in new plant and equipment, houses, and state and local government securities.

Examples in the recent past of the failure of the national debt to work toward more stable economic conditions at a high level follow.

During the three months prior to the Korean War, E-bond redemptions were $668 million, and purchases $909 million. This was a period of deflationary tendencies in the economy.

During the first three months of the Korean War, E-bond redemptions totaled $1,038 million, and new purchases $832 million. This was a period of strong inflationary pressures.

During the normal to deflationary period, there was a net purchase of $241 million of E-bonds. During the highly inflationary period, there was a net redemption of $206 million of E-bonds. This same unstabilizing tendency became apparent again in 1953 and 1954 when the economy was experiencing deflationary pressures. Savings bond sales rose and redemptions fell.

In the Spring of 1953, the inflationary pressures of the economy were strong and the Treasury determined to market a security maturing in 20 years. In order to sell a long-term security at this time, it was necessary that the Treasury offer a relatively high interest rate—$3\frac{1}{4}$ per cent. Within a few months of its sale investment began to decline, and deflationary pressures became apparent. To many economic commentators, the decline of business activity was due to the Treasury's absorption of savings by the security offering it had made in the Spring of the year.

At the time this is being written, inflationary signs have returned. The inflation is especially evident in the rising prices of common stocks. Again the Treasury's debt-management policy is being criticized, for during the past year, in order to combat the deflation, it has been offering securities which have been purchased largely with commercial bank credit.

It is difficult indeed to adopt a national debt-management policy which will be free of criticism. But as long as the criticism is constructive, it is helpful to those having this thankless job which could always be done better by second-guessers. The types of comments which are not helpful are those which conclude that the Treasury should abandon its attempts to improve economic conditions by way of its method of debt management.

DEBT-MANAGEMENT PROPOSALS

SUGGESTIONS to improve the management of the national debt have been offered by the informed and the uninformed. Two lengthy Congressional Hearings, one headed by Senator Paul H. Douglas of Illinois (1950) and the other by Congressman Wright Patman of Texas (1952) have been held to consider possibilities for improving national debt management.* The concensus of the testimony at both hearings was favorable to the efforts made by the Treasury with the help of the Federal Reserve System to manage the national debt with the end in view of assisting to achieve the goals of the Employment Act of 1946.†

Use of Consols

The word "consol," taken from the "British Consols," is used to designate a perpetual bond. Some economists recommend that all Federal government debt be issued in the form of consols. Under this scheme refunding issues would never have to be sold, and the change of the market value of the securities with a change of the interest rate would be maximized.

If the government wished to spend more than it received as revenues and was unwilling or unable to borrow through the sale of consols, it would simply print the necessary money.

The advantage of the scheme as seen by its advocates is that money would be clearly distinguished from debt, and the confusion of "issuing moneys, practically moneys, and near-moneys under other names"‡ could be avoided. Those favoring this administrative procedure would transfer all outstanding debt issues into money or consols as rapidly as the maturity dates of debt outstanding permit.

---

*Senate Document No. 129, 81st Congress, 2d Session; and Senate Document No. 123, 82nd Congress, 2d Session.

†See pp. 170–173.

‡Henry Simons, *Economic Policy for a Free Society* (Chicago, University of Chicago Press, 1948), pp. 220–230.

Use of a Purchasing-Power Savings Bond

A purchasing-power savings bond is a savings bond with an added provision which would assure that its purchasing power at maturity would be equal to the purchasing power of the money used to purchase it when it was issued. The redemptions of this type of security would tend to be high when a fall of the price level was expected and low when a price rise was expected.

The purchasing-power savings bonds has the advantage, its advocates claim, that savers, while acting in their own best interests, would also be acting to stabilize national income. They would tend to increase their holdings of national debt during inflation and reduce them during deflation. This, of course, would be the reverse of the way in which the size of the holdings of savings bonds now being sold changes.*

Tax-Exempt Bonds

Prior to 1942 the interest paid to holders of Federal debt, along with that paid to holders of state and local government securities, was commonly exempt from all income taxes. Since 1942 the interest received by owners of government securities issued since that date has been taxable income. The recommendation has been made that the Treasury be permitted to use its discretion in determining whether or not a new security issue should be tax exempt.

If the recommendation were adopted, its advocates believe that the Treasury would be able to attract and hold funds during an inflation period without offering the high rate of interest which was necessary, for example, in the Spring of 1953. Also, if the country is entering into a war inflation period with its concomitant high taxes, those owning tax exempts are more likely to hold them than are those owning taxables. This stabilizing effect is expected because tax exemption becomes more valuable with higher tax rates.

CONCLUSION

BORROWING and debt-management activities of the Federal government are very closely associated with the functioning of the monetary system. This close association arises because the

*See Sumner Slichter, "Curb Inflation with Purchasing Power Bond," *Commercial and Financial Chronical*, March 15, 1951, p. 1121; and Clark Warburton, "A Hedge Against Inflation," *Political Science Quarterly*, March, 1952, pp. 14–17.

Federal government has the power to print or create money. Therefore, it issues debt obligations and contracts to pay interest to the holders of these obligations only because, for one reason or another, it has decided not to increase directly the money supply.

Involved in the decision to borrow by any level of government are the reasons why it spends more than it collects in taxes. Mixed into spending and taxing decisions are many political, psychological, and economic considerations entwined so completely that separation is almost impossible. However, there is little doubt that a modern government will always give much more than passing consideration to the effects on the whole economy of borrowing, debt repayment, and administration of the debt outstanding.

QUESTIONS AND PROBLEMS

1. From whom does the government borrow? Why does the source from whom the government decides to borrow make a difference?

2. Compare the economic effects of compulsory government borrowing and tax payments.

3. In what ways other than those in this chapter could the growth of the national debt be shown. Using the *Statistical Abstract of the United States* or some other source of data, use one of your bases to show the trend of the growth of the national debt.

4. Why might a larger Federal government debt be preferred to a larger state and local government debt. On what basis could the reverse position be justified?

5. How does government borrowing increase prices and employment?

6. Make an economic analysis of the change in the ownership of the national debt between 1945 and 1954. If the national debt were to remain at approximately the same size until 1963, what additional shifts would you expect in its ownership? Why? If it were to increase by $40 billion within a two-year period, how would you expect the ownership of the additional $40 billion to be distributed? Why?

7. Explain the different effects to be expected from the Treasury repaying debt owned by the Federal Reserve Banks, commercial banks, and others. Give the "why" in each case.

8. How would the issue of consols, purchasing-power savings bonds, and Federal tax-exempt securities tend to assist the Treasury in meeting its debt-management goals?

CHAPTER 11

The Government's Budget Balance and the Determinants of National Income

THIS, the last chapter of this book, is aimed at presenting what is called the aggregate, or the macroeconomic, or the national income, or perhaps most accurately, the monetary approach to fiscal policy. As the discussion proceeds, it will become apparent why each of these designations possesses a certain amount of appropriateness.

BALANCED BUDGET

MOST of the chapter is concerned with the effect of a government deficit on the private economy's two components of national income—consumption and investment. However, the possibilities of affecting national income within the framework of a balanced budget are always in the wings. To bring them out onto the stage for a moment, they are included as the prologue— to continue the metaphor of the theater—of the discussion of the monetary approach to fiscal policy.

Balanced Budget Theorem

One widely publicized relationship between national income and an increase in government expenditures which is equal to an increase in revenues bears the label "balanced budget theorem." This theorem states that any increase in government expenditures which is balanced with a tax increase has a multiplier of one. It does not matter what type of expenditure is made or what type of government revenue is used. However, no change in the propensity to consume and no change in the willingness of private investors to absorb savings is assumed. This increase of national income is equal to a balanced budget expansion be-

219

cause private disposable income is not decreased as a result of the levy of the tax. Therefore, the expenditures of the private economy remain constant while the total expenditures, or national income increase by the amount spent by government.

Private expenditures do not decrease by the amount of the tax because private incomes are also increased by the amount of the tax. That is, the private income decrease caused by the tax is made up by the increase of private income caused by the government expenditures.

The analysis thus far does not demonstrate a multiplier of one; it demonstrates only that income is not changed. To complete the analysis, the increased expenditures of the government must be included. This increase in government expenditures is, of course, equal to the increase in government revenues; and when it is added to national income, the multiplier turns out to be exactly one. The increase in income will be in real terms if employable unemployed factors exist.

The simple relationship assumed to exist by this theorem can be shown by still pictures at various stages of an expenditure process in constant movement.

Prior to the balanced budget expenditure increase of 15:

$$\text{I. } 100 \text{ (C)} + 20 \text{ (I)} + 20 \text{ (G)} = 140 \text{ (Y)}$$

After the tax increase of 15 and after the government expenditure but before this expenditure becomes a part of private income:

$$\text{II. } 90 \text{ (C)} + 15 \text{ (I)} + 35 \text{ (G)} = 140 \text{ (Y)}$$

After the tax and government expenditure increase of 15 becomes a part of private income:

$$\text{III. } 100 \text{ (C)} + 20 \text{ (I)} + 35 \text{ (G)} = 155 \text{ (Y)}$$

Government expenditures have increased by 15, and national income has increased by 15. According to the theorem, the picture which catches government expenditures after having been made but before being received (the relationship shown in II) is unreal, but the picture which catches government expenditures after having been made and after having been received (the relationship shown in III) gives a useful idea of the effect of government expenditures financed with taxes. In other words, the theorem assumes that government revenue collections and expenditures are made at the same time as the expenditures of the private economy, the disposable income of which has not changed because of an equal income and tax increase.

The balanced budget theorem in this form has a bit of the magical about it. The magic is related to the timing of expenditures made by the private and public economies. Revenues collected and spent by the private economy are assumed to be made in a constant period of time, whether or not government collections and expenditures are superimposed on them. The theorem thus simply states a particular way in which the speed of the expenditure of money could be increased.

Variants of the Balanced Budget Theorem

Sometimes the balanced budget theorem terminology is used to refer to a change in the average propensity to consume when government revenues and expenditures are increased. Under this method of considering a balanced government revenue and expenditure increase, the amount of the expansion of national income resulting from the increase is uncertain, but that there is an increase is certain.

The reasoning that an increase is certain is that the government has a propensity to consume of 100 per cent whereas government revenues are collected from sources which have a propensity to consume of less than 100 per cent. The cigarette tax is an example of a revenue source which is to a large extent paid by persons who would have spent the money paid as tax for consumption purposes if the tax had not been collected. However, some of the cigarette tax is paid by persons who would have increased their savings if the tax had not been collected. The assumption is realistic and is used as the principal underpinning for the next step, which is that an increase in government expenditures increases the average propensity to consume.

If the average propensity to consume is increased, the multiplier effect with all expenditures is also increased. A large multiplier effect with all other factors remaining constant causes an increase of national income.

Another frequent interpretation of the way in which a balanced increase of government revenues and expenditures increases national income is based on the assumption that a portion of the saving arising in the private economy will not be used for investment and that therefore (using the period type of analysis) the national income of the next period will be reduced unless these savings are reduced. These savings can be reduced by increasing taxes and expenditures by an equal amount, for all common taxes will be paid at least in part from savings.

The final way in which an equal government revenue and expenditure increase can increase national income involves the expansion of bank credit. It is assumed that all the income of the private economy is being promptly spent for consumption, investment and taxes. Under these circumstances the revenues of the government are increased, and the government spends its increased revenues in such a way that they have the same effect on national income as when spent by the private economy. However, because of the additional revenue payments to the government, the private economy must borrow from the commercial banks to maintain its desired level of consumption and investment. These loans cause an expansion of the money supply and an increase of national income if everything else remains constant.

Under all these different groups of assumptions, the national income is increased through an increase of government expenditures completely financed with revenues. The increase in national income would be in real terms if unemployed labor were put to work, or if the hours of work were increased, or if new people could be induced to enter the labor force. The increase in national income would result from inflation if labor were already fully employed.*

UNBALANCED BUDGET

THE budget, as you have learned, can be out of balance and the deficit covered in such a way that prices are not likely to increase. However, a government deficit always tends to put an upward pressure on prices. The following analyses assume that a government deficit results in a situation approximately equivalent to an increase in the money supply.

This expanded liquidity is considered in regard to its effect on national income. Because national income is the sum of investment, consumption, and government expenditures, the reasons why consumption, investment, and government expenditures are large or small are also the reasons why national income is high or low. The whole is equal to the sum of its parts.

Consumption

The largest component of national income is consumption, and because government is being considered separately, these

*This cause of inflation bears little resemblance to that expected by Colin Clark, but both do arise from taxes and government expenditures.

consumption expenditures consist almost entirely of household expenditures. The size of consumption expenditures made by households is determined by how rich the households are, the needs of the family as seen by the family itself, the new types of goods being offered, expected price trends, and the like. Aggregate fiscal actions of the government can affect consumption, and therefore the size of consumer expenditures, largely by making households more or less rich. Fiscal actions can also affect consumer expenditures by affecting prices of particular commodities and the general price level. Our analysis here will show that the relation between consumer expenditures and the general price level is of the same nature as the relationship between how rich consumers are and their consumption expenditures. The relationship between consumption expenditures and the level of particular prices affected by fiscal actions of government have been considered (Chapter 5 & 7), and the remaining great variety of factors affecting consumption are related to fiscal actions so indirectly that they cannot be considered. This leaves for analysis here a single relationship, that between the affluence of consumers and their consumption expenditures.

Consumers are rich if their assets are of much greater value than their liabilities and if their expected income is large and certain. Consumers are poor if their assets are of little greater value than their liabilities, or perhaps even less, and if their expected income is small and uncertain.

By borrowing the money they spend, governments can increase the assets, without increasing the liabilities, of households. After this type of transaction is completed, households own government securities directly, or indirectly through a financial institution, which they previously did not own; and they have not acquired a compensating liability. The government acquires the liability, i.e., owes the debt; but households do not consider the debt of the government when they total their assets and liabilities. Also, the government did not reduce the income of householders as it would have if it had levied additional taxes on their income. Therefore, after this transaction, consumers are richer because their assets have increased and their income has not decreased.

The increase of private debt is not as effective in making households richer as is the increase of government debt for the simple reason that all assets arising from private debt (bonds, mortgages, and perhaps demand deposits) are liabilities, either directly or indirectly, of other households, whereas those arising from government debt are not. Private debt makes households richer because it increases their income; whereas, government debt increases both the income and the net assets of households.

Net assets of households are increased when the Federal government issues money and when any level of government increases its indebtedness. An increase in money and/or government debt also increases income; and if the quantity of goods on the market have not increased at least as rapidly, prices will rise. On the other hand, a decrease in money and/or government debt (net assets) decreases income; and if the quantity of goods on the market for some reason have not decreased at least as rapidly, prices will decrease. This, then, is the relationship between the general price level and the fiscal actions of government. This relationship is important to our consideration here because the movement of the general price level affects the volume of consumption.

If national income were considered too low to provide a sufficiently high level of employment and if it were decided to use fiscal acts to increase consumption so that national income would be larger, the above analysis provides a framework for action.

The relationships which have been discussed, between net assets, prices, and income, on the one hand, and the level of consumption, on the other, are shown by Diagram 11-1. The vertical axis is an index of net assets, prices, and income in money terms, and the horizontal axis is an index of all consumption in real terms.

The line DD' is drawn so as to equate changes in the index of net assets, prices, and income in money terms with changes in the index of consumption. The line DD' intersects neither the vertical nor the horizontal axis because, of course, neither index could ever drop to zero. When the index of net assets, prices, and income increases from M to M', consumption increases from C to C'. The increase of the consumption index is the greater because it is assumed that resources are unemployed; and under this assumption, the net assets and income portions, but not the price portion, of the index measured on the vertical axis increase.

When fiscal actions have caused the index measured on the vertical axis to move from M' to M'', the consumption index increase is much less than that of the index of net assets, prices, and income, because most of the resources which could have been used to increase consumption are already in use. Furthermore, all elements of the index measured on the vertical axis, and

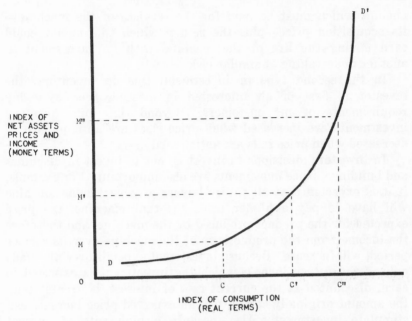

DIAGRAM 11–1. Relation of consumption in real terms to
an index of net assets, prices, and income in money terms.

especially prices and income, would be moving up. Finally, at this point the change of the index measured on the vertical axis would cause resources to flow into investment and government expenditures as well as into household consumption expenditures.

Investment

Investment expenditures, the second component of national income, can also be affected by monetary type fiscal actions. The quantity of investment is determined by the return expected from funds used to produce more goods or to hold goods. The first type of investment, to produce more goods, is that made in machines and buildings. The second, to hold goods, is that made in inventory. Because government is being considered separately, investment does not include expenditures to build government-owned structures or to hold government inventories.

In the first type of investment, that in machines and buildings, the investor is interested in the length of time for which the machine, for example, will be used—its service period. He is interested in the market value of the machine's productivity over this period. And he is also interested in comparing the amount which must be paid for the services of the machine—its acquisition price—plus the return which this money could earn during the life of the machine with an investment in another undertaking of similar risk.

In the second type of investment, that in inventory, the investor is first of all interested in meeting the day-to-day requirements of his customers. Beyond this, his inventory investments are increased when price rises are anticipated and decreased when price falls are anticipated.

In investors' decisions to invest or not to invest in machines and buildings, price movements are also important. For example, if it is expected that all future buyers of a particular machine will have to pay a higher price for that machine, the price expected for the product produced by the machine, and therefore the income from the productivity of the machine over its service period, will increase. Because investment expenditures are made only if the future income which the investment is expected to earn, discounted at the current rate of interest, is greater than the amount originally committed, an expected price increase can stimulate investment. Also, because a high rate of current interest decreases the value of all future income below what it would have been at a low rate of interest, a high rate of interest can discourage investment. Future expectations of rising prices and current low rates of interest are therefore very stimulating to investment.

The difference between the total expected money return from an investment during its life and the total money expenditure (excluding the interest cost) is the prospective yield of an investment. When this prospective yield of an investment is divided by the number of years of its life, and this quotient is divided by the amount invested, the result is the marginal efficiency of capital ratio. This marginal efficiency of capital ratio must be greater than the interest rate if investment is to take place. For example, assume that a capital good costs $1,000, that it can be used for ten years, and that its prospective yield is $2,000. The marginal efficiency of capital ratio is calculated as follows:

$2,000—$1,000=$1,000—the total prospective yield of the
investment

$1,000÷10=$100—the yearly prospective yield of the
investment

$100÷$1,000=   .10, or 10%—the marginal efficiency of
capital ratio

Under these conditions the investment would be made at a rate of interest up to 10 per cent.

The ability of an investor to sell the product of his investment for a price high enough to make his investment worthwhile is determined by the willingness of consumers to purchase a sufficiently large quantity of the product of the investment at a sufficiently high price. As described in the discussion of consumption, the willingness of consumers to purchase is determined by their richness. Their richness is decreased if the taxes they pay are increased and increased if the taxes they pay are decreased. Because of these relationships, increased tax collections decrease investment, and decreased collections increase investment.

One other point must be mentioned, which is really only a reminder of what has already been said. An increase in the richness of consumers causes prices to rise, and a decrease in the richness of consumers causes prices to fall. Therefore, tax collection expectations affect price expectations; the expectation of higher taxes reduces price rise expectations. Also, as discussed previously, additional tax cuts of certain types can be particularly encouraging to investment, and tax increases of certain types can be particularly discouraging to investment.

A low interest rate increases investment expenditures. An expectation of rising prices increases investment expenditures. An expectation of a steadily increasing willingness to purchase the product of the investment increases investment. The reverse of these conditions reduce investment. These general relationships are illustrated in Diagram 11-2.

In Diagram 11-2 the vertical axis shows the interest rate as a percent of a change in the price index. At point R the rate of interest is equal to the annual percentage price increase, while at point S the rate of interest is 1.5 times the annual percentage price increase. The closer to zero on the vertical axis, the smaller is the interest rate as a percent of the increase in the price index.

The horizontal axis measures the quantity of investment in real terms. It shows, therefore, the number of machines or the number of buildings and inventories as quantities; i.e., it shows the amount of investment in constant prices.

Line B shows the quantity of investment that would be made with different ratios of percentage price increases to the interest rate. Line C shows the same relationship if there were a general decrease of taxes, and line A shows the same relationship if there were a general increase of taxes. With all other factors re-

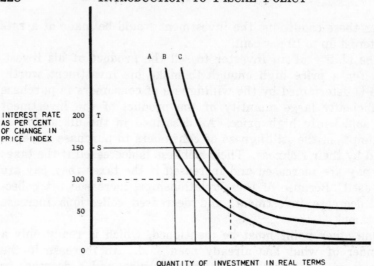

INTEREST RATE
AS PER CENT
OF CHANGE IN
PRICE INDEX

QUANTITY OF INVESTMENT IN REAL TERMS

DIAGRAM 11-2. Relation of investment in real terms to interest rate as percent of change in price index and level of taxation.

maining unchanged, an increase in taxes will always tend to decrease investment, and a decrease in taxes will always tend to increase investment.

Fiscal actions operating within the framework of this analysis could increase investment expenditures by reducing the level of taxes, by stimulating prices, and by lowering the interest rate. The investment-decreasing tendency of high interest rates could be counteracted by price rises. Also, lower taxes could avoid the necessity of higher prices or lower interest rates to reach a desired level of private investment.

It is sometimes said that rising prices are not stimulating to investment because the price that must be paid for a new machine to replace the old one will have risen by the same percentage as the price of the product produced by the machine. This argument appears reasonable, but it neglects a very important factor. The investor is only obligated to repay to the lender the number of dollars invested in the machine when prices were at their lower level, and the new higher price only affects his willingness and ability to invest in this later period.

This relationship can be seen more clearly when it is stripped of unnecessary appendages, and the simple case of a businessman investing in a new machine with the proceeds of a term loan from a commercial bank or of a loan from an insurance company is considered.

For our example it is assumed that at the beginning, the businessman borrows $1000 and that with it, he purchases a machine. At the end of ten years, he has completely repaid the loan. The businessman then requests another loan to purchase a new machine to replace the old one which has worn out. His loan-repayment record is good; in addition, assuming that prices have risen during the ten-year period, the dollar value of his assets has increased. Therefore, his request for a loan of $1100 to purchase a new higher-priced machine is granted. This loan is even more readily granted than the previous loan, and the businessman is even more willing to borrow. This favorable attitude of both the lender and the borrower toward the investment is derived from their previous experience, in which (1) the loan contract held by the bank was promptly and completely fulfilled and (2) the businessman found it easy to fulfill the contract terms; and both conditions were facilitated by the price rise.

Government Expenditures

The final component in the analysis of the determinants of national income are government expenditures. In the discussion which follows, the factors determining the amounts which governments spend are not considered. This procedure is justified on the basis that these factors are outside the general economic relationships—prices, taxes, profits, the interest rate, and the like—of the private economy. However, to avoid the problems inherent in setting arbitrary quantities of government expenditures, it is assumed that the amount spent is constant but financed in various proportions with taxes and newly created funds.

Diagram 11-3 is drawn in such a way as to show the general effect on national income of a given quantity of government expenditures which are financed with varying proportions of tax collections and newly created money, ranging from financing completely with tax collections to financing completely with created money. The change in the income effect is measured on the horizontal axis, and the portion of the expenditure financed with taxes is shown on the vertical axis. Line TQ represents the change in the income-creating effect of a given government expenditure financed with changing mixtures of taxes and created money.

Line TQ is drawn on the assumption that a basic multiplier or leverage effect exists for all expenditures, government and

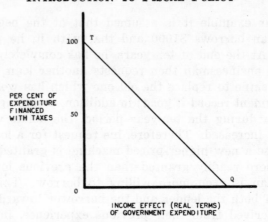

DIAGRAM 11–3. Relation of government expenditures to national income, assuming varying portions financed with taxes.

private; therefore, there is no income gain when expenditures are transferred from the private to the public economy or vice versa.* It is further assumed that the larger the portion of an expanded expenditure that is financed with created money, the greater the expansion of national income, i.e., the larger the multiplier. The increase of national income will be in real terms if the creation of money takes place under conditions of unemployment. This increase is measured along the horizontal axis, with the maximum multiplier existing when the additional expenditure is completely financed with created funds, at the point where TQ intersects the horizontal axis.

Here again is the aggregate or monetary type of fiscal analysis, the key to the change that takes place is the richness of consumers. A government expenditure completely financed with taxes has an uncertain impact on national income, the impact depending on the type of taxes used, the reasons for unemployed factors, and the like. With the approach used here, these variations cannot be separately considered. Only the relationship between the portion of the expenditure which is tax financed and the increase in national income is considered. In other words, the impact on national income of a government expenditure is dependent on how the expenditure affects the richness of final purchasers of goods and services. When only a minor portion or none of the government expenditure is tax

*Ralph Turvey, "Some Notes on Multiplier Theory," *American Economic Review*, vol. 18, June, 1953, p. 276. This is also the general position developed by Joshua C. Hubbard in *Creation of Income by Taxation* (Cambridge, Harvard University Press, 1950).

financed, its impact on national income will be maximized because the richness of the purchasers of goods and services is most favorably affected—increased the most—under these conditions.

Along with the increase in the richness of private purchasers as a result of the increase in their net assets, the expansion of consumer liquidity provides a sound basis for price increase expectations.

CONCLUSION

THE size of the national income is determined by the amount that people spend for newly produced goods and services. People—families and businesses—spend more willingly—they feel richer —if, in the light of their future income expectations, they have all the money, or liquidity, that they feel they need. In making families and businesses richer, fiscal activity is performing in a manner similar to that of a monetary activity; i.e., it is increasing net assets which have a high degree of moneyness. Governments expand the richness (liquidity) of consumers through the fiscal act of spending more money than they collect in taxes— deficit financing.

The increase in net assets which attends government deficit financing increases national income in many ways. First, after a point, consumers no longer add to their cash balances. As a consequence, a more rapid turnover of money takes place—i.e., a given amount of money is used to purchase more goods and services—and the result is an increased national income.

Second, the expansion of liquid assets under these conditions must bring forth an even *greater* increase of goods and services, or prices will rise. Expectations of rising prices are another important stimulant to the purchase of goods and services.

Finally, expenditures for goods labeled investment are greatly stimulated by another effect of an expansion of liquidity—lower interest rates. The rate of interest is an out-and-out monetary concept, but it is affected along with prices—another monetary concept—by a fiscal type of decision.

Fiscal activity can also increase the national income when additional government expenditures are completely covered by additional revenues. This could occur because (1) the average propensity to consume is increased, (2) the private economy is induced to increase the money supply by increasing bank loans, (3) the average speed of spending is increased. However, here again, part of the total impact is likely to result from price increases.

Suggested Library Reserve Reading List

ABBOTT, CHARLES CORTEZ. *The Federal Debt: Structure and Impact*. New York, Twentieth Century Fund, 1953.—The most recent and complete study of the national debt.

BARNA, TIBOR. *Redistribution of Incomes through Public Finance in 1937*. Clarendon, Oxford University Press, 1945.— This technical study has contributed a great deal to the analysis of the possibilities of fiscal activities. The data used are nearly entirely British.

BEVERIDGE, SIR WILLIAM H. *Full Employment in a Free Society*. New York, Norton, 1945.—This study, along with that by Hansen noted below, provides the framework within which democratic fiscal policy must operate. The study is comparatively free of technical analyses.

BOND, FLOYD A., et al. *Our Needy Aged*. New York, Henry Holt, 1954.—A very readable study of old-age assistance in California with many references to the national picture.

BUTTERS, J. KEITH, THOMPSON, LAWRENCE, AND BOLLINGER, LYNN. *Effects of Taxation: Investments by Individuals*. Boston, Harvard Business School, 1953.—This study concludes that high individual income taxes do not mean that individuals in the high income brackets are unable or unwilling to invest.

BUTTERS, J. KEITH, LINTNER, JOHN, CARY, WILLIAM L., AND NILAND, POWELL. *Effects of Taxation: Corporate Mergers*. Boston, Harvard Business School, 1951.—Taxation can affect the competitiveness of the economy, as this study indicates.

CHANDLER, L. V. *Inflation in the United States, 1940-1948*. New York, Harper, 1951.—Useful primarily as an historical account of the World War II inflation.

CHUBB, BASIL. *The Control of Public Expenditures*. Oxford, Clarendon Press, 1952.—Refers to British practice and experience. The conclusions, pp. 240-260, are very interesting.

CLARK, JOHN MAURICE. *Economics of Planning Public Works*. Washington, U. S. Government Printing Office, 1935.—This study, made for the National Planning Board of the Federal Emergency Administration of Public Works, and that by the International Labour Office, listed below, are much the best in the field. The exposition is easily understood.

COMMERCE CLEARING HOUSE. *Tax Systems.* Chicago, Commerce Clearing House, Current.—The only single source of information on state tax systems.

COMMITTEE ON POSTWAR TAX POLICY. *A Tax Program for a Solvent America in 1947.* New York, Ronald, 1947.—Presents the businessman's attitude toward taxes.

DOANE, ROBERT R. *The Anatomy of American Wealth.* New York, Harper, 1940.—Contains considerable wealth data.

DOBROVOLSKY, SERGEI P. *Corporate Income Retention: 1915-1943.* New York, National Bureau of Economic Research, 1951. —A basic study of the characteristics of that very important segment of private savings—corporate savings.

DUN & BRADSTREET, INC. *A Survey of Taxes Paid by Business in 1938.* New York, Dun & Bradstreet, 1939.—This study has developed very nearly the only data available regarding the variation in the tax burden borne by different businesses.

FABRICANT, SOLOMON. *Trend of Government Activity.* New York, National Bureau of Economic Research, 1952.—A study of the expansion of government expenditures in the United States. Includes many useful analyses and comparisons.

GROVES, HAROLD M. *Postwar Taxation and Economic Progress.* New York, McGraw-Hill, 1946.—Expresses the C.E.D. enlightened attitude toward the effect of taxes on business activity. Contains excellent analyses of many important tax problems.

HAIG, ROBERT M. *The Financial Problem of the City of New York.* New York, New York Mayor's Committee on Management Survey, 1952.—Examines the fiscal resources of New York City.

HANSEN, ALVIN H. *Economic Policy and Full Employment.* New York, McGraw-Hill, 1947.—This study, along with that by Beveridge noted above, provides the framework within which democratic fiscal policy must operate. Students will enjoy reading the book.

HARRIS, SEYMOUR E. *Economic Planning.* New York, Knopf, 1949.—The best single source available on the problems and possibilities of economic planning. Draws on both American and foreign experience.

HARRIS, SEYMOUR E. *The National Debt and the New Economics.* New York, McGraw-Hill, 1947.—Analyzes the Federal debt in terms of Keynesian economic relationships. Abbott's study should be read also.

Hart, Albert G. and Brown, E. C. *Financing Defense*. New York, Twentieth Century Fund, 1951.—An analysis of the fiscal possibilities existing at the time of the Korean War.

Heller, Walter W. *Savings in the Modern Economy: A Symposium*. Minneapolis, University of Minnesota Press, 1953. —The first chapter, by Harlan A. Smith, titled "The Savings Problem: A Survey," is excellent. Many of the other chapters examining segments of the problem are also good; for example, Chapters 5, 8, and 14.

Hubbard, Joshua C. *Creation of Income by Taxation*. Cambridge, Massachusetts, Harvard University Press, 1950.—Examines very carefully, but in a somewhat technical fashion, the various ways that taxation can increase the national income.

International Labour Office. *Public Investment and Full Employment*. Montreal, International Labour Office, 1946.— By far the best study available regarding the administration of government expenditures.

Kimmel, Lewis H. *Taxes and Economic Incentives*. Washington, Brookings Institution, 1950.—Chapters 1 and 10 summarize the findings and point of view of the author.

Lerner, Abba P. *The Economics of Control*. New York, Macmillan, 1944.— Contains a complete development of the ideas of functional finance.

Millikan, M. (ed.). *Income Stabilization for a Developing Democracy*. New Haven, Yale University Press, 1953.—Analyzes many aspects, including fiscal, of the problem of economic stabilization.

Ostheimer, Richard H. *Student Charges and Financing Higher Education*. New York, Columbia University Press, 1953.—A fiscal problem that is close to home.

Paul, Randolph. *Taxation in the United States*. Boston, Little, Brown, 1954.—A thorough and readable discussion of the development of our fiscal system and the job it has to do. Includes an excellent discussion of the tax developments at the Federal level since World War II.

Piser, Leroy M. *U. S. Government Bond Market Analysis*. New York, New York Institute of Finance, Publications Division, 1952.—If the student inserts current data, he will have completed an excellent analysis of the principal factors affecting the availability of investment funds to hold Federal government securities.

Rhys-Williams, Lady. *Taxation and Incentive*. New York, Oxford Press, 1953.—A very clear discussion of the problems involved in the state's guarantee of a decent standard of living to everyone.

Rolph, Earl R. *The Theory of Fiscal Economics*. Berkeley, University of California Press, 1954.—In Chapters 4, 5, 6, and 10, the discussion of the treatment of government by our national income accounts is very helpful.

Ross, James Stirling. *The National Health Service in Great Britain*. New York, Oxford University Press, 1952.—An accurate and complete picture of the problems and accomplishments up to the date of publication.

Sanders, Thomas. *Effects of Taxation on Executives*. Boston, Harvard University Press, 1951.—This study is based largely on interviews and has the weaknesses of this type of analysis. However, it is very informative.

Simons, Henry C. *Economic Policy for a free Society*. Chicago, University of Chicago Press, 1948.—Chapters 8, 9, 10, and 13 present a lucid discussion of how a free market society should function.

Simons, Henry C. *Federal Tax Reform*. Chicago, University of Chicago Press, 1950.—The definition of taxable income recommended and the treatment of capital gains advocated are of special interest.

Smith, Dan Throop. *Effects of Taxation: Corporate Financial Policy*. Boston, Harvard School of Business, 1952.—Considers such interesting topics as "Retained Earnings," Chapters 4 and 8; and "Capital Structure of New Corporations," Chapter 7.

Somers, Harold M. *Public Finance and National Income*. Philadelphia, Blakiston, 1949.—Chapters 2, 3, 4, 5, and 6 are excellent in developing more completely the relationship between government spending and national income.

Tax Institute. *Financing the War*. Philadelphia, Tax Institute, 1942.—Each chapter is written by an expert, and the result is a superior discussion of the many problems faced in financing World War II.

Tax Institute. *The Limits of Taxable Capacity: A Symposium*. Princeton, Tax Institute, 1953.—A careful consideration of this rather vague concept.

Tax Policy League. *Property Taxes: A Symposium*. New York, Tax Policy League, 1940.—Best discussions of the property tax available in a single volume.

Temporary National Economic Committee, Investigation of Concentration of Economic Power, Monograph no. 3. Tarasov, Helen. *Who Pays the Taxes?* Washington, U. S. Government

Printing Office, 1940.—The basic study of the distribution of the United States tax burden.

TEMPORARY NATIONAL ECONOMIC COMMITTEE, Investigation of Concentration of Economic Power, Monograph no. 4. Goldenthal, A. J. *Concentration and Composition of Individual Incomes, 1918-1937*. Washington, U.S. Government Printing Office, 1940.—The basic source of data regarding United States income distribution.

TERBORGH, GEORGE W. *The Bogey of Economic Maturity*. Chicago, Machinery and Allied Products Institute, 1945.— Largely a criticism of Hansen's writings prior to World War II.

U. S. House of Representatives, Monopoly Subcommittee of the House Judiciary Committee. *Study of Monopoly Power*, Part 1, 29, 2B. Washington, U. S. Government Printing Office, 1949. —The most recently published study of this subject.

U. S. Treasury Department, Tax Advisory Staff of the Secretary. *Federal-State-Local Tax Coordination*. Washington, U. S. Government Printing Office, 1952.—The most recently published study of this perennial problem.

WALLICH, HENRY C. *Public Finance in a Developing Country*. Cambridge, Massachusetts, Harvard University Press, 1951.— Based on relationships observed and analyzed in Latin America.

WHITE, MELVIN I. *Personal Income Tax Reduction in a Business Contraction*. New York, Columbia University Press, 1951.—An excellent analysis of the Possibilities inherent in this type of policy action.

WRIGHT, D. McC. *The Creation of Purchasing Power*. Cambridge, Massachusetts, Harvard University Press, 1942.—Discusses "Redistribution and Purchasing Power Creation" in Chapter 3, and defines "Inflation" in Chapter 4. Chapter 7, "Purchasing Power Injections," is long and stimulating.

Current Issues of:

Board of Governors of the Federal Reserve System. *Federal Reserve Bulletin*.

United States Department of Commerce, Bureau of Foreign and Domestic Commerce. *Survey of Current Business*.

The American Finance Association. *The Journal of Finance*.

The National Tax Association. *National Tax Journal*.

Index

237